THE LAST VOYAGE

The Story of Schooner Third Sea

by
Harold Stephens

with an Introduction by
Robert Stedman

i

THE LAST VOYAGE

Copyright @: 1997 by Harold Stephens

Front cover: 35mm Ektachrome by Harold Stephens

Photos by Harold Stephens and Robert Stedman

Published in the USA

ISBN: 0-9642521-3-9

Library of Congress No. 96-060117

Published by
WOLFENDEN
U .S. A.
P.O. Box 789
Miranda, Ca 95553-0789
Tel: (707) 923-2455 Fax: (707) 923-2455

Book cover design by Robert Stedman Pte Ltd. Singapore

Also by Harold Stephens

Who Needs a Road,
with Al Podell
Discover the Orient
Destination Singapore
Wander with the Wind
Turn South at the Equator
Malaysia
Asian Portraits
Asian Adventure
At Home in Asia
Three Decades of Asian Travel & Adventure

This book is dedicated to all those who assisted with the construction of Schooner *Third Sea*, and to those who faithfully helped sail her through Asian waters and the oceans of the South Pacific.

The events portrayed here did not necessarily take place in the order given, nor is there any chronological order to the text. All the people are real and no names have been changed, although some have been omitted.

Some of the incidents given here have been previously published in part in the *Bangkok Post, Signature, Accent, Discovery, The Asia Magazine, Cruising World, Asia Boating, Off-Duty* and Thai Airways International's in-flight magazine *Sawasdee*. Stories and newspaper articles have been re-edited to fit the text.

The author would like to thank all those who sent their condolences upon hearing of the loss of *Third Sea,* and for those who encouraged him to write his story for all to remember. He would like also to thank those who have assisted with the publication, and in particular Douglas Ingold for his encouragement and editorial contribution.

TABLE OF CONTENTS

SONG OF THIRD SEA

Life begins for us around sunset
when we gather on the deck
and watch it fall behind Moorea

When we do nothing more
serious than talk and sing
and drink wine in the mild June weather

Yes, I'd sooner be on a schooner
with my good friend Harold Stephens
than to be in a hundred other places

That I know of; to lie in the bowsprit net
like a gilded fish
beguiled by the orchestration of the sea

While skipper Steve fusses over his boat,
gentle, laughing, with jungles
and lost cities tangled in his eyes

And crew Dave and Judy Loomis
of Williamstown, Massachusetts,
love the boat to spic and span

Dave singing his songs of sailing
in the Galapagos and the Java seas,
rocking to the rhythm of the wave
Hoe Ana E...Hoe Hoe Hoe...Hoe Ana E

Urge the sturdy rowers
in their long canoes
skimming by the starboard side
Hoe Ana E...Hoe Hoe Hoe...Hoe Ana E

Beyond the breakers
they cross the channel to Moorea
as stars break over the water
Hoe Ana E...Hoe Hoe Hoe...Hoe Ana E
O let us mortals defy our fate,
encourage the great drums,
the *toeres* throbbing the air

The Fete is almost here,
so bring on the wine
and bring on the wine

I want to be like the bronzed
pagan men in the long canoes,
be free to run with the mahi-mahi

Spend my years remaining
away from the din of cities,
the world's affairs

So why set my heart of strife?
Come bring on the wine
and bring on the wine

Goh Poh Seng
Tahiti-Penang
December 1980

From book of poems: *Bird with One Wing*

Schooner *Third Sea* rests quietly at anchor in the South China Seas.

FROM CABIN BOY TO FIRST MATE

by Robert Stedman

I must have been about twelve years old when news reached our family that my uncle Harold (only our immediate family called him Harold) was building a sailing boat. We were at the dinner table—my mother, father, brother and two sisters—when my grandmother phoned. They were all disturbed, especially my grandmother. My uncle had been roaming around the world, from Tahiti to Bangkok, for a good number of years and all my family thought it was about time he settled down and gave up his wandering ways. He was always up to something. If it wasn't driving a jeep across Russia or floating on a raft down the Amazon it was building an adobe ranch house in the mountains overlooking the Mojavi Desert to living in a grass hut on a beach in Tahiti. I should say everyone was against him, except me. Uncle Harold was my hero. But I couldn't admit it.

The books my uncle wrote about these distant places, and the adventures, could not match seeing him in person, and letting him tell his tales. It seems we all have admiration for travelers and adventurers, and we admire them when we see them on TV or in the movies, but when they are members of our family, well that's something altogether different. "What good did a college education do him?" I remember my father asking. My mother didn't have an answer.

I remember when the boat was under construction in Singapore (what a romantic sounding name) that Uncle Harold came home for a short visit. He was on his way to Vancouver in Canada to confer with his boat designer and he invited me to join him. My mother refused to let me go. I guess she thought he might be a bad influence. But no amount of scoffing would discourage my uncle. "There's a magnificent world out there for anyone who wants it," he would whisper to me and go on doing what he set out to do. He was enthusiastic, and didn't care what others thought. He seemed to have some secret about the world that no one else knew. But he was under criticism constantly. "What do you know about boat building?" "Do you know how to sail?" "What about navigation?" There were all kinds of questions. His answers were to the point—"I'll learn!" And when they asked him, "What about money? Where are you going to get all the money?" He merely replied, "I'll find a way!" He did.

Once when he was visiting home, Uncle Harold asked me to accompany him to buy boat parts. He was looking for electronic equipment. "Can't get everything in Singapore," he said. I was thrilled. I had won an award in my science class in school and this was now my chance to show him what I could do.

We bought a depth sounder, and to test that it worked, my uncle suggested we use the toilet. We did, and blew it up. Everyone laughed, but my uncle thought it was the funniest thing he could have done.

He returned to that mysterious far off place. "You know where Singapore is, don't you," he said to me before he left. "You want to go? I'll take you there one day."

The boat was launched. Letters kept coming, with strange stamps and markings. They became more exciting as time went on. They came from distant places, Hong Kong, Borneo, Bali, New Guinea, the Solomons, Tahiti. Tahiti, my uncle was in Tahiti aboard his boat. No one ever goes to Tahiti. You only read about the place in books and magazines. My uncle was there. How exciting.

Years passed. Schooner *Third Sea* was sailing the high

seas, making news and a name for itself, and everyone forgot what they had said, that it couldn't be done. Now they looked for other faults. "He's crazy. You can't sail a schooner up the Sepic River in New Guinea. That's impossible!" When he did it they would find something else to criticize.

I never really thought I would see the schooner. But then, no one back home ever thought they would see it either. To most people she was a myth and no more.

Then a telegram arrived. My mother had passed away and my uncle asked if I wanted to join him on a writing assignment in Southeast Asia, and then would I like to help sail *Third Sea* from Samoa to Hawaii. I accepted. We toured Asia and then I flew ahead to Samoa. I signed aboard as a deck hand. My uncle, the captain now, showed me no favoritism. The voyage over, I returned home, knowing now that he had been right. There was another world out there. A year later another telegram arrived. Would I accept a position as First Mate aboard *Third Sea*. Would I! I sold everything I owned and flew to Hawaii where the schooner was waiting.

One thing I learned aboard *Third Sea* is there's no such word as can't. Nor is there a task that's impossible. My uncle learned it from his father, my grandfather, and he passed it on to me. "You can do anything you set your mind to," he would say, "except, maybe, if you want to be a ballet dancer." Today, when I hear someone say they would like to go to sea in their own boat, if they only had the money, I tell them about *Third Sea*. The schooner was the greatest influence in my life. It had an effect upon everyone, me and the many hundreds of others who sailed about her. *Third Sea* taught us all about this wonderful world we live in. All one needs do is go out and find it. And there is nothing except yourself to hold you back.

Stephens takes the helm of schooner *Third Sea*'s during her maiden voyage down Thailand's Chao Phraya River en route to Singapore.

Chapter 1

THE LAST CHAPTER

On January 27, 1975, the *Sunday Magazine* of the *Bangkok Post* published an article I wrote titled "How not to build a boat." It told how, with little capital but a lot of determination, I built *Third Sea*, a 71-foot sailing schooner that for some eighteen years would carry me from the Gulf of Thailand and the South China Sea to the far-flung islands of both the North and South Pacific. It was the first of many sea stories that the *Post* and various other magazines published over the years.

I had shared with readers these adventures, the happy moments, like a Tahiti landfall, and the struggles, fighting storms and typhoons and battling pirates. Adventures they were, and somehow we always managed to survive. Until now! For those who have followed the voyages of *Third Sea,* and for those who have sailed aboard her, I feel compelled to write that last chapter, as painful as it might be.

It began, or should I say it ended, when I was visiting northern California and news reached me that a hurricane was approaching the Hawaiian Islands, possibly the worst storm to hit the islands this century. I could only imagine the worst. My schooner *Third Sea* was anchored in Ke'ehi Lagoon near the airport on the island of Oahu.

Aboard *Third Sea* was a young couple and their two children. I had left the schooner in their charge, as caretakers, until I returned. I could hardly expect them to stay aboard and battle a hurricane while I was taking a vacation back on the mainland. I had to get back to Honolulu as quickly as I could, but to my horror, when I tried to

1

book a flight, I learned that all flights to the islands had been cancelled. Nor could I telephone. Lines were jammed and communications with Oahu were at a standstill. But the public was not without the latest news. Television networks had cameras on the scene and were sending live coverage reports showing Hawaii preparing for the coming disaster. Indications were that the storm would reach the islands the next afternoon, striking the western shores of Oahu and then moving on to Kauai. One report that caused some concern told the world that movie director Steven Spielberg, along with his film crew and actors, was stranded on Kauai. He was halfway through filming a science fiction drama about extinct dinosaurs coming back to life. The film was "Jurassic Park."

Spielberg may have had his problems, but my worst experience ever was about to begin.

Two days passed before I could book a flight to Honolulu, and when the seat came available, I made it to San Francisco as fast as I could get there. I still hadn't had any word about *Third Sea,* and as I winged my way across the Pacific I could only hope for the best. Then, as the jet liner approached Honolulu and dropped down through the clouds, I caught my first view of the shoreline. There were debris and fallen trees everywhere. Some roof tops were gone and palms trees stood naked with their foliage stripped away. The jet made a wide circle and as it banked far to starboard I looked down at Ke'ehi Lagoon. I was looking upon a nightmare. There remained but a very few vessels standing upright in the harbor, and *Third Sea* was not one of them. We dropped lower to make our approach; my eyes fell upon the seawall that marks the end of the runway. The entire wall was one continuous graveyard of ships—sail boats, yachts, cabin cruisers. They were all jumbled and piled up upon one another. I searched among the ruin and devastation but I could not see my *Third Sea*.

There was still hope!

The arrival hall at Honolulu International Airport was in chaos. It was impossible to find a taxi. In desperation I ran out to the main road in hope that I could flag down a taxi, but hundreds of others had the same idea. I began walking, and then half ran down the road to Nimitz Highway that led towards Ke'ehi Lagoon. My mind was not clear. A thousand thoughts blurred my vision. I was in a kind of daze. All I knew was that I had to get to *Third Sea*, as if her very survival depended upon me.

I was aware of a car stopping, my getting into the front seat and my repeating, "My boat, my boat, I have to get to my boat!" I can't recall one thing about the car or the driver. If I were to see him again I would not know him. But whoever he was he must have understood. He drove me to the gate at the yacht harbor at Ke'ehi Lagoon. I leaped out and ran to the quay. "She's down," were the first words I heard.

People quickly gathered around, mostly yachtsmen, and they all seemed to speak at once. The couple I left aboard had abandoned *Third Sea*. "There was nothing they could do," someone said. "There was nothing anyone could do," someone else repeated.

There wasn't anything anyone could do. Were these just empty words, words to console me? But had I been aboard, could I have done any better? I knew without an experienced crew I couldn't have taken *Third Sea* out to sea, which many large sailing vessels do when storms of this magnitude approach. I didn't have a crew and there was no one there to help *Third Sea*. Other yachtsmen, those who elected to stay aboard their vessels, had their own battles to fight.

One yachtsman who had remained aboard his own

vessel told me what had happened.

"We couldn't see the wind," he said. "We could only hear it. It began with the rigging. The stays and shrouds started to hum, softly at first, gradually growing louder until it reached a deafening roar. Soon halyards broke loose from their cleats and stood out from the masts rigid as iron bars. Other lines began to part."

With increasing wind, the sea began to rise, swelling, building up in mountainous crests. Soon the hurricane was upon the helpless yachts in the lagoon. They were at its mercy. "The wind choked the air from me," the man said. "My eyes felt like they would pull from their sockets. Even buttons tore loose from my foul weather jacket."

From his own doomed yacht he watched the bow of *Third Sea* bury itself into each oncoming sea, and when it did, tons of churning white water flooded the deck, covering even the main cabin. And always faithfully, the bowsprit proudly lifted up and the ship shook itself like a dog shakes water from its back.

But no relief came, no lull in the storm. Instead, its strength only intensified. There was no sky, no horizon. Visibility was limited to as far as one could reach. The unrelenting wind brought torrents of rain with its driving force. Even those things that were securely tied down suddenly began to tear loose. "The front hatch blew off," the man said, "and I watched it go flying down the deck like a playing card tossed to the wind."

The man insisted that nothing could have held against that wind. Nothing! A yacht still pulling on its anchor came swishing by and nearly crashed into *Third Sea*'s starboard beam. The yachtsman was fighting his own battle when he next looked toward *Third Sea* she was gone. Between sheets of driving rain he saw other vessels break loose from their moorings and vanish in the fury.

What every yachtsman feared happened to *Third Sea*. She began dragging. She had two storm anchors out but they were not enough. The proud schooner was carried by the hurricane-force winds across the lagoon to the seawall facing the airport.

The odds were stacked against *Third Sea*, against any vessel that attempted to stand up against that storm. Winds reached 170 mph, with a driving sea that broke twenty feet above the seawall. Nearly every vessel in the lagoon was driven helplessly toward the seawall.

"Where is she now?" I asked.

"On the reef," they said. "She's breaking up."

I didn't want to hear any more. I asked where I could get a skiff to take me out to *Third Sea*. I had to be with her one last time.

As I waited for someone with a small boat to appear, I kept asking myself why this storm and not all the others? This was not the first hurricane, or typhoon, *Third Sea* had to face. In the past eighteen years *Third Sea* and I had weathered two violent tropical storms and countless smaller ones. We fought raging seas from the coast of China to the eastern Pacific islands. I had built *Third Sea* with the specific purpose in mind of withstanding storms and wild tossing seas. I had built her for a good reason.

Third Sea was more than a ship; she was an idea, a dream. She fulfilled in me, and countless others who have sailed with me, everything we wanted from life. She had carried me to all those places I had read about in my youth, to the fabled islands of the South Seas, to the exotic ports of the East, across wide seas and up savage rivers. And now was I going to watch her die?

As I paced, waiting for a boat, I thought about all these things, the people, the places, the dream that had become real. This is the story of schooner *Third Sea*.

5

Schooner *Third Sea* under full sail in Hong Kong.

Chapter 2

ON READING JACK LONDON

I guess I've always wanted to own my own boat and go searching for the rainbow's end, at least as far back as I can remember. For a farm boy raised far from the sea this certainly was an anomaly. There were no seafarers in my family, no grandfather or wayward uncle with a sea chest hidden in the attic. My only connection with the sea was through reading. As a youth on the farm, without other kids to engage in sports and play games, I did find solace in reading adventure books. I have no doubt that's what spurred my imagination. I recall in vivid detail reading about two brothers who sailed their yacht *Discoverer* to the far South Pacific. I can't remember their names, nor the name of the book, but I do remember their photographs in the book. One in particular stands out in my mind: the two brothers, in yachting caps, are standing on the quay at Papeete in Tahiti. Oh how I longed to be there with them.

A name I do remember, and the books he wrote, is Jack London. What school boy doesn't know him! Reading London was like driving spikes into my heart, and the only way to heal the wounds was to follow his footsteps and go to sea, to the South Seas. *The Cruise of the Snark*—I was twelve when I read it—became part of my subconscious. Jack London built his own boat; I had to build my own boat. Jack London made an impossible passage from Hawaii to the Marquesas; I had to make the same passage; Jack London sailed to the remote corners of the South Seas; I had to follow suit. Only I wasn't aware of it until later in life when I reread *The Cruise of the Snark.* I realized then what an affect London had had upon me.

And thus, I continued to dream about sailing boats, about owning my own boat one day. I remember once when I was in the Marines, standing guard duty at night. To keep my wits, I paced out in the sand the outline of my imaginary ship, and then I would walk the deck. I began to plan seriously about my boat. I wrote to all the brokers listed in the yachting magazines. One schooner in particular caught my fancy; it was everything I wanted. The only thing that held me back was money. Big money! On a marine sergeant's pay, it would have taken me— provided I gave up cigarettes, beer and liberty—some sixty-two years to save up enough money to buy that schooner.

Jack London and his wife Charmaine on the deck of *Snark.*.

But dreams don't go away just because they seem impossible. Over the intervening years I did the next best thing: I crewed on boats whenever possible. Still, the dream just wouldn't go away. I wanted to own my very own boat.

About this time trimarans, those three-hulled light displacement sailing craft, became the rage, and I seriously considered building one in my back yard in California. But then I discovered with trimarans weight is a major consideration. A trimaran can't carry extra weight, and certainly not cargo; they are a far cry from trading schooners. Back to my old dreams.

Then one day a small incident, a casual remark, changed everything.

I was in Honolulu doing a story for a magazine about a Canadian adventurer, Stan Rayner, who had found an old, rotting hull on the docks, rebuilt it and turned it into a romantic-looking trading schooner. It had taken him more than two years of hard labor.

"Was it worth it?" I joked.

"If I had to do it all over again," he said, "I'd build in concrete."

Build in concrete! Was this his joke?

But Rayner was dead serious, and a few days later he introduced me to John Samson, a man who was to completely change many ideas about boat building. Samson was in Honolulu to study the design of Rayner's schooner, which he was going to incorporate in his new book of plans for ferro-cement boat construction.

John Samson gave me my introduction to cement boats, but it took a great deal more reading and homework before I could come to accept the idea. I've always been somewhat a traditionalist, never even really caring for fiberglass boats. And now cement—floating sidewalks they called them.

But as time went on I became more and more intrigued by this medium. I discovered that ferro-cement construction is nothing new. The very first one, a rowboat still in existence on a lake in Switzerland, was built back in 1848. There were scores of others, some now in museums in Europe.

In 1941, Italian architect, Professor Pier Luigi Nervi, began experimenting with ferro-cement construction for boats. His method, basically the same one used today, was to place many layers of wire mesh over small-diameter reinforcing rods and then plaster over this with a rich mortar of cement. The results are a "skin" of forty per cent steel and sixty per cent concrete. When combined this way the material has properties that make it unique. It is a classical case of the whole becoming greater than the sum of its parts. No one, not even the experts, knows why this phenomenon works, but it does.

At last, I could have my own schooner. Jack London struggled to build the *Snark*, and he succeeded. So why couldn't I? But my decision was not one I made overnight. It was only the matter of finally finding a method and means of realizing the dream.

The ship I had in mind was a schooner, unfortunately the kind of vessel that went out of vogue a hundred years ago. To my way of thinking, and it is purely personal, those old style schooners have real character. What finer vessel can there be than one with classical lines, a jutting bowsprit, rope ladders to spreaders above, high decks, chain plates and deadeyes, and all the rest? What I really envisioned was a romantic looking South Sea island trading schooner. And that is exactly what my schooner *Third Sea* became.

For her design, I knew exactly what I wanted. I didn't

find it, however, from reading any particular set of plans nor seeing any one boat that caught my fancy. It was a combination of a number of things, but mostly from years of climbing aboard hundreds of sailing vessels, from studying endless yachting books and from reading every story about cruising and sailing I could lay my hands on. Little by little the image became complete, blending into one impression that became my own creation. Later, when I looked at a hatch or the way the bowsprit was mounted aboard *Third Sea*, I could not recall where the original idea came from.

There is, I discovered, much more to consider when designing a boat to live aboard than there is to designing a house. Every single detail must be considered, with every inch of space put to some use. And I wanted more than the average boat had to offer. Since I would be spending most of my days in monsoon climates, I wanted, for example, a large main cabin. I also had to have open spaces below decks and areas not chopped up and divided into small compartments. I wanted to be able to carry cargo.

Nor did I want to waste space above deck. With weather permitting, outdoor living is a necessity. This meant a cockpit with a large seating arrangement, and a table for dining. Awnings were a must, for protection against sudden rain or the fierce afternoon downpour of tropical sun while at anchor.

Now came the big question, how could I pay for it all?

Had anyone known that I was attempting to construct a 71-foot schooner and that I had no money, they would have thought I was insane. Completely! But then maybe I was. Nevertheless, what I lacked in capital I made up in determination. I had a little money coming in from the guide book to Malaysia that I had completed, and a few magazine editors owed me for stories. Nothing else; no rich uncle, no inheritance, and no lottery. It meant that I had to labor all day in the yard, and burn the so-called "midnight oil" at night at my typewriter. Fortunately, publishers were interested in my stories. Tony Waltham at the *Bangkok Post* began publishing my weekly articles, about everything and anything, adventure, travel, interviews, opinions. A dozen other magazine editors in Asia also took up the cause and accepted my stories. Roy Howard at Thai Airways International agreed to sponsor my book on the lives of expatriates in Southeast Asia. And John Samson at Samson Marine responded to my offer that I help promote do-it-yourself boat building. I agreed to write a book for him about sailing which we called *Wander With the Wind*. In exchange he took my rough sketches for the schooner design and turned them over to Ce Norris, his chief naval architect at Samson Marine.

Newspaper articles that appeared in the *Bangkok Post*.

Only the skilled, trained eye of a naval architect can point out a novice's faults in design. I had to do a lot of arguing, a lot of compromising, but in the end I had a boat, or the plans for a boat, that would work.

Third Sea was about to become reality.

There remained, however, two big questions that I had to find some answers to. First, where should I build? And second, who would I get to help me?

I explored all the possibilities for a building site. In the end I ruled out the U.S. It would have been too costly for both labor and materials. I considered the South Pacific. A long time ago I had fallen in love with the islands but the obvious problem was the islands' lack of materials. Finally I turned to the Orient.

To my surprise I found ferro-cement boats under construction in most large ports: Taipei, Manila, Hong Kong, Bangkok and Singapore. In Bangkok an enterprising American expatriate had set up a ferro-cement yard on a small canal south of the city. In Singapore a British company had turned out half a dozen fine boats. I checked prices of materials and labor, and decided to build the hull in Singapore, motor to Bangkok and outfit there. I moved into a house in Singapore, found a yard that would rent me a small area and sent off to Samson Marine in Vancouver for my plans.

Now came the second question, who could I get to help? I needed help but I didn't have the money to pay for it.

I found the answer while I was living in Kuala Lumpur, writing a guide book on Malaysia. There I met a U.S. Peace Corps volunteer, Jim Mathews. Jim had taught school for a few years in a small village in Malaysia and his time was up. He was getting out of the Peace Corps. He didn't want to return home immediately so when I offered him accommodation in Singapore for help at the yard he accepted. Jim did more than accept. He spread word that I was building a schooner in Singapore and for those who had nothing to do and wanted to help out on weekends and holidays, they could have free room and board in Singapore. I rented a big house and hired a cook. In the months that followed my house became a hang-out for volunteers looking for something to do on their time off. Many were skilled in their professions—engineers, mechanics, electricians and just about every skill you can imagine. I kept a record of everyone who put in time, and in exchange offered them free sailing when the schooner was launched. They came by the scores from all over Southeast Asia to help with the construction.

Don Maclean, an engineer teaching in Malaysia and on his way to Borneo on leave, stopped to see what we were doing, and never made it to Borneo. Every vacation and every weekend after that he came to Singapore to help out. A year later he left the Peace Corps and joined the crew as my first mate. He sailed the South Pacific with me for two years and remained aboard until we reached Honolulu the first time. Bret Anderson, a math teacher, helped on weekends and when his tour with the Peace Corps was over, he too joined the crew, as ship navigator. Russ Vogel was with family planning, and Mimi Beams was teaching home economics. Both gave their time to *Third Sea*. Mort Rosenblum was the Bureau Chief for Associated Press. When he was on line with a news story and couldn't come to help, he sent his wife Randi. There were other women too who got caught up in the dream. Star Black, a writer-photographer, was working on the *Insight Guides* and Wendy Hutton was editor of *Silver Kris*, the in-flight magazine for Singapore Airlines. They too got involved.

And another woman, a most unlikely candidate, was a very pretty Chinese woman named Peggy Lou. She was engaged to a Peace Corps volunteer who, after his tour of duty, had returned home to Boston to arrange for their wedding. Peggy was waiting in Singapore for him to send for her when she heard about the boat building project and came out to the yard one afternoon in her Saks Fifth Avenue high boots and a leather jacket. She saw that we needed help and didn't hesitate to offer us her services. Before long she took over. She spoke several dialects of Chinese and ordered hardware and supplies, argued prices, bargained with shop keepers and instructed drivers and delivery men where to unload. Nothing slipped by her watchful eyes and she was able to get us the best deals in town. She remained through the whole building, saw us through launching and was standing on the dock waving goodbye when we sailed away.

There were others, non-Peace Corps, who volunteered their services. Adrian Nunis was a young Eurasian office worker who came to the yard one Sunday, became fascinated and asked if he could help. He took off work on Monday, then Tuesday and finally he quit his job to help out. He stayed until we launched. Then, as mysteriously as he appeared, he disappeared, and I have not seen him since. Kurt Rolfes was a photogapher who had covered the war in Vietman and after the war began to wind down he settled in Singapore. Kurt's dream was to own his own boat and sail around the world one day. He gave me every weekend he had free. There was Gope who had a camera store, who also came on weekends. Beno Anciano was general manager of a plywood factory. He felt so sorry for me typing my stories on a wooden crate at dockside late at night that he provided me with an office to use in the evening. He also sold me a great old Chinese truck for three hundred Singapore dollars. The truck, they call them lorries, became our mainstay.

The only paid labor I had was Mohan, a Tamil Indian, who introduced us to the mysteries of Asia. After work every day we went jogging, to keep in shape, all except Mohan. One day, unexpectedly, he joined us, and came shooting by, running backwards. We never asked him to join us again.

Up until I actually began building I could not think of a suitable name for my schooner. We were all sitting around after dinner one evening, throwing out names, when someone said, "What about Seven Seas?" Others protested, claiming it was a name over used. Then Jim Mathews sounded out, "Okay then, what about Third Sea!" The name stuck. We decided then and there to call her *Third Sea*. It wasn't until I later reread *The Cruise of the Snark* that I learned why Jack London called his vessel *Snark*. "We named her the *Snark*," he said, "because we could not think of any other name."

Chapter 3

HOW NOT TO BUILD A BOAT

The difficulty of building a cement boat in the Orient, I was soon to discover, was one of simply adapting to local conditions. Living in the Orient and working with orientals are two different things. The Orient can be very pleasant, relaxing and satisfying—with plenty of excitement whenever you want it. But when you try to introduce a new concept to the oriental mind, it takes some doing.

For example, in the Orient traditional trades such as boat building haven't changed in a thousand years. It's incredible the trouble you can get into when you try to break the rules.

I was building on a wooden mold which would be removed afterwards. I went to a lumber yard and ordered my timber. "Something inexpensive," I explained.

"No, for boats you need something better," the salesman insisted.

"No, you don't understand. I'm going to cover it with cement."

It didn't work. I had to go to another yard and tell them I was building a house.

In the beginning I planned to hire two carpenters to help me build the wooden mold for the hull. But when I explained that I was using very cheap wood since I would cover the mold with chicken wire and cement, they quit. They thought I was insane and wanted nothing to do with it, even after I offered top wages.

But that was only the beginning. Opposition came from all sides, even from the owner of the yard. "A cement boat!" he cried. "What will my neighbors think?"

"It's too heavy," the foreman at the yard laughed.

"It will crack," someone else added.

"It will sink," they all agreed.

"And my neighbors," the owner repeated. "Who will pay to haul it away?"

They too all thought I was mad. I tried to explain. The tensile strength of ferro-cement approaches that of steel. But it's better than steel in many ways. It's resistant to marine borers, ice, shock, impact, explosion and fire. The Chinese listened and nodded. I could have been telling them about green elephants on Mars.

I gave them more: Ferro-cement absorbs sound and vibration better than steel, aluminium or fiberglass, has no odor, and is cooler in summer and warmer in winter. It's lighter than steel and most wood vessels of comparable size and, without the need for heavy ribs, the interior has fifteen to twenty-five per cent more usable space.

"Yes, but what happens if you get hit?" they smiled.

I explained a dent can be repaired in minutes.

"But it will sink."

As a boat builder I soon discovered that what I would not be short of was advice, free advice from hundreds of so called experts, whether I wanted it or not. It can be very infuriating. Early in the game I learned how to combat all the free advice. At first I put up a sign saying this was a cement boat, and yes it would float, and no I didn't need any advice, but it didn't work. It only seemed to spur people on to ask more questions. But eventually I found the solution. When anyone came near, whether they were yard laborers or neatly dressed office workers, I would say, "Can you please hold this for a minute," and would then hand them a hammer or a heavy crowbar. If I needed something moved, I would say, "Help me carry that board over there." Often times they were too dumfounded not to help, but the next time they came around, they stood far in the background.

Advice from even seasoned boat builders and owners often did not help either. For example, I wanted portholes and windows in the main saloon that opened. These experts insisted that there is yet to be designed a porthole or window that is completely waterproof. I agreed, but I still wanted portholes and windows that opened. My solution, and I didn't know if it would work, was to install drain boards below the windows, with channels that drained into the bilge. They did work and whenever we were in port we had a free flow of air through the vessel. The drip boards collect any sudden rain.

Another item of conversation was what would be the best fuel to use for cooking. Almost everyone will agree that low pressure gas is the best, but also the most dangerous. Gas bottles cannot be stored below decks, and when kept above decks, they present a not-so-attractive sight. "Build a box around them," someone suggested. "But you lose too much space," someone else insisted.

I solved the problem by finding a barrel maker along Victoria Street in Singapore. I had him fashion two teak barrels which fitted on top of the gas bottles. No ugly rusting bottles to put up with now, except our arrivals at new ports caused custom officers to take notice. "Are you carrying whiskey?" they demanded. I grew tired of explaining, so on one barrel I printed WHISKEY and on the other RUM. For some reason it ended the queries. Never after was I questioned by a custom officer.

Aside from the two WHISKEY and RUM barrels, I had on deck two large Shanghai jars engraved with dragons. They make perfect storage for shoes when people come aboard and for skin-diving gear which can make a mess on deck when left about.

In his backyard in Singapore, Stephens laid out the first frame. When assembled, frames, some as wide as the road, were transported with his Chinese truck to the building site at the shipyard.

They first had to build a wooden hull which they then covered with mesh and re-inforcing bars before they plastered. Miles of re-bars were used, and enough wood to build a small house.

Help came from anyone and everyone, but mostly from Peace Corps volunteers. From the time we lofted the first frame to the day we launched, the complete hull construction took nine months.

One problem of building a boat in Singapore was the unwanted advice that bystanders gave. To solve the problem, Stephens put up a sign. It did no good. Advice still came from everyone who watched.

I spent the first month lofting and cutting out the frames in my backyard. When that task was finished, I then rented out the yard. But not without incident.

When assembled the frames for a 71-foot schooner measure fifteen feet wide and seventeen feet high. It took some maneuvering to load them on to my small Chinese truck and get them through the narrow streets of Singapore to the yard. We congested traffic and stopped cars and lorries for blocks. I didn't realize how strange we must have looked until a large lorry pulled up next to us and stopped for a light. It was piled high with live squealing pigs in wicker baskets. Sitting on top of the pile were two old toothless Chinese women. When they looked over at us they started pointing and broke up with laughter. If it had been someone in a Mercedes I may have understood but two old women sitting on a heap of squealing pigs was too much.

Conditions did not improve at the yard. People continued to stand back, to gawk, and laugh when something went wrong, which was often. Once we had all the heavy frames set up in place on the strongback, it took days to align them, and none were off more than an eighth of an inch. We removed the braces to tack them in permanently. Across the canal, from out of nowhere, I saw a whirl wind twisting and picking up dust and debris. It swung and turned in our direction, so slow and easy like, and at the last second, just when we thought we were doomed, it swerved away from us, touching only the first frame. We sighed; it had been close. But that last frame, it wavered, slightly, and then slowly fell backward, striking the next frame and that frame the next one, until all frames, like a row of dominos, came tumbling down. Splinters of timber flew in every direction. I escaped being crushed by diving down between timbers in the strongback. "Think of those distant islands and quiet lagoons," I had to keep telling myself as we started rebuilding, to the tune of wild laughter from all around the yard. A few more weeks of work lost.

The weekends were exciting, with dozens of helpers, but the week days were lonesome. I often worked alone. I made it my policy never to walk around the boat, for then I would see how much more there was to do and become discouraged. If I were working on the stern section, I remained there until whatever I was doing was finished and then would move on.

Building in the tropics had its drawbacks. There was the problem of the hot, tropical sun. I had to construct a scaffolding and put up a sun roof. Then there was the monsoon. It came earlier than expected and we were forced to keep everything under cover. And then there was always the totally unexpected, like the time when I arrived one morning and found the Indian watchman in a highly excited state.

"No, master, don't go near the boat!"

"Nonsense, it's my boat," I said angrily, and started to climb over the strongback. He muttered something about "snake" and I stopped in mid-climb.

It happened that a king cobra had found a home under the cool, dark strongback. It took two days for the watchman and his family to smoke out the snake and kill him.

In spite of the long hard hours of tedious work, progress went smoothly. Almost too smoothly. I began now to wonder if we were doing things properly. There was no one in Singapore, or in all Asia, as far as I knew, who had built a ferro-cement boat upside down on the wooden frame method. (Most are built right side up, a more difficult method for amateurs, I felt.) So there was no one I could consult with. No one to talk things over.

Plastering *Third Sea* (top and bottom left) was only part of the difficult task that lay ahead; another one was turning the schooner over once it was plastered (bottom right). Two heavy cranes were needed.

Once the schooner was turned over, the wooden hull mold had to be stripped away before interior work could begin. Bottom right, Mort and Randi Rosenblum, ready to get to work, look on.

But I was fortunate. John Samson in Vancouver was conducting a six-week boat building school in which a few dozen builders were traveling to the yard to construct, of all things, a schooner. He invited me to join them. I left Jim Mathews to keep shop and flew to Canada.

To my extreme delight I found that my hull mold was just as good as any the professionals built. I returned to Singapore elated.

Before I began construction, I bragged to John Samson that I could complete construction and launch in six months. Six months came and went. It was almost a year later that the final plastering day arrived, the most important day in building a ferro-cement boat. The delay had been costly. The monsoon had arrived.

"Don't worry, Tuan," Mohan said. "It won't rain."

And why wouldn't it rain? It was raining every day, so why won't it rain the day we are to plaster?

"I've agreed with my gods at the temple that if it doesn't rain I will carry *kavadi* at Thaipusam."

Carrying a *kavadi* during the Thaipusam festivals meant putting long, thin spikes through his body and carrying the *kavadi* (a heavy fan-shaped religious ornament) suspended above his body on the spikes. It is, without doubt, the most gruelling, self-mortification that man or woman can endure. Indian devotees pierce their bodies with hundreds of sharp spikes and hooks. Mohan made a promise to his gods that he would carry a *kavadi* to a cave in a mountain top.

The day we plastered it didn't rain, and shortly after I was at Batu Caves in Malaysia when Mohan fulfilled his obligations to his gods. He carried his heavy load, with spikes in his body, up three hundred and sixty steps to the cave in the side of the mountain.

The day for launching had finally arrived. Although

28

everything had been done according to specifications, there were still doubts and uncertainties, not that it wouldn't float, as all our Chinese kibitzers had predicted for the past six months, but that it would sink below the water line with too much ballast, or perhaps it would list to one side.

We sort of tried to sneak her into the water, after dark, but word had gotten out. My friend, Mort Rosenblum, from Associated Press was there with his wife Randi, but I didn't mind him coming. He had a bottle of champagne. As can be expected, there was noise and confusion, but when the crane started to lower *Third Sea* into the water, the entire dock area suddenly grew still. It seemed most eerie, and quiet, more like a funeral than a launching.

As she began to sink deeper into the water, the thought crossed my mind that she could end up half stuck in the mud. But she didn't settle into the mud! She splashed down and came up riding high, well above the water line. Shouts came up from everyone lining the shore. There was no more doubting. We did it! A tug was standing by to tow us to the Republic of Singapore Yacht Club where we would install the engine and deck gear and prepare to motor to Bangkok to outfit there. Our hard knocks were only beginning.

Standing high and mighty, schooner *Third Sea* is ready for launching. Once the engine was installed, we motored to Bangkok where we stepped the masts and began the interior work.

Chapter 4

LOSING FRIENDS

Those who know Singapore best either love it or hate it. There seems to be no in between. I happened to be one who likes the place and over the years I have spent as much time there as I could. For a writer, there are few better places to live. Most important, things in Singapore work. You dial a telephone number and you get through. You drink the water from the tap and you don't get sick, and you can eat from any fruit stand or at any food stall and you don't have to worry. There's no crime, no graffiti and no drugs. Libraries are in English and the museums are stacked with reference material. *The Straits Times* has newspapers on microfilm that date back a hundred years. And the mixture of races—Chinese, Malay, Indian and European—makes it exciting. And, for certain, these mixed races serve up some mighty fine food, from Chinese steamboat to hot Indian curries served on banana leaves. And it's a great place to build a boat.

But it's not a place to keep friends, that is, if they are Asian, and in particular, Chinese, and you are building a boat with your own hands. You are certain to lose face.

Over the years in Singapore I made many friends among the local Chinese. We got along well. They invited me to lunches and dinners, and for holidays, like Chinese New Year or the Moon Cake festival, they asked that I join them. Weddings and births called for special occasions, and I was "Uncle Harold" to more kids than I can ever remember. When I announced I was going to built a boat, my Chinese friends were impressed. Wealthy Towkays all have boats, plus expensive Mercedes and sons at Cambridge and Eton. I too must be a wealthy Towkay.

Then came the crashing blow. When I actually began building, I lost all my Chinese friends. I was an embarrassment to them.

In Asian cultures it's improper for an educated person to use his hands, to do menial labor of any sort. Do-it-yourself is unheard of. You want something done, then hire someone to do it for you. When my Chinese now saw me with dirt on my hands, dressed in baggy shorts and straw hat, I was a persona non grata to them. And when I appeared driving around town in my bright red Chinese truck, I was completely ostracized by them from their society. I had a lady friend in Kuala Lumpur whom I was keenly interested in. She had her own model agency, lived in a grand apartment and drove around in a flashy sports car. She came to Singapore to visit me soon after I began to build *Third Sea*. She came out to the yard, saw me grubby and dirty, got tears in her eyes and left. I never saw her again. Only foreigners and expatriates understood.

Kurt Rolfes understood. He was a long time friend, a photographer, married to Mae, a lovely Chinese girl with two purposes in life—one to make her husband happy, and her other, to play mahjong. Kurt was a great sport and helped me whenever he could, and the more he helped, the more Mae was able to play mahjong. Everyone was happy, especially me.

Mae never came to the yard and she never saw the schooner, that is, until I came back from Thailand. *Third Sea* was at her best having been completely outfitted with shiny teak woodwork, new sails and a bright outlook. I was looking forward to showing her off to everyone and invited Kurt and Mae aboard for dinner. They accepted and I met them at dockside in my dinghy. Mae wasn't the least bit impressed with the dinghy. It didn't have a motor and I had to row it. But never mind. I thought that would soon change when she saw *Third Sea*, catching the rays of the setting sun anchored off Clifford Pier. She did look great, pulling gently at her anchor, her bowsprit jutting out proudly into the wind. As we approached, Mae looked around at all the ships at anchor, and I announced, proudly, "Well, there she is, Mae, the *Third Sea*." The expression on her face flashed from expectation to one of horror. She couldn't believe it. This was my boat! It had masts, like the Chinese junks that came to Singapore a century ago and brought her ancestors. The past is something the modern day Chinese of Singapore want to escape. Mae was expecting an Onassis yacht. She reluctantly climbed aboard and couldn't wait until she got ashore that night. She never came back.

A boat requires sacrifices. Sometimes you question if it's worth it. Peter, my teenage son, came to Singapore after I had launched and intended to sail the Pacific with me, but the outfitting delays were long and I had little time to give him. He felt neglected and left in a huff and returned home. He didn't join *Third Sea* again until years later when I was sailing the Pacific.

Then there was the day that I had two cranes at the yard to turn the hull over after it was plastered, with a dozen workers standing by. A messenger came and handed me a telegram. I was too busy to read it and stuffed it into my pocket. I fell asleep that night, exhausted, and it wasn't until the next morning that I remembered the telegram. I quickly tore it open only to discover my father had died the day before. It was too late for me to go to his funeral.

In time *Third Sea* became a living thing, and I treated her as though she were. I never cursed her, I talked to her gently, like one does to a lady, and I never let others scorn her. I established rules aboard, like no whistling, no departing on long voyages on Friday, and paying tribute to Neptune when crossing the equator. Superstition, perhaps, but it worked. Something was in my favor. We sailed the great oceans together and never had even a minor mishap. But there was a price I had to pay. I had to play Captain Bligh when I didn't want to.

Chapter 5

MISTER PETERSON JOINS THE CREW

I was greatly pleased with both the construction and the cost of *Third Sea*. Expenses were greatly reduced since I didn't have to pay for labor, except for Mohan, a cook and the plasterers. I learned that necessity dictates; it's surprising how much you can learn to do by yourself. Welding, carpentry, metal work—they all come with determination, and besides, there's always someone about who is willing to teach you if you show interest.

I calculated that the project took 4,500 man-hours and we used nearly four miles of steel bars, enough chicken wire to fence in one square mile, 80,000 staples, and enough wood to build a small two-bedroom frame house. And, to encourage free weekend labor, I estimated that I poured enough beer to float the finished hull.

But that was all I had after nine months at the Republic of Singapore Yacht Club, a floating hull. I did have, however, the engine installed and all the water and fuel tanks in place. There was a rudder but no wheel or binnacle. I had to fashion a tiller arm that measured eight feet long. It would suffice until I got to Thailand. An American expatriate, Bob Stevens, ran his own ferro-cement boat yard on a small canal near the mouth of the Chao Phraya, and it was arranged that I motor *Third Sea* the thousand miles up the South China Sea to the Gulf of Thailand. We would follow the coast of Malaysia and by anchoring off shore could make frequent night stops. The date for our departure was set. We had two weeks to get ready.

Don Maclean and Bret Anderson signed aboard as permanent crew, as both had left the Peace Corps and were looking forward to sailing the South Pacific. Others joined the ranks to help us motor to Thailand—Ray Kaufman, a school teacher working in Japan; Captain Keven Yeland, a 747 pilot with Singapore Airlines; and Mister Peterson.

Mister Peterson was not what you might call an average crew member. Let me explain. I have to go back a few months to when my son Peter was still in Singapore.

To outfit *Third Sea* I did my procuring and buying equipment in downtown Singapore in the shophouses along Victoria Street and Beach Road. One street that connects the two streets is Rocher Road. Among the many shops on Rocher Road were several pet shops.

What a menagerie these dreadful shops kept: parrots and parakeets, mynah birds, rare hornbills, mongoose, pythons, musangs, monitor lizards. I even saw a three-hundred-pound Komoto dragon. And always there were monkeys. Small leaf monkeys, Maraqueses, white-handed gibbons, rheses monkeys and one very unhappy looking little fellow, a young siamang.

Living conditions for the unfortunate animals in these shops were dreadful. Cages were small, cramped and uncleaned. Piles of rotted fruit gave the place an added stench. In one such cage I saw the siamang. I had never seen a black ape before and had to ask the shopkeeper what he was. He called him a siamang, a name that didn't mean anything to me then. The little guy looked up at me with sad eyes and stretched his little hands through the bars for me to hold. It was very touching. He was so young, less than a year old.

After that I made a point of stopping on Rocher Road each time I went into town. I secretly hoped the little guy wouldn't be there, that someone had bought him and had given him a home. But my emotions were mixed. I was delighted when I saw him, and I would spend the longest time holding his little hand through the bars. And when no one was within earshot, I would talk to him. You know what I mean, animal talk.

The weeks passed into a month, two months, and then three. No one bought him. For all those long months he had been cooped up in that same incredibly small cage. Each time I saw him I felt more miserable. I decided to avoid Rocher Road altogether.

In time I probably would have forgotten the little siamang had not my Peter arrived to help on the schooner. I was anxious to show him the sights and took him downtown when I went shopping. We were on Victoria Street one afternoon when I mentioned the pet shops on Rocher Road with their assortment of jungle wildlife. Peter wanted to visit the shops. When he saw the siamang looking sadly at him through the bars it was love at first sight.

Against all possible logic I bought the siamang. Not right then. Later. I had to do some rationalizing. Peter's birthday was coming, and the siamang would make a great surprise. But equally important, I would get the animal out of the wretched shop. What I didn't realize was that by buying him I created a market. A few months later when I passed there were two siamangs in the same small cage at the shop. I was aware that to capture young animals, their mothers have to be shot by hunters. When I saw them in the cage I had the impulse to buy them too, but in another month I'm sure there would have been four animals in the same cage. I had to stop somewhere.

Peter was below deck when I returned with his present from the pet shop the morning of his birthday. I was concerned that the young ape, which I named Mister Peterson (for Peter's son), might escape so I bought a small cage to transport him back to the schooner. In the dinghy when we were away from shore I opened the cage door. I reached in for his little hand.

That soft and gentle little ball of fur was no more. A huge, ferocious monster with bared fangs came leaping out of the cage. A real Dr. Jekyll and Mr. Hyde! He looked at least four foot tall! He almost knocked me overboard in his lunge to reach the dinghy's bow, and then like a gorilla with a hand on each gunnel he began shaking the boat from side to side as though he wanted to upset us. I had to defend myself with an oar.

I should have known. In my research I had learned that a siamang is a Malay term not listed in English language dictionaries. But in a reference book *Animals of Southern Asia,* a siamang is classified as a "greater gibbon." They inhabit the jungles of the Malay Peninsula. The reference further states that siamangs are the loudest and largest of the gibbons and adult males may reach eighty pounds in weight. Little is known about their habits, as none have been successfully raised in captivity. That alone should have taught me something, but it didn't.

I must admit, although I have been fond of man's hairy friends ever since I was a youngster and read *Tarzan of the Apes,* I have always been opposed to keeping monkeys, chimpanzees, gibbons, orangutangs or the likes of them for pets. Their place is not on a chain or in a cage but in the open jungle. Ironically, because of this firm belief about uncaged animals Mister Peterson came into my charge.

And so here I was, in the dinghy, rowing out to the schooner with a monster on my hands. Peter heard my shouting and rushed up on deck. When he saw Mister Peterson he began leaping up and down with excitement. I shouted warnings for him to beware, that we had a demon on our hands. Peter was too excited to hear or take warning. When he reached down for Mister Peterson, I imagined him being torn apart, maimed for life. Instead the brute gently swung up into his arms. They were friends from the very start.

Overnight our lives aboard changed. *Third Sea* would never be the same. And Mister Peterson was its master, unchallenged. He had the complete run of things.

The schooner made an excellent retreat for our boarder. The masts and rigging and miles of lines and ropes became his playground. It was like being back in the jungles. For hours each day he would swing back and forth, doing cartwheels and handstands and daring leaps from one stay to another.

You might hear that monkeys are unclean. They may be, but not Mister Peterson. From the first day he was house broken. He used the toilet as we did, but he couldn't flush it.

He never wanted to be left out. If he were, he screamed and ranted and made life miserable aboard. He joined us at drinks and parties, and he insisted in having his meals with us. We had a place set at the table for him. He sat on

Mr. Peterson, a siamang, or better knows as a greater gibbon, was from the deep Malay jungles. He had a personality all his own, and he was completely at home aboard *Third Sea.*

a waste basket turned upside down. Often if someone had something on his plate that Mister Peterson liked, it suddenly disappeared. He could snatch things away without your noticing it. He had a sneaky foot.

Mister Peterson thrived on attention. If you didn't give it to him you were in for trouble. He knew how to sidle up to someone, cuddle up, and the next thing they knew their cigarettes or lighters or whatever they had that he wanted was gone. Mister Peterson would then appear on deck trying to light a cigarette or wearing a pair of sunglasses.

He was in his absolute glory when passers-by on the shore stopped to look at the schooner. He could captivate an audience for hours on end. He performed by swinging on ropes and doing cartwheels up the stays to the top of the mast. If no one was around to watch, he sat around and moped.

Mister Peterson was happiest when there was a party aboard and when people sat around and talked and laughed. He always joined in. He didn't like it when anyone was quiet and tried to read. Suddenly he would slam their book shut and be out the door in a flash. No one could catch him. He had infinite patience and could sit on top a mast until all was forgiven. Only then would he come down.

Mister Peterson loved to aggravate the crew, especially Don, the first mate. When Don was working on a project with wrenches or screwdrivers, Mister Peterson would grab a tool from him and then leap back two or three feet, forcing Don to chase after him. There were times I thought Don would kill him if he could catch him, but he never could. Mister Peterson was always too fast. Then Don found a workable solution.

Like all tree-dwelling creatures of the jungles, Mister

Peterson hated water. When the first drops of rain began to fall, he immediately took cover and rushed below deck. He had a morbid fear of being pushed over board and he was even terrified if someone threatened to throw water at him. Just reach for a glass of water and he was gone.

So when Don settled down to work, he spread out his tools and within reach kept a glass filled with water. If Mister Peterson came too close, he got doused. The system worked. Soon on deck we started storing half filled buckets of water to keep Mister Peterson at bay. For strangers standing on shore it must have looked ridiculous, to see three or four crew running around the deck with buckets of water waiting for a defenceless monkey to come down from the rigging. But that was only the beginning. The spectacle got much worse when we discovered that water pistols worked just as well as buckets.

We bought water pistols and took to wearing them tucked into our belts. The pistols worked wonders. Slap your side like you were going to draw and Mister Peterson fell back. But our reputations began to suffer. Full grown men carrying water pistols! It was really embarrassing if we forgot and went ashore with pistols. We had a hard time explaining.

Mister Peterson brought us a lot of laughter and joy. I became accustomed to his moods and even came to know his facial expressions. When he turned up his nose, something was disagreeable. Or, if he turned his back, he didn't want to listen or be scolded. He would laugh when he was amused; he would actually throw back his head, bear his teeth and laugh. When someone told a joke, you could be sure Mister Peterson would laugh loudest.

Two months after Mister Peterson was aboard, Peter left to return home. Mister Peterson slipped into a state of remorse. It was weeks before he was back to his nasty normal self. By then we were at sea.

A week before we were to depart, Singapore immi-gration cracked down on yachtsmen. The policy had been if you were aboard your own vessel you could remain in port for an unspecified limit of time. This was the time of the oil boom in Southeast Asia. Anyone who could walk, or in some cases, swim, could get a job on an oil rig. Some yachtsmen skippered supply boats to the rigs. The pay was good, with two weeks on and two weeks off. Those who lived aboard their yachts had it made. Then for some unknown reason, the Singapore Immigration authorities realized it was all wrong. In one sweep they went to every yacht in Singapore and ordered the owners and crew to report to the court house. Everyone was given three days to get visas or move out, or else suffer heavy fines.

Someone told me about the Geneva Convention, that governments could not force a ship to go to sea that was unseaworthy. When it came my turn, I stood up in front of the judge and pleaded the Geneva Convention ruling.

"You have twenty-four hours to be out of Singapore," the judge said. I reminded him about the international law. "I regret to inform you," he continued, "but for your information Singapore is not a member of the Geneva Convention."

Every yachtsmen at the club helped us load supplies and empty our equipment stored at the club. We had hoped to make some trial runs before departing, but there was no time now. Our trial run was the real thing. With Don and Bret at the bow, I turned the key and the engine started. I revved it once or twice and put the clutch into forward. We began moving forward, slowly. I shouted at the top of my voice, "We've moving!"

Ed Boden was aboard. He was leading us through the

narrow channel to the outer roads, and there we planned to tie up to moorings and row him ashore.

Before our departure, Ed had spent the last few months teaching me and the crew navigation and boat handling. We could not have had a better teacher.

Ed is an incredible person, and one of the finest yachtsman I know. You get to know some fascinating people when you are around boats, and Ed Boden is an example. Often by their very nature, these people tend to shun public attention. They are looking for neither fame nor fortune. Their reason for doing what they do is infinitely more complex. Ed was sailing alone around the world in a twenty-five-foot boat. He was not insane nor was he a daredevil. He did have, in fact, a degree in mechanical engineering and left a high paying position with the Jet Propulsion Laboratory to see the world in his tiny boat. After ten years of sailing he saw nothing strange in what he was doing.

It was dusk when we got to the mooring. I pulled the dingy that we had been trailing up to the schooner and announced to Ed that I would row him ashore.

"The schooner isn't secured yet," he said.

"That's okay," I replied, "the crew will take care of it."

Ed didn't get into the dinghy. He called me aside so that no one could hear. "You are the captain," he said. "You are responsible for your ship and for the lives of everyone aboard. It is your duty and no one else's to make sure everything is secured before you leave your ship."

Ed's advice stuck and became my creed. Never once in the years that followed, as long as I was captain, did I leave the security to others. Only when the vessel was well moored or the anchor well set did I step ashore.

By midnight we rounded the southern tip of the Malay Peninsula at Horsburgh Light and turned northward to-

Chinese friends and friends of friends were quick to come aboard *Third Sea* when we arrived back in Singapore from Thailand.

wards Thailand. It was a splendid feeling to be at sea in a ship that I had built, even if it wasn't completed. I was beginning to feel freedom that I had never imagined possible. I was realizing that this tiny vessel was a world unto itself, and that we alone were responsible for our safety and well being. There was no drug store around the corner, no machine shop down the road, no telephone we could use to call for help. We were our own masters, and if we got into difficulty, we ourselves had to get out of it. It was that simple.

We celebrated Mister Peterson's first birthday at sea. He had grown in the short time that he had been with us. He now stood up to my waist and was strong as a bull. In the beginning when he was naughty we often put him in the dinghy which we pulled aft of the schooner. Mister Peterson would sit solemnly in the dinghy and look up at us, very annoyed. After a few weeks he was able to sit in the dinghy, take hold of the painter (rope) and pull the dinghy up to the schooner. He would then leap aboard. He could also get into the dinghy any time he desired by pulling it up to the schooner.

Mister Peterson proved to be an excellent master-at-arms. When we were anchored and a boat approached, he gave the alarm, and then jumped up and down threatening to tear anyone apart who dared come aboard without permission. Other times he might hide, and when people did step aboard, he would swoop down and in one swing remove their glasses or hats. Then up into the rigging he'd go, whooping and hollering. After the first experience people never stepped aboard unless they were invited.

The sun beat down unmercifully and we were anxious to reach the mouth of the Chao Phraya River where we were to rendezvous with Bob Stevens, the owner of the yard where we were heading.

"We have to wait until it's dark," Bob said when he came aboard.

"Dark! Why do we have to wait until it's dark?" I asked.

"Because we can't bring an unfinished boat into Thailand without a lot of papers and red tape."

"Then what do we do?"

"We sneak in!"

And so began *Third Sea*'s first real adventure. Under the cover of darkness we slipped silently up the Chao Phraya River into the forgotten world of Joseph Conrad, past government patrol boats, around a Thai Navy check point guarding the river entrance, and in that darkness we somehow found the entrance to the canal. We then slowly motored up the narrow congested waterway to our final destination, and our home for the months to come while we outfitted. It was to be one of the most rewarding experiences of my life.

Third Sea under sail from Thailand to Singapore.

Chapter 6

SOJOURN IN THAILAND

The very moment we reached Colorado Eastern, Bob Steven's boat yard located a mile or so up the narrow canal—they call them klongs there—I knew we were in for trouble.

The klong was narrow and trees reached down to the very water's edge. There would be no keeping Mister Peterson aboard now unless he was locked up or tied. For the first time I had to destroy his freedom and tie him up. He didn't like that, not at all. We had a few Singha beers to celebrate our arrival and turned in for the night. The following morning the serious work would begin.

At dawn, when all was still and workers had not arrived yet, I heard a sudden commotion on the river bank. I turned over, trying to drown out the noise, but the ruckus grew louder. I went on deck. Mister Peterson was gone! He had untied himself. I immediately knew the noise had to be his doing.

Adjoining the boat yard on the left was a chicken farm, and Mister Peterson had never seen chickens before. Until now that is. The owner of the yard, when he saw me, came screaming and shouting. He motioned for me to follow him. He entered a fenced-in yard, and there sitting in the middle was Mister Peterson, clutching a chicken, pulling out its feathers. Hundreds of chickens were fluttering all about him, feathers flying. Eggs were dumped everywhere. I knocked over nests and feeders chasing after Mister Peterson, and when I finally caught him, the owner tore into me. He was livid with rage. "I'll pay," I shouted. "I'll pay for everything." I made further promises to both him and Bob Stevens. I swore I'd keep Mister Peterson tied up securely after that. That night I put a double bowline around his waist. He managed to untie it again.

The noise the next morning was twice as loud, and this time Bob Stevens was doing the ranting. "You and that damn monkey," he screamed. "Now look what he's done."

I looked toward the chicken yard. "No, not there," he shouted. "Over there!" He pointed to an enclosed field on the opposite side of the boat yard from the chicken farm. He pointed to a papaya orchard.

Several hundred trees made up the orchard. There were papaya trees in every stage of growth, with fruit the size of walnuts and others fully grown and ripe. My heart stopped. Mister Peterson couldn't have. But he had. If he had eaten half a dozen papayas I could understand. But no! He had leaped around from tree to tree, and had taken single bites out of all the ripe papayas. He didn't miss one in the entire orchard.

We were ordered to either get rid of Mister Peterson or else leave immediately. We couldn't leave. Our work had just started.

"I'll give you a hand," a voice said during the heat of the argument with the owner of the papaya orchard. A man stepped up and introduced himself. He had an American accent. He explained he owned a charter junk at Pattaya, a beach resort down the coast. He had a pet baby gibbon who had fallen overboard and drowned the week before. The man said he would watch Mister Peterson for the next few months while we were in the yard. We were saved.

Occasionally news reached us from Pattaya. Mister Peterson was having the time of his life on the tourist junk. He had all the attention he wanted. He was a hero with all the guys. He had an act whereby he would hide when young ladies clad in bikinis came aboard, and then he would swoop down from behind and in one movement untie their bikini tops and whip them off, and then go howling to the top of the rigging. We missed the little bugger, but at least we could get work done. We'd pick him up when we sailed away.

Once secure on the klong, with a corps of skilled Thai carpenters and shipwrights working on her, at the pay of two dollars a day each, and with a stack of teak on the dock, a year's work lay ahead. *Third Sea* would have to be the very best I could make her. She didn't need fancy gear and sophisticated modern equipment. She needed to be strong, and tough. Aside from being able to sail any ocean through any sea she had to capture the spirit of adventure. And that came from putting love into her.

For a year we worked six days a week, sometimes twelve hours a day. Four and as many as eight carpenters worked full time and turned the schooner from a bare hull into a fine work of art. They took nearly three tons of

Stepping the masts without the use of a crane.

teak which they trimmed, shaped and carved to form rails, banisters, ladders, louvered doors, arched passageways, tables, seats and everything from binocular holders to door stops. There wasn't anything they couldn't do with teak.

But even more amazing were the carvings the craftsmen turned out. All custom made. It was an awkward process, but one which worked. First the boards, such as the ten-foot-long drip boards under the windows, were fitted into place, then removed. These I carted to Chieng Mai in northern Thailand by bus and train, and where I turned them over to my friend, Swiss artist Theo Meier. Theo had spent twenty-five years on Bali and the last ten years in Thailand. He was quite well known when I knew him in Chieng Mai, but it wasn't until after his death in 1983 that his fame spread. Oils that he was selling for a hundred dollars and less in Chieng Mai were now on auction at Christie's in London for $25,000 and more. I can't even imagine the present day value of the many carvings Theo did for *Third Sea*.

Even Theo had let himself get caught up in the romance of *Third Sea*. He envisioned himself and Prince Sandith Rangsit, his friend of many years, sailing with us to the Marquesas Islands in French Polynesia. Following in the footsteps of Gauguin, Theo had gone to paint in the Marquesas when he was still young, and he longed to return to visit the islands one day. He seriously considered returning aboard *Third Sea*. A few years later, when we were in the Marquesas, Theo lay dying in a hospital in Switzerland.

When I brought the teak boards to Chieng Mai, Theo sketched out patterns on them and then with his carvers he set to work. When the carvings were completed I carried them back to Bangkok by train and then put them aboard a bus that would carry me down river to the boat yard on the klong. There was never a problem on the train, and getting aboard a bus was simple. The train arrived in Bangkok early in the morning and the buses were nearly empty. But by the time I reached my destination down river, there was hardly room to stand, and the carvings, wrapped in paper, were on the floor in the isle. It was pandemonium when I tried to retrieve the boards, with everyone in a packed bus standing on top them. How I ever got the carvings out of the bus and back to the schooner still baffles me. There may have been better ways of transporting them, but I couldn't afford it.

Back aboard ship, the carpenters installed the finished products in their proper places. Sometimes attempting to cut costs actually cost me more money in the long run, like the time I made plywood fuel tanks which I took into town to have a metal smith make duplicates out of steel.

When I took the tanks back to the schooner, they didn't fit. I learned that the welders had used the plywood for molds but assembled them wrong. I still had to pay. After that, I got the workmen to do their own measuring.

A blacksmith forges a mast-head fitting for *Third Sea*. Much of the work on the schooner was done by hand, with patience and care.

Much of the work was tedious and took a great deal of patience. For example, deadeyes, those wooden blocks along the sides of old sailing ships that held the rigging in place, went out of style with square riggers. But dead-eyes I had to have. Don drew up plans from photographs of old sailing ships. Then things like weaving a net at the bowsprit and lacing rope ratlines to the schrouds required endless hours. But gradually everything began to fit into place. I did manage to keep her in traditional design, with chain plates, channels, a fife rail and jutting bowsprit— all for aesthetic reasons. And I did my best to keep the operation simple, with mechanical pumps and windlass rather than going electrical. Our lighting was by oil lamps as well as battery powered, in case of generator failure.

At last, masts went up; carved dragons were fastened to the sides of the hull; and trail boards with the name THIRD SEA on one side and HONOLULU on the other

Schooner *Third Sea* had few mechanical winches. Instead the crew made use of a fife rail with belaying pins, like ships of old.

were bolted securely into place on the bow. I registered *Thrid Sea* in Singapore with Honolulu as home port.

The day for our departure seemed to arrive suddenly. *Third Sea* was completed and stores were brought aboard. Excitement had built to a fever pitch. Our first port-of-call after leaving the Chao Phraya would be Pattaya Beach where we would pick up Mister Peterson. A dozen friends wanted to make the maiden voyage. Robin Dannhorn had helped me plan the schooner from the very beginning. Tony Waltham had been publishing my articles every week in the *Bangkok Post*, and I couldn't leave him behind. Don and Bret had awaited this day for more than a year. And there was Mike Yamashita, a Japanese American who joined the crew for the run to Singapore, and who proved to be most valuable. We were prepared; we would leave the next morning. And then Bob Stevens, looking up at the masts that towered nearly eighty feet above the klong, said, "I hope you can get under the wires."

"Wires, what wires?" I asked.

"The high voltage power lines that cross the klong down at the entrance. You must have seen them."

I hadn't see them. How could I have? It was dark when we came in. Immediately I took our dinghy and went down the waterway to investigate. Sure enough, at a village near the entrance, high voltage wires crossed the klong. The clearance couldn't have been more than fifty feet. In desperation I went to the village and looked up the headman. I explained the predicament, and asked if he could possibly remove the wires so that we could pass the next morning. He pondered it for a long time. I handed him four five-hundred baht notes, worth about one-hundred U.S. Dollars. He nodded and assured me I could pass.

The next morning, with everyone aboard, we cast off

the mooring lines, and glided gently down the klong, waving farewell to those who had worked and watched us for the past year. The tide was going out and we began to pick up speed. My heart was in my mouth. I should have checked that morning. What if the headman hadn't removed the power lines? I could electrocute everyone aboard. I hadn't told a sole aboard about the power lines. "Why so tense?" Robin Dannhorn asked. "Everything will be all right." If he had only known!

We drifted around the last bend, and dead ahead was the village. The power lines were gone! The headman had kept his promise. I looked again, and did a double take. The power lines hadn't simply been removed. The telephone poles had been blown up. Only the stubs of splintered wood poked upwards. The headman stood on the bank in front of the village and waved as we passed. I never did tell the crew what had happened.

We soon entered the mighty Chao Phraya River. The river here is wide as a lake with the traffic of Times Square—tramp steamers, weather-beaten freighters, salt junks, Bugis traders and tugs pulling long strings of heavy-laiden rice barges. It was real now; we were part of Conrad's world. Here was the same river that he had sailed and written about. His descriptions are as valid today as when he first penned them more than a century ago.

Still ahead was the treacherous Bangkok bar, a sand bar far out at sea that has to be crossed with caution. But that would come later. First we had to clear customs and immigration. We dropped anchor and decided to clear the following morning. We had dinner on deck, watching the pageantry of river life on the Chao Phraya. It was a great feeling to be afloat, like a new born baby who has been cut free from its umbilical cord. We were like that baby.

Chapter 7

DOWN TO THE SEA IN A SHIP

Clearing customs and immigration at any port is always a concern, and often a worry. Aside from a crew list, the ship's papers must be presented, and if everything is in order, including all port fees paid, a port clearance is then issued. It is impossible to enter any foreign port without such a clearance from the last port. It's the first thing the authorities want to see. Now came the big question, how difficult was it going to be for me to get my clearance? Bob Stevens had registered the schooner in Thailand. Although the hull was laid in Singapore, *Third Sea* was registered as a Thai-built vessel. Then came the question I was told I would be asked.

"Who's your captain?" the officer asked sternly. He was dressed in a white naval uniform. His gold epaulets sparkled.

"I am," I replied, rather proudly.

"Your papers," the officer then said.

"Papers, certainly," I replied. "My master's papers."

I breathed a sight of relief and handed him my papers. He carefully checked them over and slid them back across the counter. The papers were official. I had been worried, needlessly. Bob Stevens was right. I didn't have to worry.

Several weeks before we departed, I had learned that any vessel registered in Thailand, whether private yacht or commercial vessel, has to have a captain aboard who is in possession of a valid master's certificate. Anywhere else in the world the skipper of a cruising yacht is not required to have a master's certificate. Not in Thailand. And to hire a skipper to take *Third Sea* out of the country was impossible. I didn't have the money to hire anyone.

Bob Stevens had an accountant working for him who I was told could arrange anything. "Your papers, get your master's papers," he said when I asked what I can do.

"I want to leave in two weeks," I said. "I don't have the time to study for my master's certificate."

"You don't have to," the accountant said and reached for the telephone. He dialed a number, mumbled a few words in rapid Thai and then dialed another number. The conversation went on for ten minutes. Finally he hung up. "Okay, Monday morning at nine," he said. "We have to be at Naval Headquarters near Krung Thon Bridge." He hesitated, and then added, "It will cost you fifteen hundred baht, about seventy-five dollars."

At nine o'clock at Naval Headquarters that Monday morning I was ushered into a room where three stern Thai Naval officers sat behind a long table. They were all in uniform. The officer in charge spoke up. "You have your papers with you?"

I had not the slightest idea what he was talking about. I looked around for the accountant but he was nowhere to be seen. "Papers, I don't know what you mean," I said.

"Your master's certificate. You want your U.S. license to be certified by us, don't you?" he asked gruffly.

I had to think of something quickly. Obviously there had been a mistake. The accountant must have thought I already had my papers. "I didn't think I needed to bring them," I said, not knowing how else to respond.

Just then the accountant entered the room from a back door and briskly walked up to the officer in charge. He then handed him an envelope. The officer peeked in the envelope, then opened a drawer and shoved it inside.

"Well," he said. "No papers. I'm afraid you must take a test." He opened a book on the table and then shoved it toward me. He flipped to a marked page. There were hundreds of little circles on the page. "Tell me," he continued, "what letter do you see?"

"The letter G," I said. Any child who wasn't color blind could have seen that. I suddenly realized what was happening; it was all beginning to fall into place. The officer had received the money but he had said I would have to take a test, and he couldn't loose face. He had to give me a test. This simple color blind test was the solution.

He stood up, followed by the other two officers, and held out a hand. "Congratulations," he said, "you passed. You can pick up your papers in a few days."

The accountant led me out the front door and down to the river ferry landing. "You mean that's all there was to it?" I said. "I now have my master's papers, that simple!"

"It cost you fifteen hundred baht, didn't it!" he replied.

I thought for a moment. "What if I wanted my pilot's license, maybe to fly a 747," I said jokingly.

"Oh," he said, "that would have cost you a lot more."

Stephens, left, studies the rigging on the maiden sailing voyage from Thailand to Singapore; while crew, right, checks the ratlines.

I did wonder about the validity of my Thai master's papers. A few month's later I found out. I had accepted a charter with a group of high school students from the American School in Singapore. *Third Sea* passed the inspection, and then I was asked if I was a certified master. I produced my Thai papers. They were accepted.

And so, on a bright sunny morning on the Chao Phraya, we weighed anchor. It was a happy day to sail through Conrad's world down river, "past the rows of low attaps and great gilded Buddhas," cross the sand bar at the mouth and enter the Gulf of Thailand.

Once we cleared the bar, we raised sails. First was the main staysail, then the staysail jib. *Third Sea* responded magnificently. With all hands on the halyard we raised the main sail next. It seemed to take forever to reach the top. *Third Sea* now heeled to port on a broad reach. Next we hoisted the main jib, and then the fisherman at mid ship. She heeled farther to port. Last, we raised the flying jib. All six sails billowed in the breeze as we sailed onward toward Pattaya. At sunset we anchored a hundred yards off shore.

The next morning I went ashore to find the tourist junk that had Mister Peterson aboard. There was no tourist junk anywhere. We learned after a long inquiry that the owner, the man whom we gave Mister Peterson to hold, had sold the boat, and Mister Peterson went with it. The boat and our siamang were gone. For years after that, every yacht I encountered, I looked to see if Mister Peterson might be aboard. We were never that fortunate.

The voyage to Singapore was our shake down cruise. It was not without incident. We discovered what effects currents can have upon a sailing boat with a deep keel, and how to take advantage of them. We also learned you can never trust your anchor.

I recall reading in a yachting magazine about an interview with a yachtsman who has just completed a circumnavigation of the world. The reporter asked him which were the most violent seas he had encountered—the Horn, the Roaring Forties, the North Alantic. None of these. He said the worst seas he had witnessed were in the Gulf of Thailand. At the time I found it was hard to believe such a statement. But after I sailed the Gulf aboard *Third Sea* during the northeast monsoon, I believed the yachtsman. It took us a week of continuous pounding, and then with periods of no wind, to reach Songkhla on the coast of southern Thailand. Here we rowed Tony Waltham ashore. I regretted seeing him leave. For a year he had faithfully published my stories every Sunday in the *Bangkok Post,* and he looked forward to joining *Third Sea* on her maiden voyage. Later when we did have good sailing, and oftentimes didn't have to trim a sail for days, and sometimes not even touch the helm, I often thought about Tony. He

Schooner *Third Sea* on her maiden voyage heels far to port to a stiff breeze on her southernly course from Thailand to Singapore.

did, however, continue to publish my stories, about diving on the *HMS Repulse,* searching for Jack Kennedy's PT-109 and living with cannibals in the New Hebrides.

After fighting bad weather for a week, and saying goodbye to Tony in Songkhla, we entered Malaysian waters, and seeing what looked like a peaceful island on the chart, we decided to put in for the night. We needed a rest. The island was Redang, some fifteen miles off the Malay coast. It had a small harbor and fishing village at the water's edge. The harbor was jammed with fishing boats, leaving us with no choice but to anchor off shore in fifteen fathoms. It was much too deep for us, as our anchor scope was not much more than two to one, but there was little else we could do. We didn't want to let out more chain for fear of swinging into the fishing boats.

We should have known something was about to happen when all the fishing boats suddenly dropped their moorings and began leaving the harbor. Minutes later the wind began, and then the chop. With each swell the bow rose high into the air, and then dropped, like an elevator whose cables had broken. Suddenly we heard a loud snap! We knew immediately the anchor chain had broken. The bow swung around and now the wind drove us head on towards the rocks. Don switched on the engine and threw it into full throttle. We missed the rocks by mere inches, and it was all we could do to clear the point at the harbor entrance before we reached the open sea.

At one time, when the wind was at its worst, I went below deck to warn the others that we were in danger. A few days before at Songkhla, we had picked up a young married couple who wanted to sail to Singapore with us. The woman looked up when she saw me enter the cabin. "I want you to know it's bad out there," I began, but before I could continue, she spoke up.

"If you are coming to cheer us up, you don't have to. We are not concerned. We know the ship is in good hands."

"I just wanted to check," I said and went back on deck where Don, Bret and Mike were battling the elements. I was glad someone had confidence in us.

We had to return the next day after the winds had abated to try to retrieve our anchor. We had no scuba gear, only masks, snorkels and flippers. It looked hopeless, free diving in ninety feet of water. Everyone was ready to give up, except Mike. He made one last dive and this time succeeded in locating the anchor and chain. He made a second dive and tied a line to the chain. We were able to pull the anchor and chain aboard. Mike was our hero.

With the bad weather behind us, we sailed a leisurely course south along the Malaysian coast, but we became increasingly more anxious to return to Singapore to meet friends and show off our *Third Sea*. We sailed past a string of beautiful islands—Tioman, Sibu, Rawa, Tinggi—and

The southern tip of Tioman Island off the east coast of the Malay Peninsula as seen from the deck of schooner *Third Sea*.

neared the southern tip of the Malay Peninsula as night fell. It was one of those black, evil nights when there is no moon. It was impossible to tell where sky and sea met, except, when in the far distance streaks of lightening lit up the skies in blinding flashes. Other than the flashes, the only light came from the dim red glow of the binnacle reflecting on the face of the helmsman.

Tension began building in all of us. We knew that only a short distance ahead were some of the most dreaded rocks and shoals in the South China Sea, and yet there seemed no way of avoiding them. For five thousand years seafarers have feared this same passage, down the Malay coast and around the tip of the peninsula to Singapore and the Malacca Strait beyond. But unlike those early navigators who had to rely on chance and luck, we did have an aid, a lighthouse somewhere out there in that black void. We searched hard for that light, scanning the blackness when suddenly it appeared, ever so brightly. Could it be reflection! A glare! We waited, binoculars gripped tightly—eight seconds, nine, ten. "That's it!" I shouted almost jubilantly to Mike at the helm."That's it, every ten seconds. Horsburgh Light!" We relaxed; it was clear sailing now. We altered course due west for Singapore.

Over the years that followed, I always got that same feeling when I stood at the helm of *Third Sea* and watched Horsburgh Light come into view. I'm sure for every sailor the blinking of Horsburgh has a soothing effect.

But it wasn't always this way. A little more than a hundred years ago neither Horsburgh Light nor any other light marked these treacherous shoals. Navigators before that time simply had to chance it. The odds were greatly stacked against them, as the bottom of the sea to this day will testify. On several occasions, when the weather was calm, we anchored *Third Sea* off Horsburgh Light, put on snorkels and fins and explored the sea bottom. Only a few fathoms below the surface we found the ocean floor littered with endless pieces of broken pottery, all from wrecked ships.

Few sea lanes of the world have seen more traffic than these waters. It was past these rocks, where Horsburgh Light stands today, that early Arab traders had to make their way two thousand years ago; it was Chinese Admiral Cheng Ho who managed to evade destruction by sailing his fleet of sixty-two ships with a force of 37,000 men around the point and through Singapore's Dragon Teeth Gate; and later came the early Portuguese and Spanish followed by the Dutch and the English. The number of ships that split open their sides and spilled their guts on the ocean floor around Horsburgh is anyone's guess.

The total amount of ships lost may never be known but records do show that between 1824 and 1851 there were

Searching for the Horsburgh Light at the southern tip of the Malay Peninsula. Before the light the passage was a seaman's nightmare.

at least sixteen large vessels wrecked at Horsburgh. Even during its construction a bark loaded with tea was ship-wrecked on the rocks nearby. The crew survived by swimming to the construction site.

Once we past Horsburgh Light we turned westward and aimed the bow toward the glow in the sky that was Singapore. At dawn we were all on deck to see one of the great ports of the Far East come into view. Miles before we arrived we began to pass ships at anchor, and as we drew nearer the outer roads, hundreds more appeared. It's reported that every day of the year some two hundred and sixty ships come and go, making Singapore one of the busiest ports in the world.

Much of Singapore's waterfront has been reclaimed in recent years and a bridge and elevated highway now skirt the area closing off the inner harbor to larger ships. But then when we sailed down from Bangkok, there was no bridge, and we anchored right downtown in front of the Clock Tower, in full view of everyone who passed.

A happy skipper arrives back in Singapore aboard *Third Sea* after spending more than a year outfitting at a shipyard in Thailand.

We were a mighty proud crew, with a mighty fine look-ing vessel. Friends came aboard and for a week there were parties every night. For a dollar, sampan boys sculled pas-sengers back and forth. All someone had to do was walk along the quay and a sampan boy would yell out, "*Third Sea,* you want go *Third Sea?*"

Jim Mathews who had worked so hard helping me build *Third Sea* was planning to rejoin us in Singapore for our sail across the Pacific, but he had met a lovely English lass and they had married and gone to live in Hawaii. And Peggy Lou, her fiance had sent for her and they married. A few years later she gave birth to a son, and the last thing I heard she was giving Chinese cooking lessons on TV. Mort Rosenblum and his wife Randi were also gone; he left the AP to become Editor-in-Chief of the Paris *International Herald Tribune.* And I couldn't find out what happened to Mohan nor Adrian Nuinis. The only good friend left was Beno Anciano. He had resigned from the plywood company and set up a telephone an-swering service in town.

Mike Yamashita left us in Singapore but I wished he could have stayed aboard for our Pacific crossing. He was an excellent crew but he had other things he wanted to do. We would miss him. While he was aboard, he did his best to keep *Third Sea* shipshape. He made sure lines were coiled, that things were stowed properly and that laundry was left out to dry no longer than necessary. He had a purpose. He was a very serious photographer, one who worked hard at his profession, and was constantly taking pictures. When he first came to the schooner at Colorado Eastern he said he would like to sail with us. I admit I liked him from the start for he was sincere with dogged determination to do well. He had given up a career in the family business to become a photographer. I introduced him to a couple magazine editors in Bangkok. He sold his first photograph for fifteen dollars. Twenty years later the name Mike Yamashita is a household word in the field of photography. It has appeared in photo captions in every major magazine in the U.S., and a half dozen times his photographs have been used to illustrate feature pieces in the *National Geographic.* He and a staff writer for the *Graphic* spent a year on the Mekong River tracing it from its source deep in the mountains of China to its mouth in the Mekong Delta of Vietnam. He is one of the highest paid photographers in America today. *Third Sea* was his springboard.

I longed to take *Third Sea* to the South Pacific, but there was still a lot of cruising in Southeast Asia that I wanted to do. One place was the Malacca Strait, all the way from Singapore up to Phuket, the island in southern Thailand, on the Andaman Sea side, that has become world famous as a tourist resort. We also had opportunities to do chartering in both Malacca and Phuket which would help add a few dollars to our ship's coffer. We now turned towards the Malacca Strait, one of the most interesting stretches of water in the world.

Schooner *Third Sea* on a port tack in the Malacca Strait.

Andaman and the South China Seas, cruising waters for *Third Sea*.

Chapter 8

VOYAGING THROUGH HISTORY

Cruising yachtsmen are forever arguing which is the greatest sailing passage of the Pacific? Is it the Molokai Channel between the islands of Oahu and Molokai in the Hawaiian group? The Uturoa Pass between Raiatea and Tahaa in French Polynesia? The Torres Strait between northern Australia and New Guinea? I've sailed each of them aboard *Third Sea*, some more than once, but the one I favor the most, and which many skeptics may disagree, is the Strait of Malacca between the Malay Peninsula and Sumatra. Yachtsmen who sail from Singapore to Phuket in Thailand make the passage through the Strait as quickly as they can, not bothering to stop en route. To them the Strait is a sailing hazard and they want to get it over as quickly as possible. It is one of the busiest shipping lanes in the world. But there's also another side to the Strait of Malacca.

For centuries for as long as man has taken to the sea in ships, no body of water in the world has seen more action, more drama and, perhaps, more bloodshed than the Strait of Malacca, where the Indian Ocean and the South China Sea meet. To sail through the Strait is to make a voyage not only forward over leagues of water but also one that takes you back through the pages of history. And what a history!

Five hundred years ago, in 1406 to be exact, Admiral Cheng Ho, envoy from the Emperor of China, sailed through Dragon Teeth Gate (which is Singapore today) and up the Strait of Malacca with an armada of sixty-two ships and thirty-seven thousand men to Malacca.

Imperial China's display of strength certainly must have impressed Sultan Mansur Shah of Malacca. Admiral Cheng Ho, history tells us, was a "Three-Jewelled" eunuch, meaning he had all his private parts amputated, and thus he became the Emperor's most trusted envoy. He had to be trusted. He was carrying a very special cargo, Princess Hong Lim Poh, the daughter of the Emperor of China, whose hand in marriage had been promised to the Sultan. She arrived, unharmed, with no less than five hundred ladies-in-waiting, all of them great beauties.

For reasons which still baffle historians, soon after Admiral Cheng Ho's seventh voyage, China isolated herself and withdrew from world trade, but another force was soon to change the face of Asia. In 1511, Malacca fell to the Portuguese.

Again, it was the desire for trade, in this case for spices, that drew the nations of Europe to the Far East. What birds' nests and agar-agar did for the Chinese, nutmeg and cinnamon did for the Europeans. Once Europeans felt the fineness of silk, once they adorned their homes with glazed ceramics and tasted spices from the Far East, they could not turn back. They wanted more, at any cost. In the early days before the shipping lanes were known, spices from the Far East were so valuable in Europe that a small bag of peppercorn might pay for the cost of outfitting a caravan and sending it across the Persian land routes to Asia. And so it began, with Malacca the focal point. The Dutch came in the wake of the Portuguese, followed by the British and then the French. Soon all the nations of Europe were going to war with one another for control of the rich spice routes to the Far East.

Over the years I had visited Malacca many times; now I was anxious to see it from the sea, from the deck of my own schooner. I had aboard translations of Admiral Cheng

Ho's chronicles. Another book I had read over and over, and earmarked the pages, was the *Golden Chersonese* by Isabella Bird, an elderly British lady who had cruised from Singapore through the Strait of Malacca to Penang aboard a rusted tramp steamer a hundred years ago. The book was compiled from her detailed journal of her voyage. I found as we cruised up the coast we could use Miss Bird's book as our own guide. It was history come alive.

The most difficult part of the passage is rounding the southern tip of the Malay Peninsula at Kukup before entering the Strait. Head winds are generally strong and currents run swift with many eddies. Nevertheless, by clearing at Finger Pier in Singapore in the morning a sailing yacht can reach Malacca in two days.

We arrived at Malacca in late afternoon and anchored off shore. We could easily identify the same landmarks Admiral Cheng Ho noted in his ship's log five centuries earlier. But what was most interesting was Miss Bird's comments: "I was greatly interested with that first view of Malacca, one of the oldest European towns in the East, originally Portuguese, then Dutch, and now, though under English rule, mainly Chinese."

At the time of Miss Bird's visit, the European population of Malacca was twenty-three males and nine females.

Cruise ships and visiting yachts anchor at sea near the mouth of the Malacca River. When the Portuguese arrived and captured the town from the Dutch back in 1511, the Malacca River was navigable, and as one observer reported, it was larger than the Genoa and Venice of its day. The river was still used by fishing boats when we arrived, so why not *Third Sea*? It was a mad idea, but wasn't that why I built the schooner!

Entering the river was not the problem; turning around was. The entire river is no more than a mile or two long.

Barges load and discharge their cargoes from godowns near the entrance where the river is at its widest—less than eighty feet. When it came time for us to turn around, we found we had only had inches to spare. Nevertheless, we spent a splendid week on the Malacca River, bathed in history.

One thing we hadn't considered was rats. They were a serious menace and infested the waterfront in hordes. At night they took over and had complete control. We had to close the hatches and the portholes next to the quay when darkness fell.

On our return voyage to Singapore several months later we were not so fortunate when we sailed up the Malacca River for the second time—and our last time. Rats did get aboard but we didn't discover them until we were back in Singapore. Getting rid of them became a near impossibility. We tried everything—poison, traps and even a smoke bomb. Nothing worked. Finally, Doug Tiffany, a fellow yachtsman, came up with a solution. A hunk of cheese on a piece of plywood, surrounded by sticky glue. It sounded like an ingenuous method, and he was kind enough to fashion the board for us and place it on the floor in the galley. It worked. The next morning we found a live rat stuck on the board. Doug rowed over to us, jubilant. He took the board, with the rat still stuck, and tossed it overboard. But instead of landing in the water, the board landed in his dinghy. The jolt jarred the rat loose and the animal was now running freely around the dinghy. Doug quickly jumped into the dinghy, and taking his oar began swinging at the rat. The rat was too quick. In a mad fury Doug made a mighty swing, brought the oar down as hard as he could, missed the rat and broke his oar. He upset the dinghy, knocking him and the rat into the water. The rat swam to shore. We pulled Doug out of the water.

Unfortunately, there was another rat still aboard *Third Sea*. Something had to be done. What I did next was not quite ethical but then we are not talking about ethics but about survival. Living aboard their junk at the Yacht Club were a couple of Australians. They had just purchased the vessel and were outfitting it on their own. I had a portable generator aboard which they asked if they could borrow for a day or two. I suggested they pull along side and tie up, and we could stretch an extension cord from *Third Sea* to the junk. They came along side. That night I opened my portholes facing the junk. The next morning I suggested they take the generator aboard and go back to their own mooring. They did. A few days later when they returned the generator, they said, "A strange thing happened; we got a rat aboard."

"He must have swum," I said. "They can do that, you know." So much said for rats.

North of Malacca the Strait narrows and becomes congested with shipping. Sometimes you can see dozens of ships at a time. Fortunately yachts and sailing vessels can hug the coast and keep clear of the busy waterways.

The South China Sea and the Indian Ocean meet in the Malacca Strait where *Third Sea* has anchored below the Rochado Lighthouse.

Less than a day's sail from Malacca is Cape Rochado with Port Dickson ten miles beyond. The Cape Rochado Lighthouse is one of the oldest and most colorful lighthouses in Asia. We anchored beneath its shadow and our crew climbed the rocky cliff to the top. Monkeys inhabit the forest around the lighthouse and come in swarms to pester visitors for handouts. The view from the summit is superb. Twice a day, when the tides change, you can actually see where the Indian Ocean and the South China Sea meet. They say that a hermit lives in a cave somewhere below the lighthouse, but he keeps well to himself. I have yet to see him.

Another anchor stop I always liked to make was at a small bay a few miles north of the cape. High on a cliff overlooking the Strait lives an Englishman, John Willoughby, his lovely Malay wife Ijah, and their three sons. As soon as I could set the anchor and row ashore, I'd follow a path that leads around the cliff to their home. Here on the verandah we would have rum punches, while *Third Sea* rested quietly at anchor far below. She made a splendid sight. John admired the schooner as much as I did; he had followed her construction from beginning to the end. In fact, *Third Sea* so inspired John that he built his own seagoing catamaran and began making yearly cruises with his family to Phuket. He and Ijah sailed with us from Port Dickson to Port Klang on our first journey up the Strait.

After Port Dickson came the Klang Estuary. Sails down now; engine on. Each time I chugged up the river past the maze of waterways that make up the estuary, I imagined myself reliving a Joseph Conrad novel. After a hundred years, the estuary is still much the same way Miss Bird described it: "Entering Klang, on either side are small rivers densely bordered by mangrove swamps. At low water the mangroves are seen standing close packed along the shallow and muddy shore standing five or six feet high on their own roots, but when these are covered at high tide they appear to be growing out of the water."

Countless small islands, some too tiny to name, make up the estuary. None seem more than a dozen feet above water. Casuarinas and scrub brush blanket the land down to the water's edge where the mud flats and mangroves begin. There's one island I like to visit above the others. It's called Ketam. It's a settlement with 16,000 Chinese inhabitants, ninety percent of whom are engaged in fishing. The town, constructed entirely of wood, is built high above the water on stilts, and when you walk the wooden plank streets, you have little idea that the sea is below.

A few of the other islands in the estuary are no less interesting. Lumut is inhabited by Malays with some Orang Asli living there. Orang Asli are the "original man" and the first inhabitants of the peninsula. On Lumut they are excellent wood carvers. Another attraction is Carey Island, settled by early English tea and rubber planters and now run by Tamils who emigrated from India in the last century. A third island is a bird sanctuary, but it's closed to visitors.

The main river, upon which Miss Bird found her steamer "occasionally dragging heavily over mud banks," has been dredged, and today even large supertankers and container ships steam up the river to Port Klang. In the roads near Port Klang great steamers and freighters and tour ships drop anchor, all with exciting and mysterious names. *Jaladharma* from India, *Orchard Garden*, Singapore. *Hana Maru*, Japan. And the luxury cruise ship *Island Princess* churns slowly through the waters en route to Penang and Sumatra.

Klang is one of the great ports of Asia. Until recently

it was called Port Swetenham, after the British resident who founded it little more than a hundred years ago. The construction was almost abandoned because of the heavy toll of lives lost through malaria. In 1901 it was saved, in part, by a British surgeon, Sir Malcolm Watson, who had seen similar problems in the construction of the Panama Canal. He had the swamps drained and almost completely eradicated the malaria-carrying mosquito.

But Miss Bird had arrived long before Dr. Watson began clearing the swamps. "I am dreadfully bitten on my ankles, feet and arms," she wrote, "which are so swollen that I can hardly draw on my sleeves, and for two days stockings have been an impossibility, and I have had to sew up my feet." We aboard *Third Sea* were somewhat more fortunate than Miss Bird.

Visiting yachts tie up to moorings at the Royal Selangor Yacht Club. We moored for the night, and enjoyed hot showers and dinner at the Club. At dawn the next morning, with the outgoing tide, we were again on our way.

We headed north up the estuary now, past small palm-fringed islands which suddenly open upon the sea, and which Miss Bird noted are "slightly green towards the coral-sanded densely wooded, unpeopled shores." And how pleasant to make the passage today by yacht, unlike the voyage which Miss Bird had made aboard the steamer *Rainbow.* But in her day there was no other choice.

"The Portuguese captain," she wrote in her book, "shouts in English, dances with excitement, and screams in Malay, while the ship rolls with the ground swells on the heated, shallow sea. The little steamer has submerged her load line and is only about ten inches above water; she is licensed to carry a hundred souls and has one hundred and fifty aboard." She and the captain dined while sitting on hen coops under an awning.

Before noon the next day we sighted the southern tip of Pangkor Island, and by afternoon we were sailing up the narrow channel between the island and the mainland, past an important historical landmark called the Dindings.

Pangkor is indented with coves and two bays along the channel. Two fishing kampongs, extended on stilts far out into the bay, look like scenes on picture postcards. At the north end of the island we altered course, tacked hard to our starboard and entered the Lumut River and ddropped anchor in front of the sleepy little Malay town of Lumut.

Lumut has one of the best yacht anchorages in all of Southeast Asia. It is well protected and tranquil, and has a small yacht club nestled in among the trees along the shore. The town has food stalls, restaurants, and rows of provision shops. And Lumut has mood. It's wholly an Asian town. Here yachtsmen can leave their boats in safety and go wandering through the Malay countryside.

Third Sea anchored at Lumut in the Dindings. The sheltered estuary offers some of the best anchorage in all Southeast Asia.

When I am anchored in front of the yacht club, and the sun is setting in a blaze of oranges and reds, I can feel Asia to the very tips of my fingers. It's a combination of many things—smells that come from the village, and sounds, the imans (Muslim priests) calling out evening prayers. I feel then that the world, our private world at least, is at peace.

But it wasn't always this way. For centuries the Dindings were the haunt of nasty marauding pirates. In an attempt to stop their raids, the Dutch had built a fort on Pangkor some 300 years ago—the ruins are still there and a tourist attraction—but it wasn't until the British arrived that piracy was finally curbed.

Piracy was rampant at the time of the founding of Singapore. Pirates had operated with impunity for decades in the China Seas from Hong Kong to the Indian Ocean. For centuries sailors trembled at the thought of passing through the South China Sea, day or night, and Pangkor Island was a major pirate stronghold, a menace to shipping in the Strait of Malacca. In a move to eradicate the pirates, the Sultan of Perak ceded Pangkor Island to the British in 1876, along with a narrow coastal strip called the Dindings. With control of both areas, Britain was able to combat the pirate problem.

The west side of Pangkor today is dotted with beach resorts. We anchored in one bay at the southern end of the island and hiked to the old Dutch fort. Chiseled on a boulder close to the ruins is the Dutch East India Coat of Arms. We gave the other bays a pass this time and with the first light of dawn sailed up the coast to the pearl of all islands—Penang.

Under full canvas we sailed up the chanel between Penang and the mainland and made a gallant entrance into Georgetown, the capital of Penang. Container ships,

Chinese junks, cruise ships, sampans, shiny yachts, rusted freighters, oil tankers—they are all part of the Georgetown waterfront. And like we did in Singapore, we sailed to the center of town and dropped anchor in front of the clock tower. Yachts can still do this in Penang, but not in Singapore.

Facing north from the Clock Tower to Kedah Point is the impressive Fort Cornwallis. It was there that Captain Francis Light anchored and decided to build a fort. But, the story goes, the Indian laborers refused to go ashore to clear the jungles. Neither cat-of-nine-tails nor threat of keel hauling would change their minds. So he simply loaded a ship's cannon with silver dollars and fired it into the jungles. He got the land quickly cleared and built Fort Cornwallis. He then claimed the island for Britain,

It's always a thrill to arrive in Penang by yacht. Having sailed the Strait of Malacca, you feel you are part of the world of adventure and not just an observer. You lower your dinghy and row ashore, and stand at the busy waterfront, and watch your little ship pulling at her anchor. Now you can understand why Isabella Bird wrote what she did when she arrived in Malacca in 1879—"These lovely Malacca Straits, this is one of the very few days in my life in which I have felt mere living to be a luxury, and what it is to be akin to seas and breezes, and to know why nature sings and smiles."

After leaving Penang, we sailed among the lovely Langkawi Islands and then continued our voyage northward to Thailand. Three days later we arrived at Phuket. I have more to say about Phuket later.

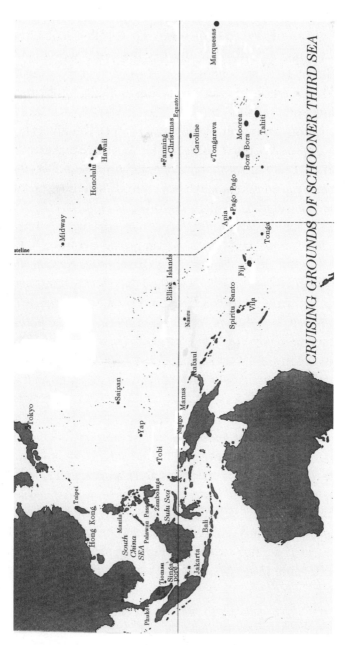

Voyages of Schooner *Third Sea* across the South Pacific.

Chapter 9

EASTWARD ACROSS THE PACIFIC

In *The Shadow Line*, Joseph Conrad wrote that any master who sailed his vessel from Singapore against the northeast monsoons to Hong Kong had to be a fool.

Perhaps he was right. I won't comment, for I sailed *Third Sea* against the very same monsoons to Hong Kong. It was a grueling difficult passage that took twenty-nine days to cover fifteen hundred miles. But then I went a step farther—I continued to sail against the trade winds and currents down through the Philippines to New Guinea and the Solomons and across the Pacific to Hawaii. It was a voyage everyone said was impossible.

To reach Honolulu from Singapore, I could have continued on around the world, across the Indian Ocean and around the southern tips of Africa and South America. Or I could have sailed northeast from Singapore to Japan and crossed the northern Pacific, or dropped south and taken the Roaring Forties. Or I could take the bull by the horns and fight my way directly across the central Pacific. Maybe I couldn't make it, as everyone said, but I could at least try. How did the early whaling ships do it? As for *Third Sea* holding up, I wasn't too worried. She was built to do the impossible. And by now I had full confidence in the schooner, myself and the crew. We could tackle most anything. Once we were back in Singapore, we began making plans and taking on supplies, using up what money we had saved from chartering.

The little things that must be done to outfit a vessel for the open seas are endless. You make a list and it seems to grow rather than diminish as new ideas are thought up and added. In the final days there were provisions that had to come aboard, enough to feed a crew of healthy eaters for months. I had to plan not days but weeks and even months ahead. And no longer could I think in small lots. I had to think in tons. We loaded two tons of food, a ton and a half of water and a ton of fuel! The crew was now anxious to depart. "How soon do we sail?" they wanted to know.

"Any day now," I answered. "As soon as the northeast monsoons end."

The monsoons were late. Usually winds begin to blow from the southwest by the end of March. This was April. "But why wait in Singapore?" everyone asked. "Could we not be at sea when they change?"

Perhaps they were right. Besides, Hong Kong from Singapore was only fifteen hundred miles. We decided to take the chance. We got port clearance and early the next morning weighed anchor. By late afternoon we were abreast of Horsburgh Light. Ahead was open ocean—the challenge!

The South China Sea rolled in from the northeast in huge swells, and the wind blew steady from the same direction at twenty knots. We were beating, hard into it, but no matter, we were free. *Third Sea* was leaving home waters for the first time.

The sea wouldn't let up and continued to pound from the northeast, day after day, unrelentingly. After a week of hard sailing we had barely covered three hundred miles. Furthermore, we were being pushed farther and farther south, toward Borneo. We were forced to tack north, now toward Vietnam. "Any day now," I kept repeating, "any day they will change." But they didn't.

In spite of the contrary winds and foul weather, it was a splendid feeling to stand on the tossing deck of my own schooner. I was learning much, about the sea, and about handling a crew. I was learning to recognize patterns in their behavior.

That excitement when new crew come aboard lasts about half a day after setting sail. It diminishes rapidly when the bow meets the first swells, and steadily decreases when the sails fill with gusty winds and the leeward rail dips deeply into the sea. For newcomers everything becomes awkward—sitting, walking, holding on. Sleeping, unbearably difficult. Cooking, an impossibility. By the end of the first day new members are convinced they can never adjust. They do, in about three days.

After a week at sea a new phase begins—boredom. One quickly learns life on the waves can be monotonous. There is a certain repetition in the sea and everything about it—the character of the waves, the colors, even the mood. Crew begin to ask themselves, "What am I doing here?" The feeling can become hopeless, filled with anxieties and deep depression, especially when one realizes the endless days and weeks ahead, and there is nothing, nothing they can do about it.

To break the monotony of the sea, a favorite pastime was to drag on a line behind the schooner, until the line broke one day.

The monotony of life at sea plays on one's mind. You look for ways other than reading to break the monotony. Before I began sailing I often thought the early whalers were very brave to chase giant whales in frail boats and with only a harpoon in hand. At sea I found it was monotony that made them do it. It was something to do.

One of our favorite pastimes was to drag from the stern on a fifty-foot length of line. It became great sport to leap over the rail and come up through bubbling, churning water in time to grab the line. Even more daring was to grasp the very end of the line with one hand and hold on. Your life was literally in your hand.

One hot afternoon I was on the helm when Bret was dangling from the stern. "Come in," he shouted, "it's great." Bret enjoyed the sport more then anyone. Often when porpoises came around, he took to the rope with his diving mask to study these sea-world mammals. Bret's call was tempting, but I couldn't leave the helm. Just then a new crew member came on deck.

"Take the helm," I said, and leaped over the rail. It was a rash move. I looked up to see the swirling water above, and grabbed hold of the line a few feet in front of Bret. But it did no good! Our combined weight, moving through the water at three or four knots, was too much for the rope. It parted with a snap. Stunned, we watched *Third Sea*, heeling gently to starboard, riding the waves, sail slowly away.

Bret and I began shouting, but the helmsman was too intently watching the compass to turn around. Again we shouted. No response. The frightening feeling of perishing alone on an empty sea took hold. We suddenly became conscious of all the horrors of the sea, of some evil demons shooting up from mysterious depths to drag us back into their dark, watery world.

Fishing not only provided protein to our diet but it also became keen
competition for the crew. We trolled day and night, in all weather.

Don, who had been sleeping in the aft cabin, heard us. He came on deck, looked around, and for a moment I thought he would go below again. Instead, he glanced back, and in the next instant turned the schooner into the wind. Twenty minutes passed before we were safe aboard.

The mishap didn't discourage us from dragging. At least not for the moment. We did stop, however, when we reached New Britain in the western Pacific. We would hook fifty-pound tunas, and before we could reel them in, we lost them to sharks. In one bite the sharks took everything but the heads.

Fishing was another favorite pastime, both profitable and challenging. We always had more fish than we could eat—tuna, barracuda, mahi mahi, yellow fin. Most of the larger fish, over four feet, we lost, until we made a long gaff and learned how to use it.

Several interesting groups of islands appear in the South China Sea between Singapore and Hong Kong. I was most curious about the Anambas, and after we tacked north they came within sight. They appeared inhospitable and steep, and offered little in the way of anchorage. Bleak and barren, the seas around them were empty. Not even a fishing vessel. Nevertheless, we decided to anchor at the southwest side of Pulau Repong, to spear lobster—but sharks came in and chased us off.

The winds and currents now carried us precariously close to the coast of Vietnam. We could see the peninsula shimmering in the distance, no more than twenty-five miles away. Vietnamese fishermen sailed by in sampans, unsmiling and unfriendly, wearing camouflage fatigues. We changed our tack to the east.

Twenty-four days out of Singapore we were less than halfway. Still the northeast monsoons continued. A little after midnight on the twenty-fifth day, the winds stopped completely. Just before dawn came a slight breeze, from the south. By noon the southwest monsoons arrived. We were moving now at seven knots in the right direction. Four days later we reached Hong Kong.

For the cruising yachtsman, Hong Kong is one of the most thrilling harbors of Asia. You know you are in Asia when you arrive. With full canvas set we sailed between Victoria and Kowloon, dodging ferries, and we couldn't resist sailing past the breakwater into the Royal Hong Kong Yacht Club located in the Causeway Bay typhoon center, only to find we were reported missing at sea.

We wanted to remain longer than two weeks in Hong Kong, but the typhoon season was rapidly approaching. With a crew of eight, including Hong Kong Editor Jim Shaw and his wife, we set sail for Manila. Now, instead of too much wind, it was the lack of it.

Left, Matts takes a high dive. With more than 7,000 islands, the Philippines has endless coves, all which offer safe anchoring and good swimming. Right, *Third Sea* anchored off shore in Zamboanga.

In the early days I refused to turn on the engine unless it was absolutely necessary, which didn't always go too well with passengers. We were becalmed for days on end. Poor Jim Shaw. He spent all his vacation at sea, waiting for wind. On our tenth day we sailed past Corregidor and entered Manila Bay. We anchored at the splendid Manila Yacht Club.

The Philippines passed in a swirl of magnificent islands, more than 7,000 of them, some inhabited, others not. We anchored in such lovely bays as Puerto Galeria on Mindoro, Romblon, the marble island, Roxas City on Panay Island and the delightful Cebu City on Cebu.

When we arrived in Cebu, Bret Anderson announced he was dropping out. He had been offered a teaching job at the International School in Singapore and decided to take it. "I don't want to disappoint you," he said, "but cruising is not really what I had expected." He was being honest. Few people will admit they don't like the sea, or fear it, and they make any excuse imaginable to quit. They phone home and say their grandmother is sick and they have to return, or their office wants them back, or their mother and father are suddenly getting divorced or they have a doctor's appointment which they completely forgot. I swear, I had one young fellow say he had a pin in his shoulder and forgot but his doctor had told him not to go sailing. I was glad to see him go. But not Bret. He had worked for almost two years on *Third Sea* and ahead were the good sailing days. He thanked us and returned to Singapore. He's director of the International School today.

We continued south to Zamboanga, a port right out of *Terry and the Pirates*. We were hoping to pick up more crew, but when we arrived the place was ready to explode, literally. No sooner had we dropped anchor than the entire thirty-six-member military staff of President

Marcos who had come to talk peace with the Moslem rebels were assassinated at the conference table.

We were told by the navy to get out immediately or the rebels would blow us out of the water. We dared not wait around to pick up crew and were considering sailing north to Cebu again when an offer came to sneak four women, wives of political refugees, out of the country. The women wanted to go to Sandakan in Borneo, a three or four day sail to the south. The problem was that our route had to border the pirate infested Sulu islands. The women pleaded with us to take them. There was nothing illegal about it, they insisted. They had their passports and they aggreed to check into immigration once we arrived in Sandakan. The price was also right. We told them to get their gear and come aboard.

A storm, one which grounded the planes at Manila airport fifteen hundred miles away, drove us close to the hostile islands. Then it happened. Under full sail, while we were doing five knots, we saw a yellow prow on the horizon. It was a Sulu boat. We watched it, hoping we would go unnoticed, but no luck. It altered course and came swooping down at us, intending to cut across our bow. Just before they did, at a hundred yards, I turned on our engine and we shot forwards, towards an approaching rain squall. The vessel now had to veer and cut across our stern, and as they did they drew their weapons and began firing. I don't believe they were aiming directly at us, but only wanted us to stop. We didn't and continued for the squall, with all hands on deck to show our numbers. For some reason, they did not continue the chase.

Sandakan turned out to be a restful retreat with secure anchorage at the Sandakan Yacht Club. After we arrived I discovered the Straits Steamship Company had service to Singapore. Leaving *Third Sea* in Don's charge, I sailed aboard *Raja Brooke* and spent a needed week in Singapore. I had to buy supplies, which included a new anchor chain, see my editors and turn in the few chapters I had completed to *Asian Portraits*, the book I was writing for my publisher, Roy Howard. The manuscript was already long overdue.

At a small hotel on Beach Road in Singapore I ran into two Scandinavians, Joop and Harns, who were leaving for Borneo that day and were eventually heading to the Pacific. I told them about *Third Sea* that was anchored in Sandakan, bound for New Guinea and the South Pacific. I didn't think they believed me, but when I arrived back in Sandakan they were there, waiting. They spent the next six months with us.

After two days in Sandakan we set sail for the return to Zamboanga. We arrived four days later. The port was still in political turmoil. For our own safety, the navy suggested we leave immediately, or we might be sunk in the harbor. Rebels were preparing to attack the town and were firing on vessels at anchor. That night we were convinced we had to leave when we watched the tracers zipping by overhead. The next morning the Philippine Navy offered us a gunboat escort through the rebel-held Baslin Strait. We decided to strike out for the U.S. Trust Territories in the Caroline Islands, less than a thousand miles away. At a shipping office in town I found a Scandinavian who was looking for passage out of the Philippines. He introduced himself. "I'm Matts," he said. I signed him on.

At dawn the next morning we waited for the gunboat at the harbor entrance. Instead, a cutter came with word that the navy could not escort us. All vessels had to remain to defend Zamboanga. We waited until dusk, and under the cover of darkness, entered the Strait with all sails set, but without engine for fear of being heard. As we silently sneaked past in the black of night, we watched silhouetted islands slip by on both quarters. By dawn we were in open sea.

A week later we sighted Tobi, the southernmost island of the Carolines. The sea was running and without proper charts we could not find an opening in the reef, so we stood offshore. Presently a native sailing craft came out, informing us that island authorities had alerted the U.S. Coast Guard that a vessel tried to enter the reef. Did we have permits to enter U.S. territory? We did not. If we did enter, they said, even as an American vessel, we were subject to arrest. It was the most discouraging news we could hear.

The natives were not lying. A U.S. Coast Guard vessel appeared on the horizon. We hoisted sail and set course south. But where to? If we continued south we would reach the Celebes and Spice Islands, but we had no sailing permits from the Indonesian government. The typhoon belt lay to our north. The only alternative was Rabaul, some two thousand miles away, across the top of New Guinea. An incredible sea voyage followed.

The world we were about to enter was far removed from anything I had ever known, or imagined. It was Herman Melville and Joseph Conrad coming alive. For a month, with the exception of the U.S. gunboat, we did not see another ship. Not another human being. But life around us there was—the sea was alive with activity. And frightening it was at times. Huge whales, larger than us, surfaced around the schooner, making gasping sounds as they did. Some passed beneath our keel, to reappear twenty yards astern. Others came leaping out of the water, and went crashing into the sea, sending up a spray as a battleship does when launched. We thought of the unknown number of yachts sunk by whales. Porpoise came by the thousands, some doing aquatic performances that kept us entertained for hours. And in these strange seas magnificent fish began striking at our lines. Large tuna and ray and squid. We hooked mahi mahi, some five feet in length, and fought them up to the gunwales, only to have them break away. We usually kept two lines out, day and night, and it was always exciting to hear the call "Fish, Fish" and have everyone rush on deck.

Our first landfall was Ninigo Island, a real tropical South Sea atoll. We needed fresh fruit and vegetables, but the reef was treacherous. For ten miles it stretched across the sea, with but one opening. Beyond the reef was a peaceful lagoon, dotted with tiny coral islands. The Sailing Directions claimed there was an abundance of wild game on the island. We decided to gamble. I sent two crew aloft to watch for coral heads and search out the opening.

Left, *Third Sea* kept a lookout aloft when negotiating reefs. Right, native islanders help free the anchor wrapped around a coral head.

From the spreaders they called instructions to me at the helm. "Five degree starboard," they shouted. "Hold it there! Steady! Steady she goes!" We reached the point of no return. The pass was twenty-five yards wide, with the sea breaking in deafening rollers on both sides of us. Suddenly the incoming swell picked us up and now our thirty-five-ton schooner was like a surfboard riding the crest of a breaking wave. It was great and exhilarating, with the wind and wave, and the crashing sea all about. And then suddenly the fury ceased; we were inside the lagoon.

Such startling beauty! All peace and calm, like the very soul of our planet. Blue, blue waters. We could see the bottom at twenty fathoms. Coral islands a few feet above water, with graceful palms nipping at the blue of sky, and dazzling white sand beaches. Black skinned natives in outriggers paddled out with fruit and young coconuts to drink. They directed us to a secure anchorage.

We rested at Ninigo for five days. We caught fish in the lagoon, dove for giant clams, speared turtles, and in the bush I brought down a wild boar that dressed in at one hundred and forty pounds. We roasted him on the beach. Nor did a day pass without lobster, basted in butter-garlic sauce, followed by rum punches.

But there was no time to write, to finish my book that Roy Howard was waiting for.

We made two more brief stops in the island chain. At Hermit Island, thirty miles away, we picked up the island chief who was ill and carried him to the hospital at Manus, a distance of three hundred and fifty miles. We found the entrance to Hermit equally as tricky as Ninigo, and to complicate matters as we prepared to sail with the chief aboard, the winds changed and we could no longer exit by the same pass. The chief knew another opening. But the Sailing Directions advised against it, saying it was

Top, Matts with the great-granddaughter of Queen Emma of the South Seas. Whenever possible the crew hunted for fresh meat. Middle, Stephens with a wild boar he shot on Hermit Island. Bottom, a grand view of Rabaul with a World War II Japanese Zero in the foreground.

Top left, Matts with a turtle caught in the lagoon at Hermit. Right, Stephens poses wearing a Japanese helmet found in a cave. Bottom, a World War II Japanese submarine is used today to carry fuel in Rabaul. The Allies were unable to capture the Rabaul during the war.

dangerous and not recommended as volcanic eruptions had blocked the pass. "Him okay," the chief said. "Me think you can go!"

The old man turned out to be an incredible navigator, and I had to have blind confidence in his ability. From the cabin top where he lay, he shouted out directions. "Straight, straight," he called, pointing with his hand. It was madness, for straight ahead was coral. It was clearly visible beneath the surface, but then without faltering he gave the signal, a sharp ninety degree turn to port or starboard, or whatever the case might be. At times the coral seemed only inches away, and I'm sure it was, but there was always enough water beneath the keel to permit us to safely pass.

Then came the final fringing reef. Our hearts dropped. Here the incoming tide looked like a swirling river in which we could not see bottom through the turbulence. "You go, you go," the chief keep shouting. Not too encouraging was a Japanese trawler on the reef to our port. She obviously didn't make it. "You go," he shouted, and I nosed the schooner into the foam, full throttle, all six sails set. We cracked through the surf and entered the open sea. The next thing we cracked was a bottle of Philippine rum, and passed the bottle around until it was gone. Three days later we arrived at Manus, left Joseph in the hospital and a week after that we were in Rabaul.

Rabaul was a delightful port, and with secure anchorage it made an excellent rest stop. The harbor is one of the most beautiful in the Pacific, surrounded by smoking volcanoes that drop suddenly into deep seas.

Rabaul was one stronghold the Japanese held in the Pacific that the Allies were unable to recapture. The town is tunneled with three hundred and sixty miles of caves; at the bottom of the bay are two hundred and eighty sunken ships, nearly all unsalvaged.

In Rabaul I was finally able to finish *Asian Portraits* for Roy Howard, not on board but in a quiet beach house an Australian family asked me to watch while they went on home leave. And while I was writing, Don built an eighteen-foot dory. It was a masterpiece of engineering and construction. We designed it so that it came apart with one section fitting into the other. Thus, we could stow it easily on deck, and if we didn't want to take time to assemble it, we had two dinghies we could use. We painted it yellow, and called it the *Yellow Peril*. Launching day called for a celebration, and a bet. How many bodies could *Yellow Peril* hold? Don won the bet. He gathered kids on the quay and managed to put twenty-seven kids aboard before she went under. *Yellow Peril* became our most trusted asset, and with her we were able to explore rivers and reefs we could never have reached.

In my library aboard *Third Sea*, I had most of James Michener's books on the South Pacific. One volume that had always fascinated me was his non-fiction *Return to Paradise*. Before I ever went to the South Pacific, I came to know the place quite intimately from reading the book, and then, when I did go, it was like living in Michener's world. At Vima's Cafe in Papeete, I met Homer Morgan; in Punaavia I talked to Eddie Lund about his music; at the Outrigger Bar in the Hotel Tahiti I had rum punches with Bill Stone—all of whom appeared in the book.

In those early years I came to know Michener's characters only by chance and through no conscious effort of my own. We just happened to be at the same place at the same time. But now as I made plans to sail across the Pacific, following the same course that Michener had taken, although in reverse, I began wondering what had happened to all those people he wrote about. Were they still alive? Many would have passed away but what about the others? Had they stuck it out or did they return home? It would be interesting to find out and now I had a chance to do so, one that few others had. I reread *Return* and drew red lines under the names of those characters whom I might meet.

In Michener's chapter on Rabaul, the name Yorkie Booth appears. In fact, Yorkie was one of the half-dozen people to whom Michener dedicated the book.

Yorkie, Michener wrote, was "as tough as they come." I heard he hung out in the Rabaul Yacht Club where I found him sitting at the bar. It took a couple of days before I could even talk to him, and a lot of drinks to get him to loosen up. After I got him to talk, he eventually accepted a dinner invitation aboard *Third Sea.* I almost wished he hadn't.

"So that's why you invited me!" he shouted when I asked him about Michener. I thought he was going to take a swing at me.

"He did dedicate a book to you," I said in protest.

"To me!" he shouted and cursed. "So you're one of those writer blokes probing around into other people's business. Well let me tell you. I never met your Michener." He began laughing. "You got the wrong Yorkie Booth. The one Michener knew died about ten years ago. You're about the hundredth person who's asked me that." He laughed louder. "You got the wrong man, mister, the wrong man."

It seems impossible that the vast and lonely South Pacific could have held two Yorkie Booths, but it did. And I had picked the wrong one. After that I was determined I would be more direct the next time I met one of Michener's characters. My chance would come when we sailed to the New Hebrides. Tom Harris was the man there, but more about him later.

More crew left in Rabaul, including Joop and Harns, and others signed on—a French couple who had been working in Japan, and Buka, a local, sixteen-year-old Melanesian boy with bushy hair and a wide grin.

Our destination after Rabaul was the Solomon Islands, where I dove without success searching for John F. Kennedy's famous *PT-109*, and then to Samoa via the Gilbert Islands, some four-thousand miles distant. I was aware after the Solomons it wouldn't be easy, bucking the trade winds and currents. We seemed to do quite well for the first week, and then we hit the doldrums.

The doldrums can be hell. No winds. Heat. Flat seas. But enormous swells. We rolled as much as forty-five degrees to port, then starboard. Back and forth. Impossible to remain in our bunks without being pitched out. Then there would be sudden bursts of wind, bringing high hopes. Maybe they would last twenty minutes. For eleven days we drifted aimlessly in the doldrums. We had but sixty miles to go to our destination in the Gilbert Islands, but we couldn't close the distance. We had to do something. We couldn't drift forever. Since we could not reach the Gilberts, there was no choice but to turn south, by motoring until we caught a favorable wind.

The charts showed the Santa Cruz Islands south of us, and still farther south, the New Hebrides islands. In the "Sailing Directions" they did not look very promising: "The islands are known for their earthquakes, active volcanoes and hurricanes, of which there are at least three devastating storms each year."

It also mentioned violent upheavals. Coral has been found at fifteen hundred feet above sea level. There was more: "The land is unhealthy; heat and humidity are excessive; the islands teem with large red ants; flies abound.

Malaria is rampant. Lizards grow up to five feet. Crocodiles live in rivers. And the natives can be hostile. They are Melanesians who are excitable and generally treacherous and should not always be trusted...."

With uncertainty we headed south. After three days of motoring we caught a wind from the east, not exactly what we wanted, but it at least did carry us away from the doldrums. Our intention at first was to give the savage islands a wide berth.

But it's amazing when you don't have fresh food how you crave it, and what you will do for it. We had been at sea more than forty days, living on canned goods, and even the thought of yams and taro was appealing. Some of the islands might even have wild game—cattle, pigs, goats, anything. We decided to chance the disease and hostile natives and put ashore.

No habitable islands on this planet are more remote and so seldom visited as the Santa Cruz. Seen from a distance they appear frightening and foreboding, black and menacing. Heavy rain clouds hang over jagged land masses, and from cone-shaped peaks, smoke clouds rise up from active volcanoes.

We watched one lonely cone-shaped island appear on the horizon. There were no sandy beaches, no reef, and not a single tree or bush. Only volcanic rock. That night we put the island on our starboard beam as we sailed past. Suddenly in the blackness of night the island exploded. Columns of black smoke and sulphur belched skyward, lighted by the glow of raging fire and red hot lava flowing down the mountain sides. There followed an awful tremble, as though our earth was doomed. And then as suddenly as it began, it ended. When dawn came and we looked back at an empty horizon, we wondered if it happened at all, or was it just a nightmare.

The next afternoon we reached Santa Cruz. We tacked back and forth along the northern coast, looking for an opening in the reef that showed on our chart. We found it and turned in through a narrow channel, with the sea breaking on port and starboard. The channel led into a well sheltered lagoon. The thick rich jungle came down to the water's edge.

At one clearing were grass huts, with outriggers pulled up on the shore. But we saw no one, not a dog or pig or chicken. Upon seeing us the natives had left, taking their prized animals with them. Only later did we learn that we had been mistaken for slave traders. It still happens.

The next morning two old men did appear, and were willing to trade. They had no fear we would carry them off to work the phosphate mines or copra plantations. They suffered from yaws and other skin infections. Swarms of flies covered their festering sores. In exchange for old clothing, they gave us breadfruit, yams, coconuts and taro. We asked about game in the hills; they only shook their heads. That night we set sail.

Winds continued to blow from the east, forcing us farther and farther to the south. A week later we were abreast of Espiritu Santo in the New Hebrides. We decided to put into Santo, the capital, and await favorable winds.

In 1942, Santo was the largest and most important U.S. naval base in the entire South Pacific. Overnight this slumbering tropical island port became a city of some two hundred thousand people. She could boast of forty-three movie houses, industrial shops, four hospitals, a steam laundry, radio station, miles of good road, hotels, barber shops, shoe makers, dance halls, and a thousand ships at any one time in the harbor.

Under full sail, and filled with excitement, we entered the harbor. We couldn't believe it. A battered freighter moored to a weather-beaten wharf was the only ship in sight. The town had a few clapboard buildings, with both French and British flags flying, and little else.

We rowed ashore and walked down the main street. The only signs of U.S. wartime presence were several old Quonset huts. There was a hotel, some bars and trading stores. One bar was owned and operated by Tom Harris, a name with a red line under it in my *Return to Paradise*.

"At Santo you'll see Tom Harris," Michener wrote. "He was a wonderful friend to the American forces, who alternated between upbraiding him for selling grog to enlisted men and awarding him letters of commendation." After the war Tom started up movie houses and bars.

While the crew was loading supplies and fuel and water, I decided to look up Mister Harris. I learned he still operated a bar in town. The bar was easy to find. It was early afternoon and there were few customers. Sitting behind the bar was a dark Melanesian. "I'm looking for Tom Harris," I said. No more beating around the bush like I did with Yorkie Booth.

"What you want 'm for?" he asked.

"I want to talk to him," I said, although I assumed he might be dead.

"What about?" he asked again. I could easily see he was going to be persistent.

"About James Michener," I said. A big wide grin came to his face.

"I'm Tom Harris," he said gleefully.

"You! You're not the Tom Harris Michener wrote about," I said.

"No, that was my father," Tom Harris said. In the conversation that followed I learned that his father, Tom, the senior, had married a black Melanesian. I gathered that Tom had adopted many traits from his father. He was a natural entrepreneur and ran his bar and restaurant with skill. However, he regreted but he had never met James Michener.

The next Michener character I wanted to look up was Aggie Grey in Western Samoa.

We lost our French crew to government jobs in Santo, which left us short-handed. Don, Matts, Buka and I set sail south to Vila looking for a crew and a wind to carry us east. Between Espiritu and Malekula Islands we ran a full gale. We lashed ourselves to the helm. Towering seas broke over the stern and so intense was the pounding that a bow cable holding the bowsprit snapped and the decorative trailboards on the bow were carried away. We limped into Vila, the capital of the New Hebrides.

Unbelievably, a grand reception awaited us. We couldn't believe islanders could be so friendly, just like in the story books and movies. Natives waved flags and jumped up and down on the quay, and a speed boat zoomed up and tossed us cans of cold beer. Then came the let down. We were instructed to move away from the dock area and to anchor at the far side of the harbor, away from everything. They discovered that we were not the lead boat in the Auckland to Vila yacht race. For a while I thought they might ask us to return the cold beer, but by then we had downed all the cans. All that day and the next we watched the yachts come in.

We seldom had difficulty finding new crew willing to pay their share of expenses. In Vila we signed on a Canadian oil field worker on vacation, a French and German couple who were teachers, an Aussie beachcomber and a destitute British painter. With full crew and supplies we left Vila for Pago Pago, American Samoa, due east at a distance of twelve-hundred miles, or a ten-day's sail. The last weather report stated winds were in our favor from the south. One day out the winds veered back to the east, the direction we were heading. I made the decision to run south to the 30th parallel, past New Caledonia and New Zealand. It would be the winter season at those latitudes. I was beginning to believe that everyone might be right after all.

We headed south, with each day becoming colder and colder. We put on shirts, trousers, foul-weather gear, socks, everything we had, and still froze. We sailed south and were nearing the treacherous "Roaring Forties" before we finally caught the westerlies to carry us eastward, well south of Fiji and Tonga.

I have no love for the cold, tossing southern seas. The radio reported two yachts were lost during the Auckland-Vila race, within two hundred miles of us. Seas were the highest ever reported. In spite of raging weather on deck, one of our crew members refused to go below and clung to the mast, praying. The barometer fell to a record low.

Fortunately we were running. The schooner was in no danger, although she was sliding down the crests of waves like a surfboard. South of Tonga we were able to turn north, and the seas calmed somewhat. Now came another frightening experience. Whales!

One leviathan that measured perhaps fifty feet came up alongside the schooner, so close we could have touched him. He rolled over and looked at us with a beady eye. We could see his scarred body, from his fights with giant squid, and we could smell him. For twenty minutes he and a half dozen other whales circled us.

We reached the island of Niue, which Captain Cook called Savage Island. The Frenchman and his German wife left us here, preferring to wait for an unscheduled island plane rather than chance the sea again. After Niue the South East Trades blew strong and it was a matter of

Top left, *Third Sea* in Pago Pago Harbor, getting her sides cleaned. Top right, crew take a swim in a mountain stream. Bottom, crew visits Robert Louis Stevenson's grave above Apia in Western Samoa.

a few days before we reached Pago Pago in American Samoa. To cover twelve hundred miles from Vila we had sailed four thousand. I had to leave *Third Sea* in Pago Pago for a few weeks while I visited publishers in Asia.

By the time I returned, we were pushing the hurricane season. We couldn't linger. My nephew, Robert Stedman, who had been traveling with me in Asia, flew ahead to help ready the schooner for our sail to Honolulu. In the mean time, my son Peter had arrived from California to join the crew. Robert welcomed the chance to sail aboard the vessel he had heard so much about for the past few years. In time he would make history aboard *Third Sea.*

From Pago it was an easy sail to Apia, where I hoped to meet Aggie Grey, another of Michener's characters. Aggie, indefatigable Aggie, was the hostess Michener reckoned to have fleeced American G.I.s out of millions. "But the best damn fleecing we ever had," he wrote.

Aggie was the most talked about lady in all the South Pacific. She had hobnobbed with stars like Gary Cooper and Marlon Brando; given advice to anthropologist Margaret Meade; received ship's captains, diplomats, heads of state and downed astronauts and, as Michener testified, entertained thousands of U.S. and Allied troops during World War II.

To visit her was a bit risky. It was late and the hurricane season was coming. But I decided to chance it, give it a few days and get out. We were the only ship in the harbor.

Aggie's Hotel is at the far end of Beach Road. The original old woodframe building, brought piece by piece by ship from San Francisco, still stands. I took some of the crew and went to the hotel. Out in the street we could hear music coming from inside. We entered and there inside the entrance we saw Aggie. She was sitting on a high fan-back rattan chair, elegant, dignified, proud, with an audience gathered around, hanging on her every word. My impulse was to rush up to her with arms out and introduce myself, but I knew I couldn't interrupt her. She might be annoyed.

"Tell her you want to do a story about her," Matts suggested when we took seats at a table nearby.

That wasn't the approach, I was sure. Aggie had probably met every journalist and would-be writer who had ever crossed the Pacific. At least one or two of the people gathered around her at that moment had to be writers. One kept scribbling in a notebook.

"Wait a minute," Matts said and stood up. Without a further word, and before I could stop him, he walked over to Aggie.

I watched Aggie stop her conversation and look up at Matts; he leaned over and whispered something in her ear. She glanced in our direction, said something to those seated around her and rose to her feet. Taking Matts by the arm, she marched straight to our table.

"That's your schooner anchored in the harbor?" she asked.

"It is," I replied, wondering what Matts had told her.

"And you braved the hurricane season to come see me?"—she didn't give me time to answer—"Any captain who does that has to be a friend of mine. Now, aren't you going to ask me to sit down?"

That was my meeting with Aggie Gray. Indefatigable Aggie. Fun-loving, humorous, generous Aggie. It was a meeting that was to last a week. In between exploring Beach Road, climbing to Robert Louis Stevenson's grave on Mt. Vaea and swimming at Vailma waterfalls, I spent my spare time in her company. She was good enough to show me all her personal letters from Michener.

"He wasn't a writer when he first came," she said. "He

was just a navy lieutenant. But he became a friend in later years. And, you know, he wasn't a bad writer either."

The tragic news came when we were anchored in Singapore a couple years later. Aggie Gray had passed on quietly in her sleep. She was eighty-six years old.

We took on food and fresh water and set sail with a fair wind. The last twenty-six hundred miles to Hawaii remained. The seas were warm and the winds favorable. We were making our necessary easting when a week out of Apia we discovered our water supply had been contaminated. It was filled with worms. When we took on water in Apia we had tied up alongside a Singapore freighter. Rather than cart water in cans across their deck, the crew on the freighter handed us their hose. We didn't know it, but we were taking on bad water from their tank.

We couldn't turn back for we would have to buck winds to Apia, and Honolulu was still three week's distance.

Left, some of the crew go ashore in the dory to look for an opening in the reef at Tongareva. Right, an island feast on Fanning Island.

I studied the charts. A hundred miles off our course was Tongareva, the northern most island in the Cook Island group. The Sailing Directions said the island had a village where we could purchase limited supplies. And, we reasoned, if there was a village, there had to be water. We altered course and pointed the bow in the new direction.

The morning of the second day brought the island into view. So striking was the approach to this lovely, forgotten coral atoll, so powerful, that it brought tears to the eyes of some of my crew. Imagine, seeing the speck of island at the first light of dawn, and as you close the distance, the island takes shape and form. Palms nip at the blue of the sky, swaying gently, and white sand beaches glitter in the morning sun. You follow the coast, searching for the opening in the reef, and when you find it you cautiously edge your way into a blue, blue lagoon. A white coral church appears, and further along the lagoon is the village nestled among tall palms.

But something very strange was going on. The village appeared to be abandoned, yet thin columns of smoke arose from cook fires in the houses. Not a soul could be seen; no one came to greet us. We raised our yellow "quarantine" flag and still no one came.

Not knowing what else to do, I sent two of my crew ashore to see what might be the problem. Through my binoculars I could see them enter the village. Presently two young children appeared, and then a few more. Soon people came from the houses, and now there seemed to be much shouting and laughing and pointing toward the schooner.

It wasn't until I went ashore that I discovered what had kept the villagers at bay. They thought we were pirates. It's true—pirates. It seems that about seventy years before we made our appearance, Peruvian slavers came to the island and carried off every male from the age of six to sixty. They were never seen again, but it's believed they were taken to work in the mines in Peru. After the incident, mothers told their children when they were naughty that a big sailing vessel would come and get them. We were that big sailing vessel. At first seeing us, even the elders believed we might be the same evil ones.

We remained less than a week, but in that short time we came to know the people and their habits, and found many friends among them. We discovered that most of their income is generated by pearl trading. The lagoon is rich with pearl shells, and some shells yield prized black pearls. My crew traded nearly all their possessions, including most of their clothes, for pearls. But I was more cautious. The pearls didn't appear to me to be that valuable. Later when we were at sea, and my crew shivered on their watches as they stood at the helm, I asked if trading their warm sweaters and foul weather jackets was worth it.

The laugh was on me. When we reached Honolulu, one crew had two pearls set into a pair of earrings. The jeweler valued the set at seven hundred dollars. I had missed my chance. I made up my mind then and there I would go back to go Tongareva, and this time with a couple chests loaded with trading goods. On my return voyage across the Pacific to Asia, I did just that. I had aboard *Third Sea* boxes of clothing and diving gear to trade. I was going to be rich, the next voyage, but more about that later.

Tongareva was the culmination of our South Seas adventure. We remained only five days, and for me and my crew it was the most memorable five days we spent in the Pacific. Here was a "South Sea Island" paradise. It had all the attributes: islanders who paddled out to the schooner with fresh coconuts to drink and pearls to trade. Island feasts of roast pig and sweet yams cooked in coconut milk. And drums in the night, woodblocks and shark-skin drums. And the fulfilment: lithe maidens doing savage dances to the beat of the drums under palms.

We indulged in all the pleasures life had to offer us, and one Sunday morning, when all the villagers were in church, we hoisted sail. There was no other way. The Tongarevans would not have let us go. When they saw our sails and the schooner about to sail out the pass, they came running out of the church. The women were dressed in long ankle-length *muumuus*, with straw sun hats and ribbons and flowers. They waved frantically, and we watched them fade into the horizon.

For the next week it was a silent crew that sailed *Third Sea* toward her rendezvous in Honolulu. Their thoughts and hearts were back on the island.

We crossed the equator and spent Christmas Day on Christmas Island, and made another stop at neighboring Fanning Island. We were quite used to nipping in and out of coral atolls now. At some atolls where anchoring was impossible, half the crew stayed aboard the schooner and stood off shore while the others went exploring with the dory. There wasn't an atoll we couldn't explore.

We passed through the doldrums without knowing it, for the winds kept pushing us steadily northward at more than one-hundred and fifty miles a day. And then, early one morning, we saw the lights of Honolulu.

We sailed into Ke'ehi Lagoon, tied up at the quarantine pier and notified customs and immigration that we had arrived. We had made it, eastward across the Pacific, twelve-thousand miles from Singapore. Don and most of the crew had planned to leave *Third Sea* once we arrived in Hawaii. My intention was to remian only a short time, find a new crew and sail to Tahiti. The best was yet to come, and the worst.

Schooner *Third Sea* moored in front of the famous Illiaki Hotel at Ala Wai Yacht Harbor in Honolulu. We made it across the Pacific.

Chapter 10

A STAR TO SAIL HER BY

No one will doubt, Hawaii is one of the most beautiful groups of islands in all the world. Mark Twain testified to this when he called Hawaii "the loveliest fleet of islands that lies anchored in any ocean."

But what you don't hear, and what tourist brochures fail to tell you, is that Hawaii is inhabited by countless thieves, robbers, liars and remittance men of the worst sort. Robert Louis Stevenson was more direct. When he visited Hawaii in 1889, he concluded, "In vile Honolulu there are too many cesspools and beastly *haoles*." *Haole* is Hawaiian for "white man" or Caucasian. Some critics say Stevenson, himself a *haole,* was perhaps a bit too harsh on fellow white men living in Honolulu. After all, some of his best friends, even his wife, were *haoles.* Nonetheless, Stevenson was simply being honest and stating the truth. The fact is that *haoles*, or foreigners, are not very well liked in Hawaii, and this "thou is *haole*-er than me" attitude has taken on a racial connotation and a slur more than simply a synonym for Caucasian or foreigner.

Casual visitors, that is, tourists, are generally not aware of the underlying racial current. They are enthralled with the beauty of the islands, the sun and surf, lofty mountains forming the backdrop, rum punches and pretty long-haired girls (most likely *haoles*) with flowers around their necks preforming the seductive hula-hula. Visitors, fortunately, don't have to do business in Hawaii; yachtsman do. That's the difference.

I didn't intend to remain long in Hawaii, only to sign on a new crew, do some necessary repairs, take on supplies and sail to Tahiti via the Marquesas. I was stopped short when we arrived at Ke'ehi Lagoon and customs came aboard and informed me that I had to pay duty for bringing *Third Sea* into the U.S.

"But I'm not staying here," I explained.

"You're an American citizen returning to America," the officer said, running his fingers over the teak carvings in the main saloon.

"I know, but it's a Singapore registered vessel," I replied. I did in fact register *Third Sea* at the U.S. Embassy in Singapore. I also changed her home port name on the stern from HONOLULU to SINGAPORE. It did little good. Before I knew it custom officers were swarming over the schooner with tape measures and pen and note books in hand. The next day I was summoned to the main Customs Office downtown and handed the tax rate schedule. They had set the value of the schooner at US$195,000, and of this figure I had to pay a tax of between fifteen and twenty-two percent. In other words, I would probably have to pay around thirty thousand dollars before I could sail for Tahiti, a sum which I didn't have. I protested. "The schooner only cost me $40,000 to build." I was talking to deaf ears. "I want to see the supervisor," I finally said. The officer looked at me like I was a criminal about to be executed.

"Come back tomorrow, at nine o'clock," he said and turned to help someone else.

What could I possibly do now? I could raise the money if I sat down and wrote hard for the next few months, but customs wanted to be paid immediately. If I didn't make payment within thirty days I could be fined heavily, as much as fifty percent of the total bill. Furthermore, the Coast Guard could impound *Third Sea* and most likely I would not be permitted aboard.

The next morning when I arrived at Customs, a Japanese American lady who worked in the front office called me aside. "You said you had it built in Singapore, didn't you?" she asked.

"Yes, I did."

"Tell them about the trade agreement. Tell them Singapore is a Third World Country." She said no more and turned to the stack of papers on her desk.

"I'm requesting a tax waiver under the rules for the trade agreements with Singapore." I said to the superintendent when I entered his office. It sounded impressive but I had no idea what I was talking about.

The man looked at me as if I had leprosy. He leaned back in his swivel chair and stroked the top of his head. He was sweating under the armpits. "You built in Singapore," he said, not wanting an answer. "What engine do you have?"

"Perkins," I said. "I have a Perkins diesel engine."

"Sorry, that's U.K. manufactured," he bounced back. "England doesn't apply to Third World trade agreements."

"But I bought it in Singapore, second hand."

"It doesn't matter. What about all your other hardware? Where did you purchase that?"

"I had it made up over there, some in Singapore, some in Bangkok," I said. I explained I didn't have winches, only fife rails and belaying pins, and that such things as port holes and deck fittings were cast in Bangkok.

He listened but I was making no headway. He was becoming more and more annoyed with each argument I put forth. Halfway through a statement he stopped me. "Look," he said. "You're wasting my time. Regardless of what you say, everything has to be documented. We need receipts, records."

"Fine," I said.

"You are prepared to furnished receipts for every-thing?" he stammered.

"I can furnish you with receipts," I replied.

He thought for a moment. "What about labor? You have a record of wages paid?"

It was my turned to balk. "I didn't pay wages," I said. "I had all free help, from Peace Corps volunteers. On their time off they helped me."

"That's not acceptable," he said and smiled for the first time. "Nothing is free, especially labor. You have to verify salaries." The meeting was over. I had three days to settle my claim.

Not all was lost. When I began constructing *Third Sea,* I kept a ledger with the names of everyone who worked on the schooner. Next to their names I entered the amount of time they put in and the job they worked on. At the end of the month I totaled the hours. I had promised everyone who helped that in return for their time they could sail aboard *Third Sea* any time they wanted once she was afloat. In addition to the ledger of names I kept receipts for ever dollar I paid out—yard rental, hardware supplies, tools, equipment, material, food bills, everything.

What did bother me was the salaries. This could be an issue. I cabled Beno Anciano in Singapore for his sug-gestions. He had salaries to pay when he was manager of the plywood company. Two days later with a cardboard box filled with receipts I went back to the customs office.

For two days I had to answer questions an accountant fired at me. What was this for? What was that for? When it came time to settle the salary problem, Beno's telegram arrived. It was official from the Singapore government labor department. It gave the figures for the pay scale for laborers in Singapore during the time *Third Sea* was un-der construction. The cost for skilled labor was less than one U.S. Dollar an hour.

"Take your papers and get your vessel documented," the supervisor said. "Pay the clerk outside."

I paid the clerk in cash, a total of fifteen dollars. I then went and got *Third Sea* documented, like he said to do. She was now an official U.S. vessel, protected under the American flag.

From Ke'ehi Lagoon we moved *Third Sea* to the lovely Ala Wai Yacht Harbor near Waikiki Beach. After being chastised by customs and the Coast Guard we now found ourselves being lauded. When we first sailed into the yacht harbor, I went to check with the harbor master. He very politely informed me that *Third Sea* was much too large for a mooring and had to anchor out. When he stepped out of the office to point out where we had to go and saw *Third Sea* with her sails neatly furled and the crew standing by, he changed his mind. Obviously, he figured *Third Sea* could add to the tourist attraction of the harbor. "As long as you agree to move when I tell you," he said, "you can tie up at the loading dock." The loading dock was at the very entrance to the harbor, directly in front of the Illikai Hotel. Every tourist and every visitor who came to the yacht harbor had to pass the loading dock.

Mister Peterson would have loved it; with the audience we had he could have put on a show that would have put Barnum & Bailey to shame. But Mister Peterson wasn't with us and we had to carry on without him. Passers-by stopped and stared. Sometimes as many as a dozen people stood there at any one time, looking over *Third Sea* from one end to the other. When we sat on deck doing rope work and other boat chores, they asked us endless questions—"You ever get into any storms?" "How many are on board?" "How much food do you carry?" "Do you ever stop at night?" "Do you mind if we take a picture?"

We had no complaints and were proud as any parents could be. *Third Sea* probably appeared in more photographs than any other vessel in Hawaii at the time. I was most pleased when Stan Rayner showed up one day on the quay and stopped to look us over. He had no idea, of course, that he was partly responsible for *Third Sea* being there, or for her very existence for that matter. He was overwhelmed when I told him the story. "I don't have *Valkerien* any more," he said sadly. *Valkerien* was the schooner John Samson studied when he was in Honolulu planning his book for ferro-cement construction for yachts. Rayner explained that after I wrote a story about him and *Valkerien* for *Argosy* magazine, a businessman had made him an offer he could not resist. He accepted a large sum of money for his schooner, and six acres of farm property on Maui. Like Jack London, Stan Rayner became a sailor on horseback, from seaman to farmer.

Our fine location at Ala Wai brought a score of people who wanted to sail to Tahiti with us. Some wanted to join immediately; others later in the year. In the meantime we would have to return to Ke'ehi Lagoon and go into drydock to paint the bottom with antifouling and prepare the schooner for her coming sail to Tahiti. I had selected a crew and they were on hand to assist. My son Peter, now in his early twenties, was among them. He planned to sail to Tahiti with us.

Ke'ehi Lagoon, however, is not the Ala Wai Yacht Harbor. We were about to see Honolulu as Robert Louis Stevenson saw it—vile with beastly *haoles*.

Had I been able to careen *Third Sea* on a beach at low tide, I would have done so and saved myself a bundle of money and time. But with few such beaches in Hawaii, this is impossible. The only alternative was to slip *Third Sea*, to go into drydock, at a healthy cost of five hundred

Third Sea in drydock in Honolulu, preparing for her voyage to Tahiti and the South Seas, with her new coat of bottom paint, bought from a con man, that peeled off the moment we went back into the water.

dollars a day, plus hauling-out charges. We had to work fast and hard.

The day we hauled out a man appeared at the site. He said his name was Sam. He may not have looked exactly honorable, but at least he wasn't as shabby as some of the derelicts who hung around the waterfront. And I must say, he was convincing. "I tell you, you can't beat it," he said. "The navy uses it for their submarines, and think what submarines have to endure." The man in question had bottom paint to sell me, and cheap. He said he worked for a shipyard that had gone bankrupt, and they were unable to pay him and the other workers when they closed shop. The yard gave him submarine antifouling paint for his lost wages. "The government pays two-hundred and fifty dollars a gallon for this stuff," he said. "I'll sell it to you for fifty bucks a gallon." It did sound like a good deal. Antifouling paint, even a cheap brand, costs at least sixty dollars a gallon. I couldn't go wrong. The cans were marked and sealed. I took six gallons off his hands, enough to paint the bottom and a gallon or two to keep as spare. After all, the price was right.

In five days, with ten crew members working twelve hours a day, *Third Sea* was shipshape from bow to stern. The last day the yard crane came and lowered *Third Sea* back into the water. We all gave a shout—"Hoot, hoot, hurray." I was at the helm and gave the orders to cast off the mooring lines, and I then put the gears into reverse.

"All clear?" I called.

One of the new crew members ran over to the rail to check. "What's that?" he shouted, pointing down to the water.

"What's what?" I called.

"All that gray stuff!"

I handed the helm to someone else and ran to the rail

and looked over the side. I couldn't believe it. The propeller was spinning in reverse, causing the water to rush back against the hull, and as it did, it carried sheets of bottom paint, our precious antifouling paint, with it. Within minutes the bottom of the hull was completely naked. Five days of work lost, and thousands of dollars. All we could do was motor to the end of the lagoon and drop anchor. By morning growth had begun clinging to the hull. Unless we slipped again and repainted the bottom, every week we would have to put on diving gear and scrape the bottom. But we had no other choice; I didn't have two thousand five hundred dollars to slip again. Before we sailed I went back to the boat yard but there was no remittance man around who sold cheap submarine bottom paint to unsuspecting yachtsmen.

With a new fresh crew, all eager hands, we set sail for Lanai and the islands to the east of Oahu. We had cleared Honolulu, and with a complement of ten crew, *Third Sea* was ready to make its passage to the Marquesas, some two thousand miles southeast of Hawaii.

Before proceeding I must confess I had a problem which I didn't want anyone to know. I couldn't navigate. Oh, across the Pacific I did sun shots, and I plotted courses, and I drew lines and coordinates on plotting charts, and I knew the stars and how they traversed the heavens, but the real navigation I left to Don, my first mate. And now Don was gone. He had found a job in Hawaii.

In Singapore, Ed Boden had spent hours of his time in the main saloon of *Third Sea*, with the fierce tropical sun beating down on the cabin top, teaching Don and me the rudiments of celestial navigation. Don with his engineer mind absorbed it all. I found myself floundering. I had more enjoyable things to read than the *Tables of Computed Altitude and Azimuth* that comes in three volumes.

It's as exciting as a telephone book. He talked about grids and coordinates, and that Dec. means Declination, GHA is Greenwich Hour Angle, LHA is the Local Hour Angle and SHA is Sidereal Hour Angle. I could understand GHA and LHA but SHA was beyond me.

Then came instruction on the *Nautical Almanac* and Bowditch's *American Practical Navigator*, the bible of navigation. *Practical Navigator* weighs ten pounds, and the *Almanac* contains such gems as "Altitude Correction Tables" and the "Increments and Corrections." With each page I turned, the hotter became the sun beating down on the cabin top, and the more insistent Ed Boden grew.

"And you must remember," he said, "if the LHA is greater than 180 degrees, then Zn is equal to Z, however, if the LHA is less, Zn is 360 degrees minus Z. Got that!"

"I got it," I said, but ten minutes later I forgot it. My problem was that mastering a lot of figures and dates didn't interest me. I never did like math and formulas. The very reason I went to the School of Foreign Service at Georgetown University was that I wasn't required to take math, and the science that I did take was Political Science. Nevertheless, I got my degree, Bachelor of Science, and still I didn't know the difference between an acute angle and an obtuse angle, nor did I know anything about tangents. How on earth could I ever possibly learn navigation?

Don was *Third Sea*'s navigator and as long as none of the crew knew how to navigate he could lord over us, which he did. Whenever he wanted to take a shot, everything had to stop, conversation, music, even meals. No one could object, after all, life depended upon the navigator. And so Don continued to make navigation on board *Third Sea* a great mystery that only he could understand and solve. I helped him by jotting down the time when he

Stephens taking a sun shot; it's easy, if the world is just like an orange.

called "mark" after getting a fix. I regularly checked WWVH for any chronometer adjustments, and I did my own plotting, but dead reckoning only. That was about the limits of my navigation.

And now, a couple of years after launching *Third Sea*, I had to master navigation. But first I knew I had to take the mystique out of navigation, and to do that, I had to do it Frank Sinatra style—my way. What had to go was sines and cosines and explanations like "think of the earth as an orange." The earth isn't an orange, and all I wanted to do was to get from A to B and I didn't give a damn about the logic of it all. What I really wanted to know was how to navigate in Ten Easy Steps. Nothing else. I was in luck. The yacht club at Ala Wai was conducting navigation courses for beginners. I got the instructor aside before the first class began and explained what I wanted. He sat me down and was kind enough to give me some time. "First of all," he began, "you must learn the basics. I want you to think of the earth as an orange."

I knew another yachtsman, an Englishman, Gordon Cook, who was sailing around the world with his family and was holing up in Honolulu trying to make a couple extra bucks to continue his cruising. I first met him a few months before on Fanning in the Line Islands and knew well he was a no-malarkey sailor. I bought a half gallon of Gallo Burgundy, rowed over to his yacht and asked him to help with my Ten Easy Steps. I uncorked the wine and he took out a sheet of paper. It took him no more than twenty minutes to jot down Ten Easy Steps, and these I put to memory. We then drank the wine.

Back aboard *Third Sea*, without any prodding from anyone, I learned simply that if I took a sun shot in the morning I would get a Line of Position which would tell me that I was some place along that line. Next, if I advanced that line in the direction which I was heading, and that afternoon I took another shot, the new Line of Position would intersect the old line, and that's where I would be. Simple! Sorry Ed Boden and Mr. Bowditch, but there's no mystery to that. What matter be it that I didn't think of the earth as an orange?

I began taking sun shots the moment we left Hilo on the Big Island. "You mean we're lost already?" one crew asked and pointed to Mauna Kea, poking its snowcapped peak through the clouds at 13,796 feet above sea level.

"No, we aren't lost," I mumbled but I didn't tell him I was checking my calculations with my Ten Easy Steps while we were still in sight of land. I was right on! Thereafter, all the way to the Marquesas, every morning, every noon and every late afternoon I took sun shots. I worked out our Line of Position and marked it on the plot sheet. Low and behold, a pattern started forming. That sun shot that I just took at 0835 this morning, how would the angle appear if I took a sun shot at exactly the same time tomorrow? Slowly, without effort and painlessly, the wonders of navigation began to unfold. At noon I could follow the sun till it reached its apex, and catch it when it began to fall, and I would know our latitude. And when the moon was out during the day, I could get a fix on it and then one on the sun at the same time and get our immediate position. Soon I was shooting the planets, and the friendly stars. I was becoming fascinated with navigation, and when I read deeper into Bowditch it all began to fit together. And then one afternoon, after taking a fix on the sun, and drawing some lines on the plotting sheet, I announced to the crew, "Tomorrow, off the port bow, at 10 a.m. you will see Nuka Hiva." At nine forty-five the next morning one crew member climbed the ratlines on the foremast and stood on the upper spreader, holding on with one hand and shading his eyes with the other. Ten o'clock came and went, and all eyes were fixed on the man on the spreader. Occasionally they would glance over at me, but it would only be a fleeting glance. Then, at five past ten the man aloft gave the call.

"Land Ho!" he shouted. "Two points off port beam." It's moments like this at sea that fill one's heart with joy.

The sighting of Nuka Hiva in the Marquesas was a most joyous moment for more than one reason. We had been at sea twenty-five days, and we had fought head winds most of the way. I had driven the crew almost to the point of mutiny. Only a day or two before we sighted land, Peter had called me aside, and as spokesman for the crew, asked if we could fall off and head for Tahiti. I knew then if I didn't relent I might be another Captain Bligh cast afloat in the ship's longboat by the first mate. The only consoling factor was that I was the only one aboard who could navigate. I asked Peter to tell the crew to hold on for a little longer.

So near, still we couldn't close the distance to reach Nuka Hiva in the Marquesas, after beating for weeks. The crew was near mutiny.

The truth was we were on an impossible voyage.

From the Sandwich Islands to the Marquesas was the way Jack London called the shot. In *The Cruise of the Snark,* he claimed there was no word at all in the Sailing Directions concerning the passage from Hawaii to the Marquesas Islands. "The reason for the lack of direction is, I imagine, that no voyager is supposed to make himself weary by attempting so impossible a traverse," he wrote. Then he went on to say that the impossible did not deter the *Snark*, principally because of the fact that he did not read that particular little paragraph in the Sailing Directions until after he had started.

I truly believe that when you read a book, and it's a good book, it becomes part of you, like the food you eat becomes cells, bone tissue, and every part of your body. I didn't know, or understand, why I was so determined to make the passage from Hawaii to the Marquesas until I reread *The Cruise of the Snark* years later. I realized then that Jack London had instilled in me thoughts and beliefs that I was not even aware of. But they were there, hiding, in my subconscious, causing me to act, or not to act, because of something that had been ingrained in me since I first read *The Cruise of the Snark* when I was in my youth.

We began our voyage with an ill start. I decided to work our way eastward along the Hawaiian islands and thus get as much easting as possible, and at the same time let my new crew get a feeling for the schooner. We did have a checkered crew. First, there was my son Peter who had sailed with me from Samoa to Honolulu; then Don Perkins and Dave Wills, no newcomers to *Third Sea*. Don was a real estate broker; Dave a forest ranger for the California Park Service. Eugene Mortensen was as unlikely a sailor as you could find anywhere. He was a lumber man from northern California, whom we called "Mountain Man."

Kevin Haapala, Paul Schofield, Patrick Anderson and Jim Tiffany joined in Honolulu. We had one female crew, a Chinese woman from Singapore, Christina Lee. We called her Kim. She was making the passage to Tahiti before resuming her job as airline hostess with an Asian airline.

I soon discovered it was a mistake to attempt to train a new crew in Hawaiian waters by sailing to the windward islands. Contrary to what most people might believe, sailing among the Hawaiian Islands is not very pleasant. The seas are not very kind. The early Hawaiians had a devil of a time getting around from island to island, and an inter-island ferry service never was too successful. The channels between these islands can be rough, especially the notorious Alenuihaha Channel that separates Maui from Hawaii, or the Big Island as they call it. Winds and seas funnel down through the narrow channel with a vengeance.

By the time we arrived in Hilo after a sloppy crossing, I thought half the crew might back out, but fortunately only one man abandoned ship, Jim Tiffany. A long distance phone call to his girl back in California made him change his mind.

On the southwest coast of the Big Island, Captain James Cook, the man credited for the European discovery of Hawaii, met his untimely death on a beach at Kealakekua Bay. Here he was overwhelmed by angry natives who stoned him to death. It's a depressing bay with a black sand beach and a gloomy rocky shore line. We made Kealakekua Bay our last anchor stop in Hawaii, to pay tribute to Captain Cook, and here our voyage nearly came to a temporary halt. Dave and Jim were rowing me ashore in the dory while I was manning the sweep, the oar at the stern. The surf was running high and cresting only a few feet from shore. The two oarsmen, upon seeing the high surf building up behind us, panicked and stopped rowing. The dory slipped sideways and overturned, dumped us into the surf and came rolling and tumbling over on top of us. In the melee I broke my left leg at the shin.

I had a friend, Fred Holschuh, who was the resident physician at the Queen's Medical Center in Honolulu. I gave him a call and he recommended a hospital. He also called a doctor friend of his, Dr. Wayne Galante, and asked him to attend to me. The verdict was that I should have my leg placed in a cast and that I should not move about for at least three weeks. "But I'm going to sea," I protested. "The schooner is loaded and we're ready to sail."

The doctor withdrew from my case and the hospital discharged me. Dr. Holschuh explained over the phone that if I insisted upon going to sea it would be at my own risk. A cast would not be advisable then, and hot compresses for the first week could take down the swelling and speed up the mending process. Definitely no moving about. I had antibiotics in the ship's medicine chest to take if an infection did set in. Dr. Holschuh wished me luck and bid me bon voyage.

The most difficult task was for the crew to get me back through the surf to *Third Sea*. Once I got along side, they stretched a sail overboard at the water line. I slid into it and they hoisted me aboard. I moved from the captain's cabin into a bunk in the main saloon, near the chart table, and Kim began the compresses, every fifteen minutes. Three times a day I made it topside, and while laying on my back on the cabin top, I did my sun shots. In a week I could get up, and in two weeks I was hobbling around. Five weeks later when we were hiking over the mountain to Typee Valley in the Marquesas I had even forgotten that my leg had been broken only a short while before.

In our first four days at sea we were able to cover four-hundred and fifty miles. On that morning of the forth day, Peter caught a forty-pound wahoo. We had sashimi, raw fish Japanese style, for lunch, and baked fish steaks for the evening meal. Fish did wonders for our diet aboard. Immediately after eating fish, raw or cooked, we could feel our energy returning.

By evening the weather began to turn foul. In the log for the fifth day I made the following entry: "Weather has been deteriorating. Seas rough and pounding. Rain squalls everywhere and lightening on the horizon. Pitch black and not a star to be seen. But we do have dolphins following; we can hear them." The next morning a whale surfaced on our starboard beam and circled us for the better part of an hour.

For the eighth day I wrote: "Log 814. Winds ENE at 15 knots. Squalls and shifting winds. Rains continuously. Difficult to cook. No more meals on deck."

Our watches were two hour durations. When a crew got off the helm, he stood by for two hours, thus there were always two hands on deck. I kept the ship's log book but I also had the crew keep what we called a "running" log. They made their entries after they got off watch, noting the course steered, the taffrail log reading, direction of wind, barometer and comments. The comment entries in the running log for the next few days tell their own story: "Clouded over with high rolling seas." "Big Roller coaster." "We want sun." "Up and down." "Dismal day." "Wet to the bone." "Lots of rain." "Down pour." By the tenth day we were only making thirty-five-mile runs.

Then came the doldrums with no wind. We tried to nurse every breath of air we could. I made my entry: "The booms swing and the sails slap—slap, bang, slap. There is no escape from the blistering sun above deck, and below in the saloon it's hot as Hades. The main sail

Stephens studies the rigging. Beating to windward made the passage to the Marquesas difficult and was hard on spirits as well as sails.

split down a seam and the crew is taking turns stitching."
It took most of the day to finish the sewing. Finally, we
had to motor out of the doldrums, which used up much of
our precious diesel. Once through the doldrums we picked
up the Southeast Trades. For the two days that they lasted
we had great sailing with wonderful sunsets. "Sailed
through the night with full sails except for flying jib. Ex-
quisite." Dave expressed his thought in the running log:
"Superlatives can't express the deep emotional feelings
of contentment on such a nite." And Kevin made his: "This
is what sailing is all about."

Our habit aboard *Third Sea* was to close the navigation book from the crew's view a day or two before we
reached the Equator. The uncertainty of when we might
cross kept them in suspense. Then very surreptitiously
we would start displaying certain items on deck—a long
plank from the storage locker, a coil or rope from the
rope locker, a life ring. The moment we reached the Equator, the ship's bell sounded and all sails came down. All
polliwogs, those who hadn't crossed the Equator before,
were ushered below deck, hatches closed and the volume
on the stereo turned as high as it would go. One by one
they were brought blindfolded back on deck, and spun
around until they could hardly stand. The ship's roll without sails up didn't help their case much. And then we
made them walk the plank. But in mind only. We would
tie a rope around their waist, guide them along the plank,
which was flat on the deck, and then give them a shove.
At that moment we would douse them with buckets of
water. It never failed; they thought they had been shoved
over the side and would begin swimming.

It was great fun and put everyone into the spirit of the
sea, and perhaps even placated Neptune. We entered the
names of new members of the club, no longer polliwogs,

into the log book and sealed the contract with Neptune with a bottle of rum. Neptune always got the first glass which we tossed to the sea, accompanied with loud cheers.

But bad times come with the good aboard a sailing ship. Unfortunately unlike a motor vessel where one can steer behind an enclosed house, helmsmen aboard sailing ships must endure wind and rain for it is the wind that makes it move. A good yachtsman must feel the wind.

The log for the twentieth day reads: "Time 1000. Log 1852. Barometer 1014. Winds from the east 15-20 knots. We still have two hundred miles to go to reach Nuka Hiva. We are running through a school of tuna. They have been with us for two hours, leaping out of the water on all quarters. But none will take the two lines we have out. Peter changed the lures three times. Mountain Man went out on the bowsprit with a boat hook and tried to land one, unsuccessfully, of course."

The next day we landed a forty-pound tuna. "Peter pulled him in on a hand line. Immediately we marinated a heaping bowl of sushimi. However, the seas are building. Had to take down the big jib and run with the jib stay sail. Reefed the main. Pounding but can hold our course."

On the twenty-fourth day I made the entry: "Tensions running high. Fortunately I estimate we should see the northernmost island, Eiao, tomorrow morning at 1000. Afternoon sun fix puts us fifty miles due north."

At five past ten the next morning Perkins sounded the call "Land Ho!" My navigation was right on. But we weren't there yet. The most difficult part of making headway aboard a sailing vessel is attempting to close a distance when the elements are against you. We fought all that day and night, and the next morning I made my entry: "Log 2068. Wind ESE 18. East southeast is the direction we want to go. So close and yet so far. The winds and current are carrying us away from Eiao."

Mountain Man lost his blue seaman's cap overboard. "My hat, my hat!" he shouted above the sound of the wind, but nothing in the world could have saved his hat. It would have been impossible for us to turn around.

The entry the next morning was even more depressing: "Still we cannot close the distance, a short thirty miles." What kept coming to mind was what Peter had told me about the crew's discontent, that they wanted me to fall off and head for Tahiti. "Hopefully the sight of land will change things," I concluded in the log.

In the library aboard *Third Sea* was *Around the World Single-handed,* a book written by yachtsman Harry Pidgeon. I remembered vaguely reading something about his arrival in the Marquesas. I took the book down from the shelf and hastily read the passage, and then quickly hid it from sight so no one might read it. Pidgeon wrote that when he was sailing into the harbor at Taiohae on Nuka Hiva, the four-masted schooner *Rosamond* from San Francisco made every effort to beat windward to enter the bay but eventually fell off and disappeared to the westward. It was two weeks before the schooner showed up again in Taiohae. Pidgeon learned that she had sailed one thousand miles to get to windward once more. This I didn't want the crew to know.

We demanded everything that *Third Sea* could give. Even with our engine running full throttle and as much canvas as she could possibly carry, we could make very little headway.

The next entry in the log reads: "Time, 2230. Seas veered from southeast to east, and Nuka Hiva is now due east at twenty miles distance. Attempting to motor directly into it with only the jib set to steady us. We can't end up like the *Rosamond*. Hopefully by dawn we will be in the lee of the island."

Dawn came and we found we were under heavy cloud and driving to the south. "The crew wants to take advantage of the wind and turn and run with it to Tahiti. We must still try! Had to heave-to while we changed a steering cable. The schooner is under great pressure, straining hard. Sometimes I think she can't take any more pounding, but she always does."

At 6 p.m. the same day I made another entry. "We are managing to close the distance. Just before dark the cloud covering lifted and we were able to take two bearings on the island. Put us eight miles southwest."

Twenty-sixth day: "Log 2218.7 Dawn and there she was, looming up ahead of us, five miles distant. The sun rose over the north of the island. Great indentured valleys and clouds hanging over the summit. Crew is lined along the rail."

At 8 a.m., two hours later, I made another entry: "When we rounded the southwest point of Nuka Hiva the full fury of the Southeast Trade hit us. We raised all six sails and turned on the engine, and we were stopped dead. We had no other choice but to tack back out to sea and will then beat back toward the island. We have been at it now for hours. We will make it! Come on, you can do it, *Third Sea,* you can do it!"

My next entry was jubilation: "Log 2243.9. Time 1230. We made it! Dropped anchor in Taiohae, to cheers of the crew. The bay is well sheltered but with a noticeable swell. High, lofty mountains, sheer to the very peaks, green all the way to summits. Three other yachts are at anchor."

With *Third Sea* well set with two anchors out, we all went ashore that afternoon, had cold Hinano beer in the Chinese shop and walked around the village. In no more than five minutes we had seen all there was to see. The islanders did not seem to be too friendly. No smiles, no cheers, no happy faces. A gloom appears to dominate the people. Are they tired of yachtsmen?

Before white man came, the Marquesas were a warlike people who practiced human sacrifice, and unlike their Tahitian cousins, were cannibals. When Captain Cook first visited the islands, the population numbered about fifty thousand. Fifty years later it fell to five thousand, and then dropped to twelve hundred. Today it has about seven thousand inhabitants. Herman Melville jumped ship from a whaler here and later wrote his autobiographical *Typee* based on his experiences in the Marquesas. Both Robert Louis Stevenson and Jack London wrote about the islands resulting from their stopovers, and Bengt Danielsson of Kon Tiki fame spent several years in the Marquesas and wrote at length about his experiences here. But the book I found to be most valuable is *White Shadows of the South Sea*, published in 1922 and written by Frederick O'Brien. I had a copy in our ship's library, and at the first crack of light the morning after our arrival, I grabbed it from the shelf and went on deck to read it.

"The healthy Marquesians had no antitoxins in their pure blood to overcome the disease with which us, hardened Europeans and descendants of Europeans, are not deadly. Here they rage and destroyed hundreds in a few days or weeks. The white man brought the Chinese, and with them leprosy, and opium. Small pox came with the Peruvian slave ships. And one of the tribe of merciless American whaling captains, having sent ashore a sailor dying of tuberculosis, the natives received him in a Christlike manner, and carried off four-fifths of the race." He also spoke out about the missionaries: "The efforts of the missionaries have killed the joy of the living as they have crushed out the old barbarities, uprooting everything, bad and good, that religion meant to the native. They have given him instead rites that mystified him, dogmas he can only dimly understand, and a little comfort in the miseries brought him by trade."

We spent five days exploring the island. I took several crew and we hiked over the mountains to Taipivai Valley where Melville sojourned in 1842 after deserting his whaler. Although we found a few temples and stone tikis, the valley was a far cry from what Melville had seen. There were certainly no happy smiling faces.

I thought often of Theo Meier in those five days we were in the islands. He wanted desperately to sail with us to the Marquesas, and instead he gave us the carvings that lined the main saloon. Theo painted here in the 1930s and wanted to re-visit French painter Paul Gauguin's grave. Gauguin died on the island of Hiva Oa in the Marquesas seventy years before, and Theo had come to follow in his foot steps. I left the visit to Gauguin's grave site for another trip.

Stephens, right, and his son Peter, stop to pose for a picture on a hike in the mountains of Nuka Hiva where Herman Melville once tread.

In Taiohae two yachtsmen who had jumped ship approached me about passage to Tahiti. Peter Forde was American; Tony Wouda was Dutch. We agreed with the gendarmes to take them as passengers to Papeete, thus we wouldn't need to secure a bond for them upon our arrival. We were reminded of Melville's experience for he too had been stranded on Nuka Hiva after jumping ship, and he too had to join another ship that carried him to Tahiti. The difference with Peter and Tony and Melville was that no savages were chasing them.

For the first time since leaving Hilo, after endless days of constant pounding, we no longer had to beat into the wind. With four sails set on a broad reach, and with no seas breaking over the deck, we averaged better than six knots for the first two days. And we had no more grumbling from the crew. Spirits were up, and now the talk was about Tahiti. "Tell us again, skipper, what is it like," they asked, and I told them, the same story over and over, like George telling Lenny about the rabbits in *Of Mice and Men.*

The winds continued to be favorable with the current pushing us along. *Third Sea* sailed her best with wind on the beam; most of the time we were able to carry both the fisherman and flying jib. I considered stopping at one of the Taumotus, the low lying atolls northeast of Tahiti, but everyone was anxious to get on to Tahiti. On the third day I made the following entry: "Time Noon. Log 319.6. Winds East at 8 knots. 3rd day run 108 miles. Had to keep an east course with wind on port quarter. Noon fix put Takaroa in the Taumotus some 120 miles to the south. Want to keep a distance of at least 50 miles. Hoping to sight Tahiti in five days. So peaceful and gentle sailing. All the world is ours. Fine bread pudding for breakfast. Kim has been typing my stories. Little else to report from our paradise in the South Seas."

Later that day I made another entry: "Forgot to mention that pilot whales followed us late last night at dusk. Mountain Man was making friends with them from the bowsprit. We could actually hear them talk, or should I say communicate for a better word. One whale had a nick taken out of his dorsal fin. He was Mountain Man's friend. Others came up to the taffrail log spinner and nudged it with their nose. When one whale came up to it and opened his mouth, and showed white teeth, we thought it was a goner but he didn't take it."

The ideal sailing conditions with light seas and a beam wind gave the crew their chance to break old records for the most miles covered in a two-hour stretch at the helm. My log entry read: "Don Perkins set the record at 14.4 miles, or 7.2 miles in one hour. Our run for today was 141.5 nautical miles." We did prove the point that a good helmsman could get more distance by keeping a vessel on even course. The key is concentration.

At two o'clock on the afternoon of the seventh day after leaving Nuka Hiva, we sighted the high mountains of Moorea, Tahiti's sister island. At last, I was returning to Tahiti after thirteen years' absence. Tahiti had been my part-time home for many years. I went there to live long before they had an airport, when the only way to get there was by ship, and now I was going back. I longed to see my old friends, Tahitians and *popaas* alike. And we were arriving now at the best time of the year, for the National Day celebrations—the Bastille Day Fete. But more important to me than anything else, I was returning with a dream fulfilled. I was returning aboard my own lusty schooner, and a trading schooner at that.

Schooner *Third Sea* tied up stern to at the waterfront in Papeete, Tahiti, with a view of Moorea in the background. Aboard *Third Sea* approaching Cook's Bay on Moorea, twelve miles from Papeete.

Chapter 11

TAHITI FOREVER

I was on deck at 4 a.m. to watch Moorea and Tahiti come into view. I couldn't miss this sight for anything. As I stood beside the helmsman, my thoughts went back to the first time I arrived in Tahiti some twenty years before. There was no airport then, not like today.

I had boarded a ship in Panama and it took two weeks to make the crossing. It was a French ship, from the old Messageries Maritimes line; it carried both passengers and freight. There were few tourists aboard. Passengers were mostly Tahitians, some French. The Tahitians were returning home after vacationing or working in France; the French were colonials, military personnel and civil servants, returning from home leave or else going to their new posts for the first time. I had never met a Tahitian before this, nor, for that matter, had I even known anyone who had been to Tahiti. And now I was surrounded by Tahitians. Although that was years ago, I remembered it all so very well. There was Afa, Chinese-Tahitian, a barber. He had become crippled from eating poison fish in the Taumotus and went to France for treatment, which was unsuccessful. There was Emile. He was part French, part Tahitian, and handsome as a movie star. He owned a couple of shops and a hair dressing salon in Papeete, and was traveling with a long-haired Tahitian beauty. We who didn't know Emile thought she was his wife, until we got to Tahiti and discovered his wife was a dour red-headed French women who worked in the Shanghai Bank in Papeete. Jacque was French and had lived thirty years on the island. He went back to his village in southern France after he retired from shipping, but he missed Tahiti terribly. He was returning now for good. There were so many more. There was Genevieve, French-Algerian, going to find a new life and to escape the turmoil in North Africa. Maggie and Margaret, two American school teachers who had saved their money for years and were on the voyage of their lives. Per Stabenfelt, Dutch-American, ran the Richanbeck California Dry Cleaner in Ponce, Puerto Rico; Per was looking for the rainbow's end.

I was hoping that some of the people I once knew might still be in Tahiti when we arrived. For certain Homer Morgan. He was one of Michener's characters in *Return to Paradise*. When I met him he was married to a lovely Chinese-Tahitian woman from a very prominent Tahitian family, and they had two daughters. And Leonie was back in Tahiti. She was one of the leading ladies on MGM's "Mutiny on the Bounty," but then she fell in love with an Australian surfer during the shooting and ran off with him to Melbourne where they got married. I had heard that Nick, her husband, had died suddenly, and Leonie was back with her four children. And there would be others, names and faces I had forgotten but would immediately recall when I saw them.

With each passing day aboard that French ship, the excitement became greater and greater. My newly made friends fired me up with wild, intoxicating stories, about love and romance and daring adventure. The anticipation became almost unbearable. The festive mood that these happy, laughing Tahitians created was infectious. Long before we arrived I knew Tahitian songs by memory, and I could already do the fiery *tamure*, a wild uninhibited Tahitian dance. We could hardly wait. Then came the announcement, we would see the island at dawn. No wonder I wanted to be on deck of *Third Sea* before it got light. Would it be the same after the passing of years?

It was impossible to sleep that night aboard the French ship. Long before dawn appeared in the east I was on deck. Half the crew and most of the passengers were there too, staring vigilantly into the darkness. Suddenly Jacque broke the silence. "There, there it is," he said, with a voice that cracked with emotion. "There, Point Venus." Indeed it was, the flashing light in the darkness marked the north-western tip of the island—the lighthouse at Point Venus.

With the first light of dawn we could see silhouettes, like paper cutouts on the horizon, long silhouettes that caught the reddish glow of morning light. Soon the sky was all ablaze, and now we could discern not one but two island masses. "That's Moorea, on our right," Emile said with his Tahitian lover at his side. We silently approached Moorea and passed it on our right.It began to take shape and form. Bays cut deep into the island, where lofty jagged mountains dropped down right to the water's edge. Greenery clung to the very summits, and cascading waterfalls tumbled hundreds of feet, sending off a thousand rainbows in the morning light. And then, straight ahead, Tahiti came into sharp focus.

That view was overpowering. All sorts of emotions begin to well up inside everyone aboard ship. And I wondered if I might not be witnessing an aberration, a fiction of the mind. I not only saw the island but I could feel it, through all the pores of my skin, through my whole body, to the very tips of my fingers. It was like a very powerful drug that weakens you, that brings tears to your eyes. I felt that I might die right there, and if I had, I would have lived my fullest.

The feeling seemed to intensify as our ship drew nearer. From a distance it was only a silhouette. Now it began to take on depth. The hills above Papeete are undulating;

higher up the shadowed sides of cliffs are deep pools of purple, and clouds and mist form on the higher ridges. The sea unrolls on velvet black sand beaches, beaches where palms meet the sea

A speed boat appeared, pulled along side, and a pilot in a white uniform took hold of a rope ladder that had been dropped over the side for him. He climbed aboard. The ship now silently slipped through a pass in the break-water and we entered Papeete Harbor. At last! It was like I knew it would be: a stone circular quay, clapboard build-ings along the waterfront, a steepled church in the center of town, and all along the quay yachts of every type— motor launches, sloops, cutters, yawls, ketches. And there were the schooners, those magnificent vessels, some tied stern-to to the quay, others anchored farther out, floating on the quiet waters. Here, with the tall-masted vessels, was all the romance of the South Seas. It was no longer a

Papeete waterfront in the late 1950s. Trading schooners await cargo and passenger which they will carry to the outer islands and atolls.

picture in a story book. It was real! Now came the exciting moment. As the ship made its turn and the mooring lines were tossed ashore, as far as I could see there were people, throngs of people, people shouting and waving, people laughing and others with tears flooding down their cheeks. They, both men and women, had wreaths of flowers around their necks, every one of them, and crowns of flowers upon their heads, like Roman gladiators, and flowers tucked behind their ears. They had garlands of flowers drapped over their arms, to be bestowed upon all the new arrivals. The entire waterfront, in fact, was a sea of flowers.

There could have been no finer welcome in all the world, for neither king, prince nor pauper. Everybody was somebody aboard that ship. There were no exceptions. That was once how one arrived in Tahiti before the airport was built.

First Moorea, then Tahiti, came into view off *Third Sea*'s starboard bow early one moring. The view was overpowering, and everlasting.

I feel sorrow for those who arrive now by air, for they do not know the thrill of arriving by sea. I don't mean that it can't be dramatic by air, with that first view of Moorea as the jetliner swoops down from the clouds and begins its descent to Faaa Airport west of Papeete—that is if you have a good window seat and are on the right side of the aircraft. "Ladies and gentlemen," a voice calls over the intercom, "this is your captain. On the right you will see the island of Moorea." Passengers strain hard to catch a glimpse out the window, but it's difficult. Four hundred people are all trying to do the same thing. Then, before you can see anything, a hostess tells you to put your seat in an upright position and fasten your seat belt. The aircraft bumps to a stop, the engines thrust into reverse, and you have arrived in Tahiti.

It's much different by sea, as my crew was now finding out. They too saw the light at Point Venus, and that view of Moorea as we sailed past was no different than when I first saw it so many years before, nor was it any different than when Captain Cook first saw it, and William Bligh, Herman Melville, Robert Louis Stevenson, Jack London and all the rest. Time has not changed that.

The first view of Tahiti had not changed, but the port itself was much different. The lovely little coconut island called Motu Uta out near the reef was no more. It had been cemented over and made into a wharf that extended all the way into town. The clapboard buildings which were once the trademark of the waterfront had been replaced with unimposing concrete and glass structures, and the lovely Vaima's Street Cafe where everyone had gathered for morning coffee and afternoon drinks had become a shopping center. Papeete was no longer a sleepy port in the South Seas. But my crew did not know Tahiti before; they could not make a comparison; and I refrained from telling them. I remembered when I was boarding ship in Panama, going to Tahiti that first time, I met an elderly American who had lived on the island for many years. He had left Tahiti disgruntled, swearing he would never return. "It's not the same," he had said emphatically. "Don't go! You won't like it. The French have ruined the place." Of course, I went, and I loved it. Now I didn't want to be like that old man in Panama telling everyone they wouldn't like it.

We dropped anchor in front of De Gaulle's statue, checked through customs and immigration, and the next day tied up stern-to at the quay right in the center of town. We ran a plank from the stern to shore, connected electricity and water, and had the finest mooring one could ever ask for. And what timing! The National Day Fete was about to begin. From all the islands, from as far away as the Rarotonga, islanders were arriving by plane, trading boat, private yacht, government launch and even French Navy gun boat. They were arriving to compete in outrigger racing, horse racing, bicycle racing, javelin throwing, fire walking, and singing and dancing competitions. Those who weren't competing were coming to have fun. Prefabricated green bamboo stalls for the drinkers and carousers were already up along the waterfront. And from somewhere far off came the sound of shark skin drums and wood blocks. Drummers were practicing for the competitions.

Gone from the Papeete waterfront was the infamous Quinn's Tahitian Hut, the rowdiest bar in the South Seas. You have to imagine an old West saloon, a Dixieland Cabaret in New Orleans, an Oriental taxi dance hall, a German beer garden and a Pigalle bistro in Paris. Combine them under one roof and then take away the liquor control board, the fire marshal, the building inspector, the health and sanitation officer, the W C T, and the DAR. What remained was Quinn's Tahitian Hut.

The noise was shattering. The place seemed to be unhinged. Music blared out into the street and along the entire waterfront. The bamboo walls pulsated and the floor bent in rhythm to the swing of frenzied dancers doing the Tahitian version of the twist. In time it became the most famous bar in the South Seas. And now it was gone forever, closed down a couple years before we arrived. There was now another bar, called the Saloon Bar, that had taken its place. It too was loud, wild and filled with drunken happy Tahitians tossing down buckets of Hinano beer. Whenever I wanted any of my crew, I was certain to find them at the Salon Bar.

Left, Quinn's most famous bar girl, Suzie No Pants, strikes a pose. Right, Quinn's Tahitian Hut, the most infamous bar in the Pacific.

We lost a few crew. My son Peter and Mountain Man flew back to California, and Kim returned to Asia to continue her work with the airlines. Peter Forde and Tony Wouda, our two intrepid castaways from the Marquesas, asked to be signed aboard *Third Sea*. When they heard we were sailing to the Cook Islands after we left French Polynesia, they wanted to join us. They both proved to be good seamen, and were affable, so I signed them on.

The day after Peter and Mountain Man left, my friend Robin Dannhorn arrived from Bangkok. Robin was as much a part of *Third Sea* as anyone. He helped me plan her from the very beginning, and he was aboard for that first sail down the Chao Phraya River. He would make the voyage with us back to Honolulu.

Finding Homer Morgan was an easy matter. Everyone knew him, and his fame came, in part, from James Michener. It was in Quinn's one night that Michener met Homer and his friend Hank Clarke. From that meeting and others later, Michener gathered much of his material for *Return to Paradise.* "Homer Morgan and Hank Clarke were looking for something to do after the war," Michener wrote. "They went to Tahiti to make a million in a shark-catching venture. They both caught the bait but never a shark."

Homer found Tahiti much to his liking and stayed on. When I first got to know him he was married to the Chinese-Tahitian woman that I mentioned. At the time he was the general manager of Hotel Tahiti, the biggest one on the island then.

Homer greeted me warmly, and over lunch filled me in on the local gossip. He had remarried, and I later met his wife, a dancer, and one of the loveliest beauties in the islands. Aside from the shop he had in Vaima's, he had another job any dreamer would want. He and his wife had their own Polynesian dance group with forty lovely dancers. Their team, he said, usually came in first during the National Day Fete competitions.

Homer told me about Michener's coming to Tahiti and their meeting in Quinn's. "No one knew Michener then," he said. "He wasn't a big-selling author. He was just another writer in town. He was with his wife and he was the sort of person you could lose in a crowd of three but in a short time he got to know everyone." Homer admitted Michener was one of the sharpest interviewers he'd ever met. "You didn't even know you were being interviewed," he said. "He got people to talk, to loosen up. He could draw a great deal of out a person without that person ever knowing it." Homer mentioned that Michener came out to their bungalow to talk to him and Hank and then, after a while, said he had to go. "I asked Michener if he was going to interview us, and he said, 'I just have.'"

Between checks from editors Stephens had to eat, so he took bit parts when Hollywood came to Tahiti. Left, as stand-in for Captain Bligh in "Mutiny on the Bounty," and right, the *Bounty* in the background.

I didn't recognize Leonie when I saw her. She wasn't the lithe Tahitian *vahine* who posed for MGM in the arms of Marlon Brando. She had put on weight, acres of it, and she called out, "Steve, where have you been?" She then introduced me to Fortuna, her Tahitian husband of half a dozen years. Later I met her four children.

Emile now had grown old, and gone was his Tahitian sweetheart. He was back under the clutches of his French wife with red hair. Emile didn't remember me. But Jacque did, and he was proud to sign a copy of a book he wrote on Tahiti. I kept it in the library aboard *Third Sea*.

Another man that I admired and wanted to see again was Bill Stone, but I was too late. He had died a year or two before. Michener wrote about him in *Return to Paradise*. Bill had flown in the Lafayette Escadrille in France during the First World War and in the 1920s piloted commercial aircraft between the US and Mexico. Tragedy struck when he was crippled in an air accident and confined to a wheelchair for the rest of his life. Rather than burden his wife and infant daughter—no social security then—he ran off and boarded a steamer bound for Australia. The steamer stopped in Tahiti. While the passengers went ashore, Bill sat in his wheelchair behind the railing, looking over the side. A young Tahitian girl waved to him to come down and, when he didn't, she ran up the gangplank to get him. When she saw that he was crippled she turned and ran, making Bill even more despondent. But the girl came back, followed by her burly brother. The Tahitian picked Bill up and carried him ashore to a new life.

Bill began writing, made a little money, invested it in property and, in time, became quite wealthy. Without his wife knowing his whereabouts— for he married the Tahitian girl who came aboard that day—he supported her and his daughter by sending them money through a lawyer in San Francisco. When his daughter Barbara was grown, she tracked down her father in Papeete. Bill introduced me to her, and I now learned that after his death she no longer came to the island. Bill had autographed several of his books which I kept aboard *Third Sea*.

The competitions lasted for six nights, and on the final night the drummers from all the teams gathered under torch light. There may have been as many as two or three hundred, in grass costumes and coral headdresses, with damp brown bodies catching the reflections of flickering light. They let loose. Not for others, not in imitation of others. They say the sound could be heard on Moorea twelve miles away.

Like it was for the crew of the *HMS Bounty* when it came time for them to leave, the crew of *Third Sea* were no different. They too had been caught up in the spell of Tahiti, and by the Tahitians. In spite of the many changes the island has endured, the Tahitians still remain a remarkable people. They have not lost the ability to smile and laugh. Life is a moment of happiness, to be felt, to be enjoyed. They may not comprehend the double meaning of a joke, but burn your tongue on a hot cup of coffee, or say the wrong thing at the wrong time, and they fold up with laughter.

Such laughter becomes infectious, and like laughter in a school room it spreads. Even when the French detonate nuclear bombs on neighboring isles and fearsome mushroom clouds rise skyward, they laugh and remark how beautiful it was.

Some things don't change, and don't disappear. The scent of lush foliage after a rain shower, the sweet smell of copra drying in a shed, the aroma of fresh coffee coming from a plantation. And the fragrant scent of flowers, frangipani and the Taire Tahiti. They are everywhere.

It's all these things, the combination of sounds, smells and sights, that create the mood that hangs heavy over the island. It awakens all the senses, and one almost becomes a savage, wanting to imbibe in its wild and wondrous madness. Sometimes the beauty of Tahiti—maybe the mist, the way it hangs over the mountains in the morning, or maybe the sinking sun at dusk, dropping over the edge of a reef—sometimes the beauty becomes so overpowering you feel you can never leave. Nevertheless, depart we must.

We had remained a month. Our plan now was to sail to the leeward islands—Moorea, Huahine and Bora Bora—and then to Rarotonga in the Cook Islands. From there we would visit Tongareva again, and perhaps take in Christmas Island on the final leg of the voyage to Honolulu. When word got around that we were sailing to Hawaii, we had a hundred people who wanted to join as paying crew. Aside from Peter Forde and Tony Wouda, we signed on a young Canadian woman, Elieen Hunter, and two Americans, Carol Schidler and Lynwood Hume. We had eleven aboard when we left Tahiti and sailed for Moorea. Leonie's young son, Charlie, was sailing with us to Moorea.

We anchored the first night in Papetoai Bay and the following morning moved to Cook's Bay nearby. Both are equally beautiful, with vertical cliffs that drop sheer into the lagoon, but Cook's Bay held the attraction for me. I wanted to visit with my friends, Harriet and Omar Darr and the three Americans who owned the Bali Hai Hotel, Muk, Kelly and Jay. We dropped anchor in Robinson's Cove and warped the stern up to the beach by securing mooring lines to palm trees on the shore. It has to be the world's most splendid anchorage.

Robinson's Cove is named after William Albert Robinson, a name well known in the annals of yachting. In 1928, he set out from New England to sail around the world in a thousand dollar, thirty-two foot ketch called *Svaap.* He returned home in 1931 to write a best-selling book about his experiences, *Ten Thousand Leagues Over the Sea,* and enjoyed the excitement of a busy schedule of lecturing and writing stories and magazine articles. He was soon a celebrity.

What he had seen in passing enroute around the world remained to haunt him, particularly Tahiti. He returned to Tahiti by steamer in 1934 and purchased the land that now bears his name.

Shortly before World War II began, he went back to Ipswich, Massachusetts and found a shipyard that built schooners for the Gloucester fishing fleet and ocean-going sailing yachts. For himself in 1941, he built a seventy-foot brigantine called the *Varua.*

The war forced his small shipyard into bustling activity with six hundred employees turning out vessels for the Navy. It was not until 1945, three months before VJ Day that Robinson received permission from Admiral Nimitz to sail *Varua* back to Tahiti where he has remained ever since. He sailed his schooner about the Pacific with his wife and a crew of two. One voyage in *Varua* was a 14,000-mile circle of the Pacific in 1951, Tahiti to Chile to Panama and back home to the Islands. Robinson described this voyage in *To the Great Southern Sea.* In a 1957 voyage he sailed *Varua* up the Chao Phraya River to Bangkok, and wrote about it in *Return to the Sea.*

I first read Robinson's *Ten Thousand Leagues Over the Sea* when I was still a teenager and could quote passages of the book by heart. My surprise came when I first went to Tahiti and saw *Varua* anchored with the rest of the big schooners in Papeete Harbor. My chance to meet him came when Bill Stone and his daughter invited me to dinner at the Hotel Tahiti. We were seated when Robinson came into the restaurant with his Chinese-Tahitian wife Ah You and their four daughters. I expressed my delight in meeting him, but he seemed not to hear me. He was rather aloof and casual. I tried several times after that to make his friendship but he always maintained his distance. When we had *Third Sea* in dry dock in Honolulu, *Varua* was anchored in Ke'hee Lagoon, but Willaim A. Robinson was not aboard. He had turned the grand vessel over to the Seventh Day Adventists Missionary Society.

Not far down the road from Robinson's Cove I looked in on Omar Darr and his wife Harriet. They owned the Shark's Tooth, a kind of gift shop cum boutique. Omar is one of the great characters of the South Seas that Michener somehow missed.

Barbara, daughter of late writer Bill Stone, and Omar Darr, go aboard *Wanderer*. Right, Omar in later years at his home on Moorea.

Omar actually hunted for sharks in his early years, but he was most famous as captain of schooner *Te Vega* which made a name in the movie "Cinerama" in the late 1950's. Captain Darr ran passengers between Honolulu and Papeete, a lucrative business before Tahiti had an airport. Sitting on his verandah, facing the world's most beautiful bay, I enjoyed his rum punches, listening to his tales about catching sharks and his voyages aboard *Te Vega* and Sterling Hayden's *Wanderer* which he once owned. Years before I had crewed aboard *Wanderer* under Omar.

Omar made the Honolulu run for a dozen years, spending only a few days in each port before sailing again. He actually raised his family at sea. To my delight he praised *Third Sea* when he saw her, and on one of my subsequent visits to Moorea asked me to sail to Caroline Island north of Tahiti to rescue a worker he had there overseeing his copra plantation.

And farther down the road was the Bali Hai Hotel, owned and operated by three friends, Muk, Kelly and Jay. The three entrepreneurs had arrived in Tahiti about the same time I did. They came from Los Angeles, looking for a good time. Muk was a graduate engineer, Kelly a successful lawyer, and Jay had a seat on the stock exchange. Needless to say, they fell in love with the islands, especially Moorea.

The new airport made easy access to Tahiti, so why not build a house on Moorea, they reasoned. Maybe rent it when they were on the mainland. They found land along the beach and built a grass house. I helped them lay the concrete slab for the foundation and cut the corner posts from palm trunks. They wove their own thatched roof.

It was lovely. They liked company and invited friends over from Papeete. Then the habit developed to chip in two dollars a day, to help with costs. It was the same price for those who brought their Tahitian *vahines* with them.

They called it the Bali Hai, and soon it became the most popular spot on the island. Space became a problem so they erected another house. But trouble began when the manger of the only hotel on Moorea put up a fuss. Even his own help started to abandon him on weekends, to join in the fun at the Bali Hai.

The hotel owner petitioned the French Governor to run Muk, Kelly and Jay out of the islands. Kelly, the lawyer, got a second petition signed by nearly every native on the island to let them stay. It was quite an accomplishment since most of the islanders couldn't read or write. The three Americans won out, and not only that, they obtained a licence to operate a hotel. They now began to grow in leaps and bounds. Unfortunately they created a situation they had tried to escape from, namely making money. Before long they had hotels on three other islands. Everything they touched turned to money. They were having difficulty finding enough eggs to supply their hotel restaurants, so Muk started a chicken farm. Soon he was supplying three-fourths of the eggs for all French Polynesia. Before we sailed, Muk took me with him on an egg delivery trip to stores around the island. The locals loved him, with his antics and gibes. They called him the "white Chinese man."

From Moorea we sailed to Huahine, a two-day passage. I felt rather proud. I read from the log of the *Bounty* that it took Captain Bligh thirteen days. We anchored in front of the Bali Hai Hotel. When it came time to depart, we motored to the wharf in Fare, the main village on the island, and took on water and supplies. We unfurled the U.S. flag, cast off our mooring lines and sailed out of the harbor with all six sails bellowing in the wind. We then set our course for Bora Bora. We gave Raiatea and Taha a miss but these two islands would come later, on other voyages. We sailed through the night, with a fine red-tinted moon that rose up behind us over Raiatea. At dawn we had Bora Bora in view. *Third Sea* entered Teavanui Pass with all sails set and anchored in the front of the new Bora Bora Yacht Club.

During World War II, the U.S. Navy had five thousand sailors and marines stationed on the island. Lt. James Michener, USN, arrived on the island as Navy historian. He was amused to find the Navy had moved all the eligible women off the island to neighboring Raiatea. On a clear day the marines and sailors could see the island shimmering in the distance, and there they longed to be. The setting gave Michener his theme for the legendary Bali H'ai in his best selling *Tales of the South Pacific,* which later became a musical hit—"South Pacific."

Left, the most striking landfall a sailor can experience is the sight of Bora Bora. Right, we found a cannon from World War II in the hills.

We had good sailing all the way to Rarotonga in the Cooks Islands. We passed many beautiful islands with romantic sounding names like Maupiti and Mopelia. The sailing conditions could not have been better. Robin took up the challenge of trying to beat the helmsman record. He was a perfectionist, adjusting and trimming sails, but it was Perkins who came out in the lead and broke his own record. He averaged 7.5 knots. He had *Third Sea* skimming over the top of the seas on a broad reach.

Avarua on the island of Rarotonga is the capital of the Cook Islands and is considered by many to be one of the great ports of the South Pacific. It was our destination. We brought up the island at dawn and by noon we were tacking back and forth across the entrance of the harbor, studying the situation. It didn't look like it was possible to enter the harbor.

Third Sea's crew explore the wreck of Captain Irving Johnson's famous brigantine *Yankee* on the windswept reef at Rarotonga Island.

High on a coral reef north of the entrance was the rusted remains of the brigantine *Yankee,* Irving Johnson's famous ship that made seven circumnavigations.

We were prepared to tack and go back out to sea when a fishing boat entering the harbor motioned for us to follow them. I pointed *Third Sea* into their wake. The pass, although well marked, was barely fifty feet wide, and a freighter at the pier seemed to take up all the room. I suddenly remembered I was breaking one of my own rules that I had learned when we first sailed *Third Sea* down the coast of Malaysia to Singapore. Then, as now, I was considering entering Trengganu, a port on the mainland. Fishing boats were running in and out with ease. I stopped a fishing boat and the captain informed me we could make it. Fortunately we were on an incoming tide, and as we began to enter we bumped bottom. It was time to turn around and get out. What local boatmen don't know is that sailing yachts have a deep keel. Ours measured seven and a half feet. But in this instance the pass was deep and we entered without difficulty. We tied up next to the freighter at the pier.

We toured the island for two days, and I was fortunate to meet the aging wife of Captain Andy Thompson, one of the great trading boat skippers of the Pacific. Our next destination was Tongareva.

With the wind from the southeast we made good on a northerly course for Tongareva and then Honolulu. We passed beautiful Aitutaki on our starboard and was tempted to stop but we would have had to anchor outside the reef. We were doing better than one-hundred and fifty miles a day. But when we were less than a hundred miles from our goal, the wind backed and came from the direction we wanted to go. We had to beat into it, tacking back and forth. Then even what little wind we did have came to a stop. We felt fortunate if we could do two knots. Once when I went to check the log line, the spinner was hanging perpendicular, straight up and down. We had a burst of wind that moved us at six knots and then it died as suddenly as it began, but in that short burst Robin was able to land a twenty-five pound wahoo. We had sushimi for an afternoon snack. The next burst of wind landed us a fifteen pound barracuda. The next morning at dawn, Paul spotted land off the starboard bow. Tongareva!

By ten o'clock we were about to enter the pass when we got hit with a powerful line squall that came whipping at us at forty knots an hour. We had no choice but to head back out to sea, and after it blew itself out we headed back. This time we didn't have to lower the dingy and go investigate the pass as we did before. We knew it well, but the new crew, when we started in, thought that their captain had gone mad.

Left, islanders on Tongareva scamper aboard *Third Sea* for a look inside. Right, no paved sidewalks only coral paths on Tongareva.

When we hit the white water on the incoming tide, *Third Sea* picked up like a surfboard and went shooting into the lagoon. We knew where the coral heads were inside the pass, and I swung hard to starboard to avoid them.

Two boats set out to greet us, for they now recognized *Third Sea*. Before we could drop anchor, dozens of kids swam out from the shore. The older boys immediately began to pull out pearls from bags attached to their waists. Then Papa Beer arrived with his wife and family, and chased the boys off. He wanted us to himself. It was a happy reunion. I only regretted that I hadn't brought trade goods with me. I never expected to stop at Tongareva on this run. Nevertheless, I was able to give them a chest of clothing and a box of old tools and enough presents to keep him and his family happy.

We spent a happy week on the island. We had Papa Beer and his family aboard for dinner one night, and Archie Pickering, the Harbor Master, another time. During the day Papa Beer took us diving for pearls, among the sharks, and we explored the wreck of a yacht that sank in the harbor a couple years before. At night the young women invited the crew to feasts and dancing on the beach. It was lovely when they strummed guitars and beat rhythm on empty five-gallon kerosine tins turned upside down. It wasn't so lovely when they wanted us to bring ashore our tape recorders, and then played Eric Clapton. The lure of South Sea island romance was lost.

A few days before we left, the weather turned foul and to keep from dragging I had let out thirty-five fathoms of chain, over two-hundred feet. When it came time to weigh anchor, we were wrapped around coral heads. It took us hours to untangle and it was near dark when we set sail. Papa Beer came aboard with presents—four beautiful black pearls, a large floor mat, two straw hats, half a dozen large pearl shells and many smaller ones, including two with pearls still embedded in them, a tortoise shell and several shell leis for around the neck. He then handed me a list he would like for my next voyage, bolts of cloth, curtain material, dishes, cups, a sea chest, diving masks and a twenty-five horsepower Mercury outboard engine.

Once through the pass, with the setting sun reflecting on the white stone church on the point, we hoisted the big jib and sat down to a spaghetti dinner on deck. The next day the winds died, and we were Coleridge's Ancient Mariner "as idle as a painted ship upon a painted ocean."

For the third day entry in the log I wrote: "Log 52.9. Wind, none. Totally becalmed. Not even a ripple." My sun shot the next morning indicated we had drifted sixteen miles to the west, a distance we would have to make up. We needed easing.

An idle ship at sea begins to play upon one's nerves. Tensions run high. A word not said right is interpreted as a hostile intent. A look the wrong way is misconstrued. Tempers flare. We begin imagining things. Or was it imagination? I entered it in the log: "Saw strange phenomena last night after dark. Ghostlike creatures, as large as pilot whales, swam beneath the surface, appearing and disappearing suddenly as though they were reflections. But there were no lights aboard, not even our running lights, and no stars, and the moon was not yet up."

The next morning I was called on deck. It was bright daylight, and there beneath the ship were the ghostlike creatures again. Sharks? A school of fish? Hardly. We couldn't tell. I made the next entry in the log: "They are slinky and shadowy and seem to glide by underneath the rudder effortlessly. It's an eerie feeling."

I remembered Herman Melville's comments. I took

Moby Dick down from the shelf. No one, sitting in the secure comforts of home, with a burning fireside at their feet and the book across their laps, no one could feel the same emotions as I did when I began reading *Moby Dick*. "Consider the sea," Melville began, "how its most dreaded creatures glide under water, unapparent for the most part, and treacherously hidden beneath the loveliest tints of azure. Consider once more the universal cannibalism of the sea; all whose creatures prey upon each other, carrying on eternal war since the world began." I shut the book and went on deck. No, it wasn't imagination—they were still there.

On the eighth day we began moving again. That evening Perkins made his comment in the running log: "Still trailed by the White Thing." Robin came up with the idea that it might be some sort of below-the-surface wake set up by the motion of the ship. Possible. There was one way to tell. If porpoise came and the "white thing" remained, then we knew it had to be a disturbance caused by the motion of the sea against the ship's hull. At two o'clock during the change of watch, we herd the helmsman call. "Porpoise," he shouted. We slammed into each other trying to get up the companion way to the deck. We could hear porpoise, the sucking sound as they breathe. They were standing their ground. We looked over the side. The "white thing" was still there. It remained until we reached the northern latitudes; we never did discover what it might have been. But we remembered Melville's lines— "dreaded creatures, unapparent for the most part."

But it was more than the dreaded "white thing" that made the crew ill at ease. Peter Forte was at the helm with several crew sitting around him in the cockpit. They heard a slapping bang, and thought at first that one of the crew had thrown something overboard. But no one was about. When they heard the second bang they rushed to the port rail. I too rushed on deck when I head the noise. To my ears it sounded like someone had thrown a plank on the deck. An eight-foot shark was attacking the ship. We saw the shark back off, linger for a while, and then coming threshing through the water and strike the port side of the hull head-on. He did this several times, striking the hull with his full force. I actually thought he might hole us but he didn't. He stayed with us for ten minutes and then swam off to the south.

We had to break the solemn mood. Robin succeeded by cooking a magnificent dinner—fish-potato cakes with banana flambe for desert, followed by rum punches with the last of our fresh fruit. We had an equally magnificent sunset that seemed to linger forever, while the crew sat along the rail and on the cabin top, listening to Beethoven's "Emperor Concerto." Later I noted the helmsman's comment in the running log: "Colorful ending to an exciting day." Beauty does follow beauty, and yet one tends to forget beauty. Upon a sailing ship, the sea and sky are infinite with beauty, and surprises. Those wonderful colors we see at dawn, as lovely as they are, they are beyond memory. They are fleeting moments of joy, never to be duplicated. The world is the sailor's imperishable painting.

The weather grew hot and the sun beat down upon us unmercifully. We had to constantly wash down the decks to cool them off. The sea about us was completely empty, seemingly void of life. Even the clouds were gone. We knew we were playing a game of poker with forces that were far greater than us. We say that we sail the seas—or climb mountains—to conquer nature. That is rubbish! We survive the sea only because it is gentle with us. The sea can take us any time it so desires. So we treat the sea accordingly. And we do become believers. If someone says he doesn't believe, we can give him a test. Ask a nonbeliever, a person who says he doesn't believe in God, ask him to swear upon it, but ask him to swear upon it when the night is black, when the sea is raging, when wind and wave are uncontrolled and his frail ship is tossed about unmercifully. Ask him to shake an angry fist at the angry sea and say that there is no God. He cannot do it. Thus, is it unreasonable that sailors are superstitious? I don't believe so.

At six o'clock the following morning I entered in the log that it was "hot, hot, hot." Never had I seen the sea so clam. No air; no horizon. The sky and the sea were one, and we sweltered without a breath of air. The next sun shot put us six miles farther to the west. I made my entry in the log: "Had pancakes for breakfast and had everyone turn to. Pulled the chain on deck and marked each ten fathoms with white paint. Repaired dory's oar locks. Divers over the side and scraped the bottom, and cursed the remittance man in Honolulu for his submarine paint. Oiled the two back stays. Placed a new block on top the main mast for the flag halyard. Painted the life rings. Fixed the klaxon. And we all went for a swim, but immediately left the water when we saw sharks."

The next morning the moon rose at four o'clock, like a Viking ship riding a wave. Dawn came two hours later with a white sail upon the horizon. Seldom do you see other sailing ships upon the open sea, but we did that morning. The wind had come up and we were ghosting along at three knots. The ship was a sloop and cut across our starboard horizon, on its way to Tahiti no doubt.

We were at sea two weeks, and less than half way to Hawaii. Perkins attributed our bad luck to the disrespect that the crew had toward tradition. They did not want to submit to King Neptune when we crossed the Equator. He may have been right. In any event, when we drew near to Christmas Island in the Line Islands we decided to make an anchor stop and let the crew stretch their legs for a few relaxing days.

I was anxious to get back to the island. On *Third Sea's* first voyage from Samoa to Honolulu, we stopped at Tongareva and then briefly at Christmas Island. I became so fascinated with the island at that time that when we reached Honolulu, I went to the Bishop Museum and did some research. I was astounded at what I found.

First, the island is not to be confused with another Christmas Island in the Indian Ocean, some eight hundred and twenty miles southwest of Singapore. That Indian Ocean island was the private domain of the Clunies-Ross family until it was annexed by Australia in 1958.

The Christmas Island we reached aboard *Third Sea* is one of the Line Islands that lie between French Polynesia and the Hawaiian Islands. It's the largest coral atoll in the world with an area of two hundred and thirty-four square miles, making it larger than Singapore, with a population of less than a hundred people. When we first arrived, other than a few statistics, we knew little about the island. We sighted her late one afternoon stood off shore for the night, and anchored at dawn the next morning. The chart revealed that the opening to the lagoon had a depth of but five feet, much too shallow for our seven and a half foot draft. The entrance had a village to the north, and another to the south, called London and Paris, respectively. We anchored in five fathoms on a sandy bottom, and two crew put on their diving masks to check that the anchor had dug in. Seconds later they came crashing to the surface shouting with excitement, "Look, look, we have never seen any thing like it before."

I thought maybe they had found a wrecked Spanish galleon or a sunken treasure but it was none of these. What they saw were schools of fish. They were so enthusiastic that the rest of us went over the side to investigate. They were right! Never had we seen anything like it before, nor, do I imagine, will we see it again.

The translucent water was like a vast aquarium where fish of the most preposterous sizes swam side by side without apparent fear of one another. Mantarays, some with wing spans that could have measured ten feet across; schools of Angelfish and other tropical fish we hadn't seen before—what a spear-fisherman's paradise. We climbed back aboard to gather our spear guns. We would have enough fish to feed the crew all the way to Hawaii.

A skiff propelled by an outboard came from the lagoon entrance with three men aboard. We could hear them shouting from the distance. They could see we were about to dive overboard with our spear guns. Evidently they didn't want anyone fishing their waters.

"You can't, you can't," we could hear them warning now. And then we heard the word CONTAMINATED.

They explained that some twenty years before, the British used Christmas Island as an atomic testing ground, contaminating the fish and every living thing with radioactivity. It was no small wonder the fish were so large and abundant: the waters around Christmas Island hadn't been fished in a generation.

We did not remain long on Christmas Island that voyage, but long enough to get my curiosity up. In Honolulu I found the answers at the Bishop Museum.

The Line Islands include Christmas, Palmyra, Washington, Fanning, Jarvis, Malden and Starbuck. What is most amazing about this remote chain of islands is that they have never had a permanent indigenous habitation.

The Polynesians of the South Pacific only used the Line Islands for temporary stopovers. At Fanning on the first voyage we did find a colony of migrant laborers from the Gilbert Islands who were producing copra under the Burns Philip Trading Company.

While Fanning is habitable, Christmas is bleak and dry. There had been a Spanish sighting of Christmas Island in 1537, but it wasn't until Captain Cook arrived in the South Pacific on his third voyage that Christmas Island became known to the world.

After sailing due north from Tahiti, Captain Cook, aboard the *Discovery* with the *Resolution* closely behind it, spotted the island after day break on December 24th. His ships made it to the lee coast and dropped anchor on Christmas morning, about the same place *Third Sea* anchored. Cook sent ashore the master of the *Resolution* to survey the lagoon. The master was Lieutenant William Bligh, then twenty-two years of age, but who later in life became a public and controversial figure in the mutiny of the *Bounty*. Bligh reported a channel into the lagoon was only fit for small boats.

The sailors also found a small island at the channel entrance which provided safe anchoring for the two ships. The island today is known as Cook Island and is a bird sanctuary. Under the command of Bligh the crews hunted turtles and in twenty-four hours captured three hundred, with the largest weighing thirty pounds. Bligh reported that "on every side of us were sharks innumerable and so voracious that they bit our oars and rudders."

Cook planted coconuts and yams on the island for future generations. Due to the inability of ships to anchor close to shore, the island has remained free of the European rat, but, as we discovered, it had something far worse—cats. Domestic cats had gone wild and become predators. They were everywhere we went, lurking in the bushes, hiding in the ditches, ready to spring upon anything that moved. They made lone walks for us dangerous, and it was impossible for the crew to camp ashore as they had planned. There were estimated to be some seventy thousand cats roaming the island.

Captain Cook spent ten days on Christmas Island. He finally set sail the first week of January with three hundred turtles aboard, and eighteen days later made one of his major discoveries, the Sandwich Islands later to be called Hawaii.

The story of Christmas Island only begins here. After Cook made known that Christmas Island had abundant fish, turtles, birds and now coconuts, every whaler and trading boat crossing the Pacific made the island a port-of-call. As a result the island was again the victim of man's destruction.

In 1835, Captain Frank Bennett wrote that he found Christmas Island still uninhabited, and gone were all the turtles and most of the fish in the lagoon, and nearly all the coconut trees had been chopped down years before. Whalers found it simply much easier to cut the trees down than to climb them for the nuts.

A year after Bennett's visit, the whaling ship *Briton* became the first known victim of the treacherous Bay of Wrecks on the windward east coast. The captain and his crew spent seven months on the island before they were finally rescued.

One country after another laid claim to Christmas, but none of them remained long. Later, Father Emmanuel Rougler, a French Catholic priest who appeared on the scene at the end of the last century, claimed the island as his own. Born in 1864 and ordained as a priest before he was twenty-four, Rougler became a missionary, then a wealthy planter on Tahiti and eventually owned not only Christmas but Fanning and Washington islands as well.

Father Rougler took a black girl from Fiji as his mistress, and it's reported that he paid 14,500 British pounds in cash for Christmas Island. He set up a baronial estate in a mansion surrounded by coconut plantations. Father Rougler was more a man of the world than a man of God. His estate was to the south of the passage; he named it Paris where today only piles of stones and a few shrubs are witness of his occupation.

The American military occupation of Christmas Island began on a winter day on November 18, 1941, two weeks before the Japanese bombing of Pearl Harbor, when eight officers, 155 enlisted men and 80 civilians landed and began the construction of an airfield. After the bombing of Pearl Harbor, the establishment grew to 2,428 soldiers and 193 civilians. It lasted until October 1948.

The defense of Christmas Island with its ninety miles of coastline presented a problem. The remains of a network of underground machine gun nests can still be traced between the airfield and the ocean shore.

There's more to the story of Christmas Island. On the quiet moring of March 4, 1956, a five-hundred-and-ninety-two-ton barge docked at London. Some six weeks later, on April 21, the first of a series of British H-bomb tests began. The first three bombs in the megaton range were dropped from bombers and exploded at eighteen thousand feet above the island. Thirty-three government staff and a score of plantation workers stood off shore aboard a gunship to watch the explosion.

The tests lasted three years and were later conducted above ground atop sixty-foot towers. Early studies claimed the only danger from the blast was to the eyes. Workers were asked to sit on the beach at the end of the island and keep their heads lowered. They were instructed not to look up until told to.

After the tests on Christmas Island, the British left and in 1970 American service personnel reappeared for the splashdown of the Apollo Thirteen crew returning from the moon. Now, on our second trip, we explored the island from end to end. Few corners of the island were not marked by the detritus of military occupation. Bulldozers stand abandoned where they last broke down. Black patches of bitumen ooze from dumps of rusted drums. A mountain of beer cans and beer bottles indicates the skeleton of a one-time canteen. Porcelain urinals stand like monuments upon the foundation of a former toilet block, and everywhere are trailing copper wires, miles and miles of them.

Buildings, the frames of offices, messrooms and workshops, are in ruins. In warehouses packing crates spill their contents over the concrete floors. In one building we found hundreds of British-made automobile engines still in their crates.

Less than a hundred islanders inhabit Christmas today, with occasional students coming to monitor the bird population on Cook Island.

The voyage was taking longer than expected, and it was playing havoc with Robin Dannhorn's schedule. He had commitments back in Bangkok and decided to hop on a plane from Christmas to Honolulu. There was a flight due in a week. We left him on the shore and set a course for Honolulu. The third day out we had a frightening experience. In the black of night, when there was neither star nor moon, we were hit by a tidal wave.

It was near midnight and Paul Schofield was at the helm ready to be relieved. I was standing in the companionway, my back against the main mast, looking out at the black void. Suddenly, I could not believe my eyes. It came so fast and unexpected I couldn't act, and I was too speechless to call a warning to the helmsman. All across our starboard quarter a wave came toward us, cresting white across the top. It stood higher than the second rung on the rope ratlines, perhaps twenty or thirty feet from sea level. It broke as it reached the ship, knocking me flat against the hatch cover, making breathing impossible. The schooner shuddered; she was completely awash. Seeing it break, Paul turned his back and held fast to the wheel. Later he said, "I didn't think it would stop. There was no end to the water." Perkins was in his cabin, ready to come on watch, when he heard the crash followed by the sound of rushing water on deck. He expected to hear our shouts but none came. He feared we may have been washed over board and came rushing topside. He was relieved to see us picking ourselves up from the deck. When things returned to normal, we listened to the weather station but there were no reports of tidal waves.

The winds for the next few days were fluky, changing from one quarter to the next without warning. For two days we had to run under a reefed main with a jib staysail only. The wind shrieked in the rigging and we pounded violently, and yet the sky was clear and the sun was out. The sea was a lovely blue and when it broke it was translucent. We were sailing upon an empty sea, with no land about for a thousand miles in any direction.

At dawn on the sixteenth day, the helmsman gave the call—"Land Ho!" He had spotted Mauna Loa towering above the clouds on the Big Island. Our morning sun shot put us seventy-six miles from the southwest tip of the island. With the sight of land soon everyone forgot the difficult sailing we had had. They forgot the endless pounding, the waves breaking over the bow, the sleepless nights, the rain-soaked watches, the hot coffee that spilled before it reached the helmsman. That was all past and forgotten. We can be thankful the mind works that way, or one would never go to sea in a small boat. The last days now were lovely and clear, and it seemed they had always been that way. And the mahi mahi were jumping again. At one hour before midnight, with the lights of Honolulu lighting the way, we slipped quietly into Alai Wai Yacht Harbor and tied up to the loading dock. We were sure the Harbor Master wouldn't mind.

We were back, back to the very spot from where we had started. We had been gone one hundred and thirty-six days and twenty hours, and had sailed six thousand nine hundred and six miles.

Over the next few years, and following Captain Omar Darr's advice, I made a half dozen runs from Honolulu to Tahiti and back. There was easy money to be made in ferrying passengers back and forth. There was no direct air service then between the islands. If someone in Honolulu wanted to visit Tahiti, they first had to fly to Los Angeles to make a connection. To make the voyages more interesting, on each passage we stopped at different islands. Once, when we were leaving Moorea, Omar Darr asked if we would stop at Caroline Island and pick up an overseer he had living there. Omar was very interested in harvesting copra on the island and had found Peter, a young Englishman, who was willing to live alone on the island and survey the copra crop there. Omar learned that Peter's mother was ill in London. We agreed to rescue him. He had been living on the island for six months when we arrived, during a violent storm. We almost lost *Third Sea* on the reef while trying to get him off the island. After seeing how Peter lived, as a hermet in a tree house away from hords of coconut rats, we carried him with us

Third Sea stopped at Caroline to rescue Peter who lived alone on the island. He poses here with a giant hermit crab we had for lunch.

to Honolulu where he caught a flight to London. A few years later Peter rejoined *Third Sea* when the schooner was anchored in Singapore.

At Fanning Island we met Bill Frew, the caretaker there. Bill was a legend. He had been living on the island for twenty-eight years when we met him. He had an island wife and grown children, and he was a raconteur who loved to tell stories. We listened to him for hours, sitting on his verandah, smoking his hand-rolled cigarettes one after the other. I found his stories so interesting that I made a point to stop at the island on my next run. Bill was no longer there. I learned that after we had left the island on our first visit, Bill got up from his chair on the verandah and went for a walk. He was never seen again. He simply disappeared, making this one of the unsolved mysteries of the South Pacific.

A man I really wanted to meet was a New Zealander named Tom Neil. He was a hermit who lived on Suvarov Atoll, a tiny group of islets on a coral reef in the northern Cook Islands west of Tongareva and a thousand miles from Rarotonga.

Tom first saw the island when he was sailing with Captain Andy Thompson aboard his schooner *Taire Taporo*. By profession Tom was a storekeeper and worked many years for trading companies on scattered islands across the Pacific. Andy was taking Tom to a new post when they saw Suvarov, uninhabited, lonely, like a new shiny pearl resting on a sea of blue velvet.

Tom could not forget that island. How fine it would be to live on such a place. He knew coast watchers had used the island during the war, and most likely they had left some buildings and other material behind. These could be fixed up into rather comfortable living quarters. There were coconuts, and unlimited fish, crayfish and other sea life in the lagoon. He could plant bananas and papaya, a vegetable garden and raise chickens. What an ideal life.

As time went on, Tom thought more and more about his island of desire. Why couldn't he survive on a desert island? But he realized his biggest drawback was that he didn't have much money. After ten years of hard work his total assets amounted to some two hundred dollars. But maybe that was even the more reason to go. He made up his mind and started making plans.

Tom eventually found an independent trader in Rarotonga who agreed to take him and his supplies for sixty-five dollars. They set sail for Suvarov and a week later the island came into sight. The crew rowed him and his supplies, along with two cats, ashore and left them on the beach. Tom watched the captain wave from the bridge. He could hear the anchor chain draw through the hawse and then watched the freighter exit through the pass and enter the open sea. He was alone.

During the months, the years of preparation, he often wondered what his feelings would be when the ship that brought him sailed away. He was fifty years old, and although he didn't fear being alone, he found himself awed by what he had done. He had often wondered what would happen if he became ill or if he had an accident. How would he cope without a doctor, or even a helping hand? But once that ship sailed he no longer thought about these things. He had work to do. What Tom Neil didn't realize was that he was about to create a world exactly the same as the one from which he had wanted to escape. A world of incredibly hard work. He found himself working harder than he ever had in his life.

By the end of the first year Tom was settled in. His island paradise was just as he had imagined it would be. The chickens were all closed in and the hens laying. The garden was producing. He had plenty of fresh fruit and vegetables for his table and there was no shortage of fish.

Tom remained twenty-one years on Suvarov, and in that time only a half dozen yachts stopped to visit him.

I had wanted to visit Suvarov but when I had *Third Sea* sailing the South Pacific, Tom had already died. But I did make a point to stop at his island on one of my runs from Tahiti to Honolulu. It was a thrilling moment.

We picked our way through the pass and anchored offshore from where Tom had lived. We rowed to the beach and set out to find the shack. It was an eerie feeling, like treading on a grave.

I expected to find his shack in shambles and the place overgrown. I was shocked to discover the shack was in fine condition. The yard swept. The garden trim. I fully expected Tom to step out of the door and say, "Welcome to Suvarov."

Tom's last request was that visiting yachtsmen respect his property. That they have done. Every yachtsman that passes makes repairs and cleans up. You feel that Tom Neil is still here.

My crew was despondent when we sailed away from Suvarov. I told them about rescuing Peter on Caroline Island a few years before. They tried hard to imagine what type of person could live alone, for the rest of his days on an uninhabited island. The agonies, the hard work just to survive would turn off most people. The only compelling force to make one stay would be to have a complete love for nature.

One of my crew gave his opinion as we watched Suvarov fade into the distance. "I could do it," he said emphatically. "I know I could do it. In fact, I'd like to. But I'd do it a little different. I'd just want a few more luxuries, a radio, stereo for music, a refrig." He went on about having a surf boat with an outboard and maybe a jeep to run around the island. Then he concluded, "Some company wouldn't be bad either, providing she—" Perhaps he was right. It wouldn't be bad, for a while anyway. But Tom Neil wouldn't have agreed.

I met some fine yachtsmen on these Honolulu-Tahiti runs. Two were Dave and Judy Loomis, a young married couple. They hired themselves out as boat keepers on yachts around the world. Dave has his master's papers. They have a farm in Connecticut and go to sea whenever they get bored, which is usually every year or two. They watched *Third Sea* for me one season when I had to return to Bangkok on business. They spent most of their time anchored in beautiful Robinson's Cove on Moorea. They have no children of their own but they love kids. When I returned from my Asia trip, I found a couple kids who had swum out from the shore. Judy explained they came to visit most afternoons. One was a pretty little girl, part Tahitian, about eight or nine. "You speak English very well," I said when I met her.

"Thank you," she replied. "My father is American."

"He is," I said. "Does he live here?"

"Sometimes," she said. By the tone of indifference in her voice, I surmised she was the product of one of those island romances that are so common in Tahiti, romances that have been going on since foreigners first arrived aboard whaling ships. The girl watched me as I checked the log book. Since the day I launched *Third Sea,* I have asked those who come aboard to sign the log and make whatever comments they wish. One of the first things I did when I came aboard was check the log.

"I signed the book too," the young girl said, and then she leaned over and began turning back pages until she found what she was looking for. She pointed to her name—Cheyenne Brando.

"This is you?" I asked pointing to her signature in bold letters.

"Yes," she replied, "Cheyenne Brando. My father is Marlon Brando."

I never forgot Cheyenne Brando, and I was especially curious about her when I saw her name again in the log as I was gathering notes about *Third Sea's* voyages for this book. I didn't have to wonder very long. I was at my desk when news about Cheyenne Brando flashed around the world one Easter Sunday morning. She had committed suicide. That poor child, so innocent in her youth. How she must have suffered since that day I met her on Moorea.

Marlon Brando met Cheyenne's mother, Tarita Teripaia, a Tahitian waitress-turned-actress in 1961, while filming *Mutiny On the Bounty*. Besides Cheyenne, Tarita also had an older son that Brando fathered, a boy named Teihotu. He might have been with Cheyenne when she came aboard *Third Sea* but I can't remember, and unlike his sister, he had not signed the log. When Cheyenne grew into womanhood—she was considered by some to be the most beautiful woman in Tahiti, and the richest—she was no longer the little girl who swam out to yachts. At twenty, she became pregnant by Dag Drollet, the scion of a prominent Tahitian family. In May 1990, eight months into the pregnancy, she told her half-brother Christian that Drollet was beating her. Christian confronted her boyfriend with a .45-cal. handgun at the Brando California estate, and in the ensuing struggle, Drollet was killed.

In a murder trial that followed, Robert Shapiro, a name associated with the O.J. Simson trail, defended Christian, and managed to get his sentence reduced to ten years for manslaughter, but with time off for good behavior.

Then on Easter Sunday morning, the world learned

that a deeply troubled, twenty-five-year-old Cheyenne had hanged herself at Brando's other estate in Punaauia on Tahiti. News reports further stated that she had tried to commit suicide three times before. She had lost a court decision to her mother denying her custody of her four-year-old son Tuki.

Third Sea made a third visit to Christmas Island. On this voyage strong westerly swells from a distant storm had built up heavy surf, breaking all along the island. We swamped our longboat going ashore and lost some of our equipment. But we were able to explore the island, and again, we were witness to the follies of man, an island totally in ruin.

On another voyage I entrusted *Third Sea* to my son Peter. He had sailed the Pacific with us from Pago Pago in Samoa to Honolulu, and later from Honolulu to the Marquesas and Tahiti. He proved to be a capable seaman and he now knew celestial navigation. He recruited his own crew and I watched him depart from Honolulu with a crew of eight. Don Perkins was his first mate, and Mountain Man was one of the crew. The schooner was in good hands. Peter did well, and arrived safely in Tahiti via Bora Bora. Unfortunately, he became restless after his crew left him to return home, and he abandoned *Third Sea*, leaving her unattended at an anchorage near the airport. I had to fly from Asia to rescue her.

As a schooner, *Third Sea* was proving her worth. I was most thankful that I had built a sturdy schooner, and a trading schooner at that.

Top two, the interior of *Thrid Sea*. Bottom, a carving by Theo Meier.

Chapter 12

WHERE HAVE ALL
THE TRADING SCHOONERS GONE

The very name "schooner" has a ring of romance about it. That more than anything else, I guess, was why I built a schooner. My love for schooners started when I was still in grade school. As kids we played "Cowboys 'n' Indians," and sometimes we were pirates, with patches over one eye, wielding wooden swords. But more than cowboys and Indians, I liked to imagine myself a buccaneer, the captain of a trading schooner in the South Seas. What an imagination, an island trading schooner! Youths today don't have the same dreams; they don't have the same stimulus as I had when I was growing up. I was raised on John Hall and Dorothy Lamour movies, movies like "South of Pago Pago" and "Aloma of the South Seas." And there was another one I can never forget, "The Son of Fury," a romantic South Sea tale starring Tyrone Power, Gene Tierney and George Sanders. How I remember that movie. I was in my early teens and went to see the film during the Saturday afternoon matinee. I watched it through several times and as a result I got home very late. I was severely reprimanded by my parents. It didn't do any good. My heart was still in the South Seas.

In his novel *Lord Jim,* Joseph Conrad said "take away that dream and you have nothing left." People were always trying to destroy that dream in me, even when I was no longer a boy. One day when I was an adult, with a responsible government job in Washington, D.C., my boss attacked me the same way my parents had years before.

"You're a hopeless dreamer! That world out there doesn't exist!'" he said and waved an arm towards an imaginary "out there." "Your problem is you read too much Michener."

We'd just finished dinner. The boss' wife had cleared the table and joined us for coffee and brandy in the living room. I knew why I'd been invited. The week before I'd announced that I was giving up my government job in Washington to go to the South Seas to live, to become a writer. I had joked about getting work aboard trading schooners. My boss was determined to talk me out of it.

"Okay, you don't believe me!" he exclaimed and went over to the TV. It was exactly ten o'clock. He turned the set on, and as the screen flickered, I sat completely bemused. How would a TV program make me change my mind? But when I heard the familiar background music and saw the titles, I wanted to laugh out loud. But I didn't. The boss and his wife were dead serious.

"There! There's your problem!" he almost shouted. "You've got to separate fact from fiction! This, my friend, is pure fiction." He puffed out his chest, victoriously.

The program was the well-known TV series playing at the time—James A. Michener's "Adventures in Paradise." Actor Gardner McKay had the romantic lead as Captain Adam Troy of the island trading schooner *Tiki*. In the opening scene the schooner, under full sail, glided softly across a tropical seascape. It did have an impact on many viewers—a trading schooner in the South Seas.

"Look at it!" my boss cried. "Just look at it! A lot of Michener romance and nothing more. Nothing else. Pure romance. Shot in Hollywood."

It was true. "Adventures in Paradise" was pure romance, and I never missed an episode. And I also admit that, like Michener's books, the program truly influenced me, much like the other movies I saw in my early youth. But nevertheless, whether or not Michener's world was real or fiction, I was determined to find out for myself. I was going to find a trading schooner and sail aboard her. My boss and his wife, even with the promise of a promotion, couldn't make me change my mind.

And so I packed my typewriter, a few books and some clothes and went to the South Seas to live and to write. I had just gone through a divorce and was free. This was my chance. As far as everyone was concerned, I had disappeared forever. I wrote to no one and no one knew where exactly I had gone until, just about a year later, on a Thursday evening at 10 p.m. sharp, television viewers back home turned on their sets.

The show that night, of course, was "Adventures in Paradise." It was the beginning of a new series and it started with a super long-shot of a waterfall cascading over a cliff on a tropical island. The camera zoomed in closer: two figures under the falls. Closer. A Tahitian girl—long hair, wet sarong clinging to her shapely body, wreath of flowers on her head—and a man in white trousers, barechested and tanned, with an arm around the girl. The camera zoomed to close-up and the man turned, faced the camera and winked. Michener's world, indeed, was real. No one could deny it now. All things can and do happen in paradise. I was the beachcomber under the falls with the Tahitian girl.

What did my boss in Washington think now, and all those who'd laughed when they heard I was going to the South Seas? What were they thinking now!

How did it happen? It was a pure accident.

I went to Tahiti not to become an actor but to sail aboard a trading schooner. I was fortunate for a few were still operating when I arrived, and I was able to sail aboard them, but as a passenger, not a deck hand that I wanted to be. Nevertheless, I sailed to the remote Marquesas and the low lying Taumotus, and as far south as the Gambier Islands, and to Rapa where the women out number the men seven to one. It was fun, and exciting, but I was not making a living. My writing was not coming easy and I knew I had to settle down in Tahiti and spend more time at the typewriter. At times I was so poor I didn't have enough money for postage for the stories that editors kept returning, but rather than give up, I took whatever jobs I could find to support myself. Tour guide whenever a cruise ship came in, and as an extra for any one of the TV and movie companies that were suddenly appearing.

Michener's books, the TV series and MGM's filming of *Mutiny on the Bounty* stirred up interest in the South Pacific. Other movie and TV companies soon followed, to compete with Twentieth Century-Fox, the producer of "Adventures in Paradise." Although much footage for the Fox production was filmed in Hollywood, many scenes and locations were shot in the islands.

After Quinn's bar the night before, Stephens and friend cool off the next morning under a waterfall, in real life and for Hollywood.

Since extras and bit-part actors were hired locally, there was always money to be made for those who wanted to stand in front of a camera.

Fox hired me for their new series. Not all the scenes I did were flattering, for sure, but their locations were real enough. The waterfalls, Quinn's bar, Moorea, Vaihiria Lake in the mountains. It took us a grueling two days to get the cameras up to the lake. Maybe paradise was a bit tarnished and corrupt but it did exist and, back home, they couldn't deny that. One lesson I did learn: Michener's world is real.

But beneath that romantic idea about schooners there were other reasons why I wanted a large vessel, and these reasons have always led me into controversy with everyone I met, especially with other yachtsmen. It was the basic question of big vs. small, and modern vs. traditional.

My reason for wanting a big vessel was not one of safety. I disagree with most critics on the subject. People are quick to attack the small boat sailor. Critics like to use the safety factor: small boats are unsafe. A bigger vessel doesn't mean it's safer. Ed Boden, the man who helped me get *Third Sea* out of Singapore, sailed his 25-foot sloop *Kittiwake* single-handed around the world, and when asked why he took such a chance, he replied, "The next safest thing to my boat is a barrel." It's true, a barrel is perhaps the safest vessel one could find. The size of a boat has little to do with its safely. Larry Nielson, another circumnavigator and friend, recalls arriving in the Bay of Island in northern New Zealand. This would be his final stop before returning to Auckland, a few hundred miles farther south, and the port that would complete his circumnavigation of the world.

Larry was resting in his bunk when he heard voices outside on the dock. "Look at that boat," a woman said.

"It says Auckland on the back. You mean it came all the way up from Auckland?"

"I guess it did," a man replied. "People take all kinds of chances these days."

Larry usually doesn't defend himself on the subject of small boats, but he did tell me about a rather tragic incident he experienced.

He was sailing his tiny ketch *Heather* across the Indian Ocean en route to Madagascar when he picked up a report that a container ship in the same waters had gone down. The vessel, some six hundred feet in length, had cracked its back and sank. "The swells were enormous," Larry said. "My tinny ketch just rode up and down with them. The freighter got caught with a swell at the bow and another at her stern. She just snapped in the middle." Larry sailed around for a week looking for survivors but he could find none, not even debris.

With our modern, Tupperware boats we have today, why go old fashion with an outdated schooner?

Boat designs too change as much as men and women's fashions. For example, when I was growing up, it was the custom for men to wear felt hats, double breasted suits with vests and wide neckties. We thought men were pretty smart in such attire. Today it's jeans and baseball caps. The same with yachts. Look at some of the old photographs of the early America Cup contenders. They were schooners, with tall mast and main booms that stretched out far over the stern. They carried miles of canvas and had fifty-man crews. Today the America Cup contenders have one stick for a mast, short booms, and all kinds of mechanical devices that reduce the crew to a minimum. The bottom line is—which vessel would you rather sail upon? My choice is the schooner.

But to like an old-fashioned schooner is one thing; to

own and sail one is something else. From Day One I had nothing but opposition to my building *Third Sea*. Only Ce Norris at Samson Marine was on my side, and that was, I imagine, that he wanted to sink his teeth into something other than what everyone was demanding in designs from him, mainly ketches.

Aside from the romance, I felt I could do more with a larger vessel, and second, I could make it support itself.

I wasn't out to win any races. I was not in a hurry. What I wanted more than anything else was comfort, and with a big boat I could have comfort. As for making it pay for itself, I reasoned that I could carry passengers and cargo and take on a paying crew. I could do research, carry diving equipment and explore wrecks and reefs. I could do charters. And when in port for a long time, I would have a decent place to live. After William A. Robinson sailed the *Svaap* around the world, he built the *Varua.* In his book *Return to the Sea,* which he published in 1972, he tells why he wanted a big vessel—"to use the ship as my home, and even at sea I liked to have room aboard for a laboratory, a workshop, and study/library."

I was looking for the same qualities when I designed *Third Sea*—airy, open, and no cramped quarters. One of the disadvantages of Ce Norris' design was that he had the interior divided into small compartments with a passage way right through the middle of the ship. After I had launched *Third Sea* and had her at the Singapore Yacht Club, doing the rough interior work before sailing to Bangkok, my friend Robin Dannhorn appeared one afternoon. I was very happy to show him what I had done. Robin, who is a frustrated boat designer—he had been drawing plans of square riggers since he was a boy in London— shook his head. "What are you doing?" he said. "Who wants to live in a coffin." I made the mistake of asking him what he would do. "If you want, I'll give you a hand," he said. I was thrilled. I had someone to help me.

I cringed, however, when he took the power circular saw, stretched out the extension cord, and then began cutting, from bow to stern. He cut away the plywood siding, made sweeping curves and open spaces. He destroyed in twenty minutes what it had taken me weeks to build. But I had to admit, it was a vast improvement. I had to thank him. "Great work, now we can begin putting it all together before we sail to Bangkok," I said. Robin looked at me askance.

"I forgot to tell you," he said. "I'm on my way to Australia."

"When?" I asked.

"This evening. My flight leaves at eight."

"But I thought you were going to help me."

"I did!"

That was Robin Dannhorn, and he was right, he did help me. The interior of *Third Sea* did look grand after it was completed in Bangkok, with its open spaces below deck and Theo Meier's carvings adorning the main saloon and passageways.

The one thing I learned about sailing the South Pacific and Asian waters was that one can make a living with a large boat. This has been made easier for boat owners only in the last few years. After World War II, every island in the Pacific was dominated by either Australia and New Zealand or a Western power. These powers controlled the islands' economy, and often they were forced to pay heavy subsidies to support the islands. Trade among the islands was regulated and restricted. Then came the call for independence. It happened quickly. All but three island groups were granted their freedom. France refused to give up the Society islands, which includes Tahiti and all French Polynesia, and her other major possession, New Caledonia in the western Pacific. The third island group is American Samoa, a U.S. posession. Washington voted several times to grant the territory independence, but the Samoans don't want it. They are much better off than their neighbors with Uncle Sam paying their bills.

On their own, the islands have very little chance of surviving in our modern world. They have no industry. They can attempt to lure tourists, but they don't have the capital nor the means to build an infrastructure for visitors; they can grant fishing rights to foreign nations, but without ships to patrol their own waters there's little they can do to enforce their legal two hundred mile territorial limits.

As a result, trading schooners have all but disappeared. Some islands don't see a ship for six months at a time; sometimes a year might pass. At Hermit Island in the Bismark Archipelago I asked Joseph, the headman, why they don't cut copra anymore. Coconuts were rotting in the sun where they had fallen. "Boat him no come," he said. I tried to explain that if they would cut copra the boats would come, but he couldn't see it that way.

On nearly every island we visited, we found islanders who wanted us to carry cargo for them. Twenty-five years ago mother countries wouldn't have allowed it. Now the island governments cry out for help. We did what we could with *Third Sea*. We carried a whole kitchen unit and a washing machine from Hawaii to the Yacht Club in Bora Bora; we carried lumber for a ship builder in Indonesia, needed medical supplies in southern Thailand, passengers from the war-torn Philippines to Sandaka; food to islands in the Bismark Archipelago, and two tons of rice to the Sulu Islands between the Philippines and Borneo. The cargo of rice proved to be the most exciting.

We were anchored in Zamboanga. I was sitting in a street cafe facing the waterfront, hot and sweaty, with my straw hat pushed back, drinking a cold San Miguel. A Muslim in a batik shirt and sarong came up to my table. In very good English he asked if I was part of the crew of the schooner anchored in the harbor. I was always prepared for such questions. In most ports I was asked to carry everything from food and building supplies to drugs to guns. I admitted I was and said no more.

"I'm from Jolo," he continued. "We need rice and the trading boats are delayed." Jolo is the capital of the Sulu Islands, and the hub of the Muslim world. It's infested with rebels and pirates, and for us to sail there would be a great risk. The man was departing that afternoon on an inner-island ferry; he emphasized if we could deliver the rice we would be well rewarded.

I hardly considered the man's offer, but I was curious how much two tons of rice would have cost me. When I went shopping the next day at the barter trade center in town, I asked a shop keeper the price of two tons of rice. He wanted to know why I was asking. I mentioned the incident. He immediately knew the man. "You don't have to pay." he said. "The man has credit here." When I mentioned that sailing to the Sulu was risky business for a foreign yacht, he disagreed. "You have nothing to fear," he said. "You are their guests."

That night a sampan pulled up to *Third Sea*. A Muslim with a bright red turban stood up and asked to come aboard. He said he was an agent for a Jolo shipping firm. He assured us we would be safe, and as he spoke he unfolded a large yellow flag with strange symbols on it. "This flag is your safety. And I will go with you."

An insane idea, but what a chance this was for *Third Sea* to sail the forbidden Sulu Sea. I accepted and the next day we loaded two tons of rice aboard *Third Sea*. The agent came aboard and that afternoon we set sail for Jolo. For two weeks we lived in another world. We were honored and treated with great respect by the Muslims of the Sulu Sea. My contact with them saved *Third Sea* from disaster a few years later.

The charter business in Southeast Asia was lucrative and at times I turned over *Third Sea* to my crew so they could earn money. But I preferred to carry passengers on long voyages. My practice was that no one aboard *Third Sea* was allowed to be idle. We made crew out of passengers; they stood watches and performed duties as regular crew did. Everyone had the chance to study seamanship and navigation, if they were so inclined. And meals were always special occasions. We encouraged, and welcomed, those who wanted to try their hand in the galley at their speciality. Those who baked bread were most welcome.

The voyage over, a happy charter group goes ashore in the dinghy.

Cargo-carrying sailing vessels have virtually disappeared from the face of the South Pacific and Asia. We did see some sailing craft in the Sulu Sea around Zamboanga but these small vessels had only room enough for a small family and, at the most, very little space for cargo. In the Western Pacific at a few isolated islands they still rely upon sail power but these are exceptions. The Tahitians sail fast outrigger canoes but these are for sport and competition. For fishing they install their Evinrude outboards. The outboard motor has replaced sails and even paddles. But there is no way the chugging of a gasoline engine will replace the romance of a wind-filled sail far out at sea.

Singapore has gone modern and even the scows and small sampans have disappeared from the Singapore River. But Singapore does have a trading port on the Pandan River on the west coast that's right out of Kipling.

An Indonesian sailing boat under sail alone makes its way into the barter port on the bank of the Pandan River in Singapaore.

The strange, proud little craft that make their way into the port are an anachronism. They are the last remnants of sailing ships that once plied the earliest trade routes between East and West. They have not changed their design in a thousand years. Nor have they installed engines or anything electrical. They come up river from distant ports without the use of navigational aids, loaded down to their gunwales with cargoes of long poles and timber. And as they have been doing for hundreds of years, they catch the wind and nurse it for every league it will take them, and when the wind stops, and if the water is shallow enough, they kedge their way forward, yard by yard.

The navigational ability of these stalwart sailors is most astounding. Some vessels come from deep within Indonesia, from distant Banka and islands in the Gaspar Strait. Their voyages take them past dangerous reefs and through difficult passes where modern vessels dare not go.

Macassar schooners tie up with their bowsprits jutting far out over the jetty at the old trading port in Jakarta where time has stopped.

The ability for them to sail and navigate comes from a hand-me-down knowledge of the sea and seamanship that is most remarkable. When I had *Third Sea* moored in the river, I talked to the skipper of a fifty-foot Rhio trader. He was from Simeulu and made the long passage through the Sunda Strait south of Sumatra to reach Singapore.

He was in his mid-thirties and had been sailing since he was old enough to swim. I doubted that he could read but when I took out a chart of the Indonesian waters he pointed to various islands and named each of them. I asked how he navigated.

He knew the currents and depended upon them as much as he used the wind. How far did he average in twenty-four hours? He took a match stick and indicated that one and a half lengths was equivalent to one day's sail on the chart. He then laughed, and in his limited English he explained it must have been difficult in his father's time. They didn't have matches to compare or record distances.

But the real tall-masted sailing ships can still be found in Indonesia. A short walk from Taman Fatahillah Square in Jakarta is the old port of Sunda Kelapa. If this were any other such port in the world, the area would be a museum piece, visited by tourists, where they could take pictures, buy postcards and souvenirs, and then return home saying how magnificent it was. In Jakarta, Sunda Kelapa is still very much in use today. It is home port for the great Macassar schooners.

In most ports of Asia and the Pacific, when *Third Sea* arrived under sail, people stopped to stare. When *Third Sea* sailed into Sunda Kelapa no one thought twice about it. We dropped sails inside the harbor, and not wanting to show off that we had engine power, we kedged up to the quay and moored between two Macassar schooners.

Some Macassar schooners measure over a hundred feet

in length; they have top masts, and when they tie up, their bow sprits jut far out over the quay. There may be a hundred or more tied up at any one time. *Third Sea* looked like a dwarf among them.

Sunda Kelapa is actually the name of the original Hindu spice-trading post which was conquered and converted to Islam more than four and a half centuries ago. All day and late into the night, laborers unload sawn timber from Kalimantan onto a wharf that has been in continuous use since 1817.

Sailing boats become legends in their time, and so do the men and women who sail them. Skippers cast romantic images that are hard to live down. Captain Adam Troy of the Schooner *Tiki* in "Adventures in Paradise" was only a shadow of such true characters as Omar Darr of the *Te Vegas*, William A. Robinson of the *Varua* and Andy Thompson of the *Tiare Taporo*. There was even a woman skipper, Emma Coe. In time she became so famous they called her "Queen Emma of the South Seas."

Andy Thompson, was the original South Sea Island trading schooner captain. He was an old man when I met him in Tahiti, retired, visiting the yachts along the waterfront. He still had the accent of a Brooklyn cab driver. The *Tiare Taporo* that Andy skippered was a schooner trading in copra and owned by A. B. Donald and Co., a trading company that's still prominent in the Pacific today. I went aboard *Tiare Taporo* when she was anchored in Papeete. Only the mate was aboard and he showed me around. The old girl must have been a beautiful ship once, but the installation of a diesel engine and the shortening of the main mast, together with a reduction in sail area, made her rather a clumsy and uncomfortable looking old boat. The piercing smell of copra did not assist in making her anything of a cruise ship. Still, back in the 1940s in her heyday, she was the only vessel to service the isolated islands of the northern Cook Island group.

Andy was a barrel-shaped gentleman, bald of head and with the hard blue eyes prescribed for sailors. Those who sailed with him told me he habitually dressed in khaki shorts and shirts, and wore a khaki solar topee. Everyone kidded him about his Brooklyn accent and many suspected that, like Maurice Chevalier, he cultivated that accent to be cherished as part of his chosen image. They say he even spoke Rarotongan with a Brooklyn accent!

Nothing fazed Andy, the threat of a hurricane, the sudden coming of a gale. Whether calm or rough, he efficiently handled his heavy-laden schooner with the skill born of years of sailing the same waters, a knowledge of the placement of reefs and the realization that this ship and its passengers were a responsibility he must and could handle. He never lost a ship or a passenger.

Some remarkable men have etched their names into the history of the South Seas—explorer James Cook, artist Paul Gauguin, buccaneer Bully Hayes, mutineer Fletcher Christian of the *Bounty* and writers Jack London, Herman Melville and James Michener, and Andy Thompson. But not all the characters were men. One was an attractive young lady, half Samoan and half American, who was run out of her native island by the missionaries and the society they created. She vowed she would return, rich and famous, and make them regret it. She did just that, by doing the impossible. She took command of a trading schooner and sailed into the cannibal islands of the western Pacific. There she made her mark.

I had not heard about her until I sailed *Third Sea* into Rabaul on New Britain. She was only a name, but then, when I began to learn more about her, I found myself being drawn to her. It was so strange, almost as though I was falling in love with someone who had been dead eighty years.

Rabaul is the center of the world's most active volcanic region where violent earthquakes are a weekly affair, but the beauty of the port, formed in part by the crater of a gigantic volcano, is second to none. And, indeed, its history is colorful. New Britain was once considered to be inhabited by the world's most fearsome and treacherous cannibals, and the memories of those past days still linger in the minds of many elders. It was here out of this wilderness that Emma built her empire. She paved the way for the Germans, who lost their possessions during World War I, and were followed by the Australians and then the Japanese.

The stories the old timers have to tell are not only about cannibals and diseases, but about German plantations and volcanic eruptions that twice destroyed Rabaul, about the Japanese taking Rabaul and holding it during the entire war years, and the return of the Australians. They like to joke about their recent independence from Australia, when the newly formed government announced to the people that on a certain day they would have "independence" and when that day came, all the natives ran into the hills. They had had too many independence days in their short but stormy past.

But the story that everyone likes most to talk about is about Queen Emma.

When we were anchored in front of the yacht club in Rabaul, and I was completing my manuscript for my book for Roy Howard, I became intrigued by the stories of Queen Emma and I wanted to learn more about her. I read what was available, and talked to those who knew her. I spent many hours at the ruins of her house, and I located her grave, forgotten and jungle covered, on the hillock overlooking the harbor. I delved into the libraries and archives, and with each new discovery, her story intensified. And later, when we sailed into Samoa where Emma was born, the story was complete. Emma Coe is the breath and soul that makes up the dramatic history of the South Seas.

She was born in Apia, Samoa, and while still an infant placed by her father in the hands of Catholic sisters to be educated. She was not yet eleven but already well developed when he sent her away to a convent school in Sydney "to save her from growing up" along the untamed waterfront that was Apia in those days.

Emma was "asked" to leave the convent when she was only sixteen, for teaching the girls in her class how to dance the licentious and uninhibited Samoan dances. Her father then sent her to live in the household of his brother in San Francisco, where she was put under some stern educational training. Part of her instructions was to learn to sew, play the piano and pour tea for the ladies of San Francisco.

But Emma's heart was not in San Francisco; it was in the islands of her birth. She longed to return, and when the chance came, she took it. She was nineteen when she reappeared in Apia, unannounced and unexpected.

In the South Seas in those days men took what they wanted and when they saw young and attractive Emma, they wanted her. She was glad to be back and she loved the attention, but her flirtatious ways did not rest well with Apia's new-found society and stern missionaries. Her father, concerned about his daughter's future, did the best thing a father could. He married her off to a prominent ship's officer, James Forsayth, who was an islander trader and captain of his own ship. Whenever she could, Emma sailed with her husband on trading voyages. She was a good seaman and became an accomplished navigator.

While Emma attended business in Apia, James Forsayth sailed on a trading voyage to China and was not seen nor heard from again. It was assumed that he was lost at sea during a typhoon off the coast of China. Emma's life now took a series of turns and twists.

Her antics became the gossip about town, but that didn't stop her from doing what she pleased. Eyebrows were really raised when she accepted a dinner invitation from buccaneer Bully Hayes aboard his famous black brigantine *Leonora.* Hayes it seems tried to seduce her, whereupon Emma merely slipped out of her dress but instead of falling into her host's arms, she dove overboard and swam ashore.

Nor did things go well with Emma's father. A new American consul had been appointed and he brought charges against Jonas Coe, Emma's father, for misappropriating U.S. government funds. The charges were false, but nevertheless, her father had to go to Washington to defend himself.

With her husband lost at sea, her father deported and most of the family property gone, Emma was at the mercy of unfair missionaries and cruel Apia society. Ridiculed and belittled, she vowed she would make those in Apia who were against her regret their words. "I am a half-cast woman," she said, "and I can do nothing about that. And I am poor, but I can do something about that." She now concentrated on fulfilling her wish. She teamed up with Tom Farrell, an Apia waterfront saloon keeper and island trader. Emma sailed away with him on his next trading voyage to the western Pacific.

When Europeans first began trading with the natives of the South Seas they lacked a common medium of exchange. It was discovered that coconut oil sold well in

Europe. Coconut oil, and later dried copra, became that exchange. Oil at first was obtained from splitting coconuts and drying them in the sun. The oil was extracted and sealed into bamboo cane containers of up to three gallons.

The early traders showed the islanders how to process the oil and then sailed among the islands offering cloth and tobacco among some of the more desirable items which they traded. The Germans, who had their headquarters in Apia, were the first to pioneer the dried coconut industry. An innovation that was about to take place was to directly change the lives of Emma Forsayth and Tom Farrell.

Most often the coconut oil gathered in bamboo containers was foul and rancid, and the Germans found they could better profit by trading for bagged copra rather than oil. The dried copra was sent to crushers. What resulted were coconut plantations on a large scale. But plantations required much labor and Polynesians would not work. Out of this need for labor came a system of recruiting black labor from Melanesia called "blackbirding."

In the beginning blackbirding had some law about it. Generally a chief, in return for trade goods, supplied a stipulated number of laborers for a certain term of years. But as the demand for more laborers grew as the Samoa plantations expanded, more often than not natives were simply trapped and carried off by unscrupulous Europeans. Blackbirding became an ugly business.

When the new plantation on Samoa opened up, Tom Farrell was one of the first to sail his schooner to recruit labor in New Guinea. Emma went with him. The year was 1877. They sailed into a little attractive harbor in the Duke of York Islands between New Britain and New Ireland. Here they established a trading post.

It was a hundred years later, almost to the day, that I sailed *Third Sea* into the harbor at Mioko in the Duke of York Islands. The only vestiges of Emma's trading post were a few concrete pillars. But here was Emma's first foothold in the western Pacific. The beauty, with its soft beaches and low palms, and water so clear we could see our anchor at ten fathoms, was unsurpassed. Sitting on our aft deck under an awning, I read the accounts of Emma at Mioko, and I could see the station clearly and the trading schooners at anchor, and both savage and white man coming to trade.

Emma had seen the vast possibilities in untamed New Guinea, but her vision was more than a rash dream. She fully understood what problems faced her. She and Tom were setting up the first trading station in no-man's land. No country nor any government controlled the place. There was no one they could turn to for help. The only laws were their own. Justice was what they made it. They had to face cannibals, loneliness, heat, earthquakes and volcanoes. Emma was willing to take the gamble.

Emma was twenty-seven when she sailed westward from Samoa. She was, by all accounts, a very attractive woman. I could picture her arrival, standing on the deck of the tossing schooner, watching for the islands to come into view, and her going ashore, wearing high boots and a long skirt, a pistol tucked into her belt.

Mioko is a beautiful island, and at a glance it might look like an earthly paradise, but in reality it was a living hell. In the jungles in Emma's day lived black savages who were more than willing to dine on stray or shipwrecked sailors who landed on their shores. Trespassers who managed to escape their cooking fires faced disease, malaria, tropical ulcers, dysentery, and a score of other dreadful maladies. Then if it weren't the dreaded diseases and fever that befell them, it might be earthquakes and erupting volcanoes.

The traders who came weren't necessarily a social group either. They were a rough breed, and they had to be. If shipwrecked, they faced shark-infested waters, and if they did reach shore they were certain to be murdered and eaten. Records show that within a five-year period over one hundred missionaries and traders were killed and most likely eaten.

But survive Emma Coe did, even after Tom Farrell became stricken with tuberculosis and had to go to Sydney where he later died. Emma carried on alone. She ran the trading store and went about armed. She took to carrying a whip which the savages feared more than her pistol.

When news spread of the trading post run by an attractive half-cast Samoan girl, ships put into the harbor. Now came a threat worse than black savages. It was drunken white sailors.

In a letter home, Emma told how she witnessed a brutal murder when one drunken sailor beat in the skull of another and threw his body to the sharks. Blackbirding schooners also put into port, their holds stinking from human cargo. Often chiefs brought captured slaves to the fort to sell to the blackbirders.

Emma knew the minute that she dropped her guard the natives would eat her and "civilized" men from trading ships would rape her. If a black man harmed any of her workers, she went and destroyed his village. When she stopped a drunken German seaman from attacking one of her Samoan girls, and he turned on her, she drew her pistol, aimed and fired. She hit him in the thigh, and had her guards drag him from the compound and toss him into the dirt outside.

Emma's vision went far beyond the trading post she

ran; it went to the fertile plains across the strait on New Britain. If the Germans were successful with their coconut plantations on Samoa, and had to import labor from here, why not plant coconuts here? She made contact with chiefs in New Britain and induced them to sell land to her. Then she began buying up islands by the score. Many she obtained for a pittance, no more than plugs of tobacco and glass beads.

Emma laid out vast plantations south of Rabaul and selected a sight for her dream house, which she called Gunantambu. Situated on a high level terrace, it looked out eastward towards the Duke of York Islands and the trading post at Mioko.

She designed a port, with jetties, godowns, government sheds and houses. In a few short months ships began to arrive from Sydney and Samoa, bringing trees and shrubs, all of which were carefully planted by her assistants.

The Germans made the port their headquarters and before long Gunantambu became a landmark that was to dominate the South Seas for more than sixty years, until the Japanese bombed and destroyed the estate during World War II.

The crowning feature of the house was a cement staircase seventy feet wide that descended down the hill to a carriage road below. Every morning Emma, attended by a secretary and a native footman, walked down the stairs to her awaiting rickshaw and was drawn by her two Buka boys along the seafront road to her offices at Ralum, a quarter of a mile away.

In the living room was a pukah fan suspended from the ceiling. She had shipped from Samoa a heavy sideboard and bits of furniture which previously belonged to writer Robert Louis Stevenson. The famed author was a friend of Emma's father and left many of his possessions to the

Coe family when he died. Carpets and curtains were imported from the Orient, and from Europe came a hot water system and lavish ornaments and decorations. She had a dinner service of gold plate and her servants wore white livery.

Another book I had in the library aboard *Third Sea* was *My Adventures Among South Sea Cannibals* by Douglas Rannie. The author describes the flamboyant and champagne-filled life that Emma led. At the time he met her, she was hosting a party aboard her steamer *Golden Gate*. She was thirty-seven, he noted, and still went by the name Mrs. Farrell.

"The steamer anchored close to us," Rannie wrote. "Mrs. Farrell was aboard the *Golden Gate* with a large party of ladies and gents. That evening I had the pleasure of meeting her for the first time at a dinner party. Mrs. Farrell, or 'Queen Emma of the South Seas,' as many call her, was a handsome woman and made a very striking figure, dressed in white satin, with a long train, which was borne behind her by half a dozen dusky little maidens. Above her jet black hair she wore a tiara of diamonds—her whole carriage was queenly. She was accompanied by a number of female cousins and other relations from Samoa, mostly part Samoan, all highly educated and beautiful women. After dinner, her little maidens stood behind her chair. Some fanned her while others rolled small cigarettes, which she smoked between sips of coffee and cognac.and afterwards dancing was indulged in until the morning's early hours."

In 1884, Germany annexed New Guinea and in the years that followed Emma Forsayth consolidated both her position and her fortune. The harassed young woman who fled Samoa with a tough, bearded blackbirder and trader, returned to her native island, now much respected, rich and much admired. Bedecked in jewels and with a train of attendants and followers, she rented the entire floor of the leading hotel, and commenced to entertain for a solid week, sparing no costs. At a party hosted in her honor by the German consul at which the London Missionary Society was obliged to attend, Emma gave a speech. She greeted the society coldly but properly, and then commented on the Samoan king, her cousin. "His birth was good," she said, "but his training I'm afraid was all wrong. I believe that his schooling came from the London Missionary Society."

Emma's keen foresight told her that Germany's position in the Pacific was not secure. If war erupted on the continent, Germany would surely lose all her possessions in the islands. A few years before World War I broke out, she sold her entire estate, including Gunantambu, to a young German planter and trader who had made a fortune in the Bismark Archipelago. She died some years later in Monte Carlo in southern France.

In Rabaul today there are a few people around who claim to be descendants of Emma Coe and her family, but unfortunately she is only a name to them. The only true remaining reminders are the stone stairs of her once great home at Ralum and the desecrated graveyard a few miles away that I mentioned. There is nothing else, except the memory of a great woman.

For the tropics, a large saloon with open windows and plenty of air, top, gave me Stephens a place to write. Weather permitting, his favorite place to read was the cabin top or the netting at the bowsprit.

Chapter 13

LIVING ABOARD

It sounds like a great life, to live aboard your own boat. And it is! No time clocks to punch, no rent to pay, and no fixed schedules to follow. And when you get bored with your scenery, or your neighbors, you can lift anchor and move somewhere else. It's that simple. After I had *Third Sea* for a couple of years, I was living the life I wanted to live and I vowed I would never change.

But there was a price I had to pay!

It never failed. I would get invited to someone's home for dinner. The food was good, the conversation pleasant, after-dinner drinks followed—and then came the big argument. I could see it coming every time, but there was nothing I could do about it. I reached the point where I hesitated to accept invitations to dinner, especially from "happily" married couples.

I often found myself in this very delicate situation. Most people who saw *Third Sea* from the dockside probably thought, "Now there's the life." And I must admit it was. I sailed where I wanted to go and I remained as long as I pleased. I anchored in undiscovered coves, explored unexplored reefs, sailed up lonely rivers. Life aboard my schooner offered all the adventure and romance I could ask for. And for a writer, it paid off.

But it's not the life for everyone. What most people don't realize is that in our modern-day world we become accustomed to conveniences, whether we want to admit it or not. Such basic things as a hot shower, running water in the kitchen, a toilet that flushes and lights that turn on at the flip of a switch are important. To live on a boat, you have to completely re-adjust your lifestyle. It isn't always that easy, or possible. Wives usually realize this before husbands do.

So, as a yachtsman who lived aboard, I did enjoy the good food and comforts I was exposed to when I was invited to someone's home. I liked the attention. "Would you like another drink?" The bar was wide open; the fridge had ice.

"Another serving of meat?" There was always a platter of roast beef that could have fed me for a week on the boat. "More wine?" "A brandy?" "A cigar?" How could I refuse? You really have to go without all these luxuries to fully appreciate them.

But trouble always came. I know that only too well. We settle back with our brandy in the living room. "Tell me, do you really like living on a boat?" the wife asks. This is it. I knew exactly what would happen.

"Yes, sometimes," I reply trying to sound nonchalant.

"Sounds like a great life," the husband adds.

"But you must miss the conveniences," the wife says.

"You get used to it," I say.

"But without hot showers and everything so cramped."

"But just think, dear," the husband interrupts, "no rent to pay, no neighbors to put up with. You just move on."

She becomes defensive. "But you have to have roots." She glances in my direction. "I don't mean for you. You, well, you like it and you don't have a family that you have to worry about."

"What does a family have to do with it?" the husband declares. "There are families who live aboard boats and love it."

"Would you?" she says, voice rising.

"Would I what?" he snaps.

"Live on a boat?" she replies.

"Hell, yes. I've always wanted to live on a boat."

"You—" she laughs now. "You are so spoiled, you can't even empty the garbage without complaining."

"Don't be ridiculous."

"Ridiculous? Who complains when there's no hot water? Who wants to strangle the paper boy when he's late, and you want to go sailing."

"That's different."

"Different? Different! If it's so different then why don't you go sailing? Maybe Stephens here has room for you!" And the battle is on. Another nice evening shot to hell.

It has happened this way not once but a dozen times. The husband keeps on pouring drinks and making apologies. "I don't know why in hell I ever got married," he mumbles. "She just doesn't understand."

It doesn't always happen exactly that way. Sometimes the wife is understanding and it's the husband who loses his cool. I remember one case in particular. Two friends, we'll call them Betty and Bob, invited me to dinner.

"It isn't that easy a life," I began to explain when they asked the fatal question. "What people don't realize are the hardships. Bad weather is one."

"You mean storms?" Betty asks.

"Something like that. When you are the skipper, you're responsible. You might not be able to go to sleep for a couple of days. You have to stick to the helm."

"You do?" Betty asks. "It must be frightening."

"Not really. You learn to cope with the situation."

"You mean you are never frightened?"

"No, I get frightened like anyone else. But you don't think about it."

"You don't! I think you're a very brave man. It sounds so exciting."

That part was aimed at husband Bob. In this case it was

Betty who was bored with life and would have liked her husband to be doing something else. She was using me.

"It's a challenge," I replied, hoping it would end. But it didn't.

"It must be fun," she sighed.

"Fun!" Bob spoke up. "What fun is there in a storm?"

"If you're with someone who is brave, then it can be fun, right!"

"Maybe you'd like to go with Stephens then."

"Maybe I would!"

I couldn't win. I accepted dinner invitations with a tinge of anxiety. I began to ask myself if it was worth it, all for a few luxuries. I thought about this on my last sail down from Phuket to Singapore. We were anchored in a small cove at an uninhabited island south of Phuket.

The sun had just set. An hour or two before we brought up half a dozen lobsters from the reef. We lit the charcoal stove on the stern and cooked the lobsters in a pot of boiling water. A young lady who was making the passage to Singapore prepared butter sauce with fresh garlic. We had cushions spread out around the stern. There was a refreshing offshore breeze.

For a special treat we opened a good bottle of white wine. I don't want to make it sound too romantic, but there was even a full moon rising behind the silhouette of the island.

The lobster was excellent. The sauce gave it just the right flavor. One of the crew baked fresh French bread. We opened the wine and I made a remark I wouldn't have made a couple of years before. "Wouldn't this be great if the wine were chilled?" I said.

See? If we'd been dining in a restaurant or a house ashore, we could have had the wine chilled.

I guess we just can't have everything.

Chapter 14

THE LONERS

Regardless of the size of a vessel, whether it's a tiny 25-foot sloop like Ed Boden's *Kittiwake* or a 71-foot schooner like *Third Sea,* there comes a time when you have to sail it alone. I was faced with this problem when we were anchored in a lagoon on Raiatea in French Polynesia. My crew wanted to explore the island and took camping gear to spend the night at the other side of the island. I was enjoying the peace and quite aboard, working at my typewriter under the aft awning, when a French Navy gunboat came along side and warned me that a storm was approaching. The captain suggested I take *Third Sea* out to sea as the lagoon was exposed to the weather and the holding ground was not that good. I stood a better chance as sea. I had to act fast. It was late afternoon and the crew wouldn't be back until the evening of the next day. I had no choice but to sail *Third Sea* alone. By the time I weighed anchor I could see black clouds gathering in the western sky, and no sooner was I clear of land than the wind went wild. Had the sails been up, *Third Sea* would probably have suffered a knock down, providing her sails had not blown out first.

The storm lasted for two days, and as long as I was hove-to, all went well. But by the time the winds and seas had abated, I was sixty miles east of the island. I had to spend another day beating against the wind, setting and trimming alone, to get back to Raiatea. But it was a feeling of accomplishment when I did drop anchor at the very spot I had left three days before. While the winds were raging and I was alone at sea, I couldn't help thinking about William A. Robinson. He sailed his schooner *Varua* with only his wife, a slender Chinese-Tahitian woman, and perhaps only one other crew, and yet *Varua* was much larger with more sail area than *Third Sea.*

It is, indeed, a lonely life at sea, by yourself, and not everyone is suited for it. I developed a great respect for single-handed sailors when I was at the Singapore Yacht Club for the better part of a year, working aboard *Third Sea,* preparing to take her to Bangkok to be outfitted there. Singapore is the crossroads between East and West for cruising yachts, and when you are at the yacht club long enough, you meet every yachtsmen making a world cruise. I found myself spending more time than I cared to, driving visiting yachtsmen around town in my Chinese truck, showing them the best places to purchase food and supplies. I met some of the best, and worst.

Solo circumnavigation started with master mariner Joshua Slocum when he sailed his ketch *Spray* around the world from 1895 to 1898. From then until 1960 only a handful of other intrepid sailors—Harry Pidgeon, Vito Dumas and Alain Gerbault, to name a few—attempted the voyage. Their motives for sailing solo were not for self-destruction or any other hidden or mysterious reasons. They did it mainly for adventure, to break up the humdrum of daily living that civilization brought upon them. They did it alone because it was the most simple, uncomplicated way to go. And they had no one else to answer to but themselves.

The average non-yachtsman might call these loners courageous, or maybe even mad. They are a bit of both. But the one thing we must admit about them—they made a trade in life, security for freedom. To survive, however, they had to develop a respect for the sea. To most of them, sailing a small boat upon a big ocean is not a contest of wood and canvas against wind and water. It is merely a way of life.

William A. Robinson, whom I have admired since I was a boy, had a biographer sum up his life after he sailed around the world in 1928-31. "To be insulated from nature to the extent which now rules in highly civilized communities is to live an artificial life, an unnatural life, a false life." Aboard his tiny *Svaap*, he found what was natural to him.

There are some who sail single-handed merely to make a name for themselves, and to make money. The question arises, where does the line separating sailing for fame and sailing for pleasure begin and where does it leave off? Does it mean one who sails for profit doesn't enjoy it? Does it mean I wrote newspaper and magazine stories about sailing *Third Sea* only to collect checks, and thus I did it for profit? I have been accused of this, but it's hardly the truth. I sailed because I wanted to sail, and then I wrote about it afterwards.

I mentioned that before 1960 only a handful of people ventured to sea in small boats. Pidgeon, Dumas and Gerbault did it because it was something they wanted to do. They had no money, at least not in the beginning, and still they did it. Harry Pidgeon invested a thousand dollars in his *Islander* that took him around the world. Robinson's *Svaap*, a beautiful little Alden ketch, cost him about two thousand dollars. Slocum's *Spray* had been a century-old oysterman that had been hauled out on the beach unused for many years and given to him as a joke. Slocum rebuilt her from the keel up, at a cost of $553.62. He set sail for a voyage that would take him around the world with $1.80 in cash.

We know it would be impossible to do the same thing today, to sail the world with little or no money. *Third Sea* cost me about $40,000 to get her into the water and sailing, but such things as a depth sounder, diving equipment and compressor and finally a satellite navigation system, didn't come until much later. But a change in yachting was about to take place, especially with single-handed sailing, when prize money was offered. From the year 1960 onward, sailing became a profit making business.

It all started with racing. In that year the first single-handed ocean race was held across the Atlantic. There were only five contestants. The fourth trans-Atlantic race that was held a few years later had fifty-five entries. As might be expected, the whole affair now turned into one of making money. High-paying sponsors added to the money prizes.

When Sir Francis Chichester made his epic single-handed voyage with only one stop in Sydney, there were those who looked for ways of doing better. Apart from simply trying to make the voyage faster, the only way of capping his achievement was to go completely around the world without stopping.

In 1968, the *London Sunday Times* sponsored the Golden Globe Race and put up £5,000 for the first person to sail alone, nonstop around the world. The course had to be south of the Cape of Good Hope, known to seamen as the Cape of storms, around southern Australia and then Cape Horn.

It was more a competitive test than a race, as boats could start any time they wanted between June 1st and November 1st from any port in Europe, as long as they returned to the same port.

Nine yachtsmen set out on what was to be one of the most incredible tests of survival and endurance a small-boat sailor could put himself through.

Predictions, of course, were made. A *Sunday Times*

news reporter favored a catamaran sailed by an Australian named Howell, known in yachting circles as "Tahiti Bill." One sailor no one was about to bet on was the unknown young Robin Knox Johnston, a twenty-nine-year-old ex-Merchant Marine officer. He entered in a scruffy little ketch named *Suhalli.*

Tahiti Bill dropped out before the race began and of the eight others only one finished. After nearly nine months at sea, Knox Johnston crossed the finish line in his thirty-two-foot ketch.

One of the first loners to enter the race but the last one to depart, was Donald Crowhurst. There was no question concerning his motives: fame and the £5,000 prize money. Eight months after he sailed, a passing ship found his boat ghosting along in the mid-Atlantic. There was no one aboard.

An incredible tale unfolded itself. It seems the *Sunday Times* was reporting Crowhurst's remarkable progress across the Roaring Forties and around Cape Horn, stating he was certain to win. However, when the log books— there were two—were examined, it was discovered Donald Crowhurst never left the Atlantic. For eight months he had sailed in circles. Deliberately. He faked his entries in one log, which he would present to the acceptance committee. Here was a man ingenious enough to invent a hoax that fooled the world, but one who was unable to endure the strain of deceiving himself. His last notation in his log read: "It is finished. It is the mercy."

Another baffling behavior of those who entered was that of Bernard Moitessier of France. Among long distance sailors he was already a legendary figure. He had sailed many thousands of miles in the Pacific and had in 1966 completed the then longest nonstop voyage by small boat—from Tahiti to Spain via Cape Horn, totalling some

14,216 miles.

Moitessier was favored to win. He rounded Cape Horn aboard his thirty-nine-foot ketch *Joshua*, and began the final uphill run to be the first man to sail alone, nonstop around the world—and win the coveted Golden Globe Race.

Awaiting Moitessier was the cash prize of $25,000, the trophy, and perhaps as much as a million dollars for books, endorsements and public appearances, not to forget the Legion d'honneur the French Government would certainly give him.

But Moitessier never won. Something very strange happened. The world was shocked, and even appalled, to learn that Moitessier suddenly changed his course, headed eastward along the Roaring Forties and in a second circumnavigation dropped out of the race. His course took him to Tahiti where he had been a recluse and silent observer for more than ten years when *Third Sea* arrived.

What happened to Moitessier? Why had he changed his mind? Had the anguish and suffering he saw in Vietnam, where he grew up, anything to do with it? Was he escaping a kind of Apocalypse Now? Did he fear the publicity? Why did he refuse to see his wife after the voyage? Over the years the rumours grew. He wrote a book about the voyage, but it was said he gave the proceeds to the Catholic church. The latest story was he wanted to become a modern day Johnny Apple Seed and plant fruit trees in the capitals of Europe. And why had he not gone back to sea again?

Before I had built *Third Sea*, I had given much thought to Moitessier's advice on "heavy weather sailing" and I incorporated his designs in the schooner. I read all his books and had two aboard. But I never really expected to meet him. No one heard much about him after the race, although he wasn't forgotten. Then one day I sailed *Third Sea* into Moorea and dropped anchor in Robinson's Cove, and there with anchor out and stern tied to coconut trees on shore was *Joshua*, in need of paint and repair, but a very sturdy boat. At last, I would meet Moitessier, and perhaps he would answer some of the puzzling questions that plagued his name.

But for the three days that we remained in Moorea, Moitessier never appeared. It was weird, as though he knew we were waiting, and was watching us from the hills, waiting for us to leave. We sailed without our ever having seen him.

From Moorea we voyaged to Honolulu and a few months later sailed back to Tahiti, and there tied stern to the quay in Papeete was *Joshua*. I hardly recognised her. She shined from bow to stern, with a new coat of red paint on the hull, her rigging freshly tarred. Moitessier was up to something.

Bernard Moitessier aboard his yacht *Joshua* in Papeete Harbor. An outspoken sailor, Moitessier was a frequent visitor aboard *Third Sea*.

During the next week I saw Moitessier several times on the waterfront but didn't know it was him. Someone had to point him out. Although he hadn't been to sea in some time, he had that weather-hardened look of a sailor about him. He was tanned and lean. He kept his hair, which was turning grey, slightly long. He wore shorts, never shoes, and loose fitting shirts with wide sleeves. He always seemed to be in a hurry.

People nodded and greeted him wherever he went, but he seldom stopped to talk to anyone. I was sure he was going to be difficult to meet.

One morning I was at the post office and noticed Moitessier at the next window. He had a stack of letters he was posting. This was a good time as any to meet him. I introduced myself. "Would you like to come aboard my schooner sometime?" I asked. "Maybe for dinner!"

"You have to excuse me," he said. "I'm very busy."

"I understand," I replied, "perhaps another time." I felt a little foolish and started to leave. Moitessier finished his business at the window, turned to me and spoke up.

"When?" he said.

"When!" I repeated, somewhat startled.

"Yes, when do you want me to come for dinner?"

"Any time, any time that you are free."

"What about tonight?"

That night Moitessier came aboard for dinner. He was carrying a Manila envelope which he handed to me. "To read later," he said. We offered him a drink. He doesn't drink, not even wine. "What about at sea, do you drink then?" I asked.

"Especially not at sea," he replied. "I get my highs from sailing."

We had dinner in the saloon and during the meal I kept the conversation light. After dinner, we leaned back and had coffee. Moitessier seemed relaxed. "You don't mind me asking you about your past?" I asked. Then he said the most extraordinarily thing.

"I wonder why you took so long," he said. "I heard you are a writer." I nodded. "Now you want to know why I quit the race."

"You don't mind me asking?"

"Not at all."

"Tell me then," I said, "did you think you were winning when you changed your mind?"

"Winning or losing, would it have mattered?" He didn't want to answer directly. "You want to know what made me change my mind. Let me tell you how I felt, what I felt, and then you can tell me why I changed my mind."

And so for the next few hours, with the flickering oil lamp lighting his damp face and all the crew hanging on to his every word, the old mariner told his story. We went back into time, to the French colonial period in Vietnam.

Moitessier was born in Hanoi in 1925 and grew up in Saigon, in a very fine house on Tu Do Street with an arbour of great shade trees outside his bedroom window. He came from a well-to-do French colonial family, and as a young man he conformed to the social conventions and rules expected of him. He was good in school, showed interest in his studies and excelled in sports, especially in swimming. He was groomed to take over the reigns of colonialism from his family, as his father had done, and his father before him.

Moitessier was too young to take up arms in World War II but he was old enough to see that changes were coming. The end of the war did not bring an end to fighting in Vietnam. The struggle for independence began, and France was not going to give up Indochina without a fight. Moitessier was twenty-five when he saw French troops marching gallantly through the streets of Saigon on their way to the jungles in the north. He watched France trying to cling unsuccessfully to its colonial empire.

Nothing made sense to Moitessier, the fighting, the killing. He refused to put on a uniform. Disillusioned he wanted to drop out. But where could he go? France was not home. He could not remain in Vietnam.

When growing up Moitessier spent much of his time at the sea shore. He often went out with local fishermen. He loved the sea immensely. The sea gave him peace of mind.

Why not go to sea, not as passenger or crew, but aboard his own vessel? He could go where he pleased, when he pleased. The sea could be his home, and he need not contend with governments and wars. He would belong to the sea.

Moitessier left Vietnam for Singapore, and there he found a suitable Thai junk which he bought for a pittance and rebuilt. He named her *Marie-Therese*, and no sooner was she completed, he took her to sea, alone.

Moitessier had no navigational equipment, not even a compass, and no charts. It didn't matter; he had no idea where he was going. He just wanted to be free, free from land and all the misery he had seen. Eighty-five days from Singapore he struck the infamous Chagos Reef in the Indian Ocean. His boat was lost.

Immediately he began planning his next boat, but he needed money. He worked at anything he could find—ship repair, wharf laborer, fisherman. He earned a few extra dollars writing about his experiences for a local newspaper. In time he was able to build a trim, twenty-eight-foot, double-ended ketch which he named *Marie Therese II*. He launched her on November 2, 1955, and soon after set out solo for Cape Town. He then crossed the Atlantic to the West Indies.

Moitessier fully intended to sail to the South Pacific, but not alone, with a lady friend from France. He set sail for Grenada where they were to meet, but he ran into a violent storm and was blown onto the reef at Grenada. He lost his second boat.

Moitessier caught the first ship he could, a tanker to Stockholm and took a job in a shipyard. Undaunted by his misfortunes, he made plans to build another ketch. This time it would be steel hulled capable of running any weather and any storm.

Moitessier continued writing and found he had an interested audience in France. People wanted to know how he did the things he did without money. An editor in Paris encouraged him to put it down in book form. He did and called it *A Vagabond in the South Seas.* I had him autograph my copy when he came aboard for dinner.

The book was an immediate success. Overnight Moitessier was the most talked about sailor in France. He became the guru of sailing, the lone sailor who advocated going to sea whether you had money or not. "Somehow you can find a means!"

With his book a financial success, *Joshua* was a reality. He met a French lady, a divorcee with three children, who showed a keen interest in sailing. They married and Moitessier had a ready-made family.

In 1963, with all France watching, *Joshua* was ready. Moitessier and Francoise set sail for Tahiti, leaving the children in France. Tahiti and the islands suited Moitessier and there they spent two and a half years. They probably would have remained but in 1965 the French turned French Polynesia into a nuclear testing site, with Tahiti the staging area.

Moitessier decided to return to Europe, by sailing eastward around Cape Horn, nonstop to Spain. If successful, Francoise would be the first woman to round the Horn in a small craft. They set out in the autumn of 1966.

It was a rough passage. They were plagued by storms for weeks on end. At the Horn they encountered eighty- and ninety-knot winds, and for fear of pitch-poling, turning end over end, Moitessier dragged heavy lines astern to slow them down. This proved unsatisfactory. In a daring gamble, Moitessier cut the lines free, and then taking the helm, he drove *Joshua* like a surfboard down the crest of a wave and around the Horn.

The voyage was the longest nonstop passage on record, some 14,216 miles, taking one-hundred and twenty-six days. Moitessier became a national hero, a legend in his own time. Another best-seller hit the stands: *Cape Horn, the Logical Route.*

Moitessier was now in demand. He was famous and had money. His every turn, his every move was watched. What could he possibly do next?

The world at this time was gripped in what the yachting world called "The Chichester fever." Chichester had won the first solo transatlantic race, and in 1965 won world acclaim when he sailed solo, at the age of sixty-five, around the world making only one stop in Sydney. He was knighted and became hero of the decade. People now looked for other heroes, and they were to find them in the *Sunday Times* Golden Globe Trophy Race. Whether he wanted to or not, Moitessier was under pressure to enter.

The rest is history. On the last leg of his voyage, Moitessier changed course, leaving the fame and glory to Robin Knox-Johnston.

"I didn't know who was in the lead," Moitessier said, sitting in the saloon on *Third Sea.* "I had no radio. I didn't even know who was in the race, but I felt confident I was in the lead." And then he said one word which kind of summed it all up—flashbulbs!

"I could see flashbulbs exploding. The Press! The stupid questions. Who was I deceiving? Myself! I was being contrary to everything I believe in. I was being dishonest. The thing that I loved was the sea, the freedom, not the winning."

After withdrawing, Moitessier's plan was to sail to the remote Galapagos but in the end he quietly slipped back into Tahiti. He wrote a book defending his position, but readers looked for some hidden meaning. "The book was agony," he admitted. "It took longer to write it than to actually do the voyage. The public makes you what they want. They called me a gifted writer. I am not a writer. I don't like to write."

I asked him if it were true that he gave all the money he received from the book to the church. "I offered it to the Pope," he said, "and if he wouldn't take it, I would give it to the Friends of Nature Society. But there were some conditions. The Pope had to use the money for humanitarian reasons rather than religious reasons. The church never accepted it, so I started planting fruit trees."

The rumors were true. For several years Moitessier wrote to ministers and heads of states, trying to convince them to plant fruit trees in their capitals. He gave money to anyone who would accept it. But he was making little progress.

I had forgotten about the Manila envelope until Moitessier had gone. I quickly tore it open. It was a letter to me, outlining his mission with the trees, and saying that he was going back to sea, very shortly.

I saw him again, several times, and we talked. Tahiti no longer held the enchantment for him that it had. He decided to sail for California.

Why California, I don't know. But I'm sure Moitessier has his reasons. But to sail there from Tahiti in the autumn of the year was not the time. North of Hawaii the weather is constant gales blowing down from the frozen north. But who was I reminding? This was the challenge that Moitessier liked. No one was prodding him into it, no wife was forcing him on. And at the end of the voyage was California, where they are perhaps as eccentric as he. Moitessier did make it and he spent the next few years in ports along the California coast. Then came the tragic news. *Joshua* was wrecked on the coast of Baja in Mexico during a hurricane. Moitessier managed to survive.

Francis Chichester did have a pronounced effect on Moitessier's decision to withdraw from the race. Late in May, 1967, Chichester sailed single-handed home to Plymouth to fame and considerable fortune. The British public had decided to create him a hero. A quarter of a million people lined up in Plymouth to watch his arrival. Every small craft in the district formed a vast welcoming armada, national television schedules were abandoned for hours of live coverage, a knighthood was hastily bestowed upon him, and the book that followed was one of the most profitable best-sellers in years.

Yet certainly Chichester's motives had to be other than a mere love for the sea. His vessel was sponsored at a quarter of a million dollars, an astronomical price then. He had a beer company backing him up and the press and television were following his every move. This to Moitessier was not what sailing was all about.

Another single-handed sailor whom I greatly admired was Tristan Jones. Tristan holds most of the single-handed sailing records in modern sailing history. Alone, he has traveled to the Arctic Circle, and has sailed the world's lowest stretch of navigable water, the Dead Sea, and had

sailed an ocean-going vessel on the world's highest waters, Lake Titicaca in Peru. He has, in fact, sailed 345,000
miles (more than the distance to the moon) in boats under
forty feet long, 180,000 miles of this distance single-
handed. He has sailed the Atlantic eighteen times, nine
times alone. And he had stayed alive on an iceberg for
fifteen months by living off seal blubber. His adventure-
filled articles and books had been translated into seven
languages.

When I was building *Third Sea* and felt depressed, I'd
think of Tristan Jones. He did all these incredible things
with little or no money. After I launched *Third Sea* I hoped
one day I would meet him somewhere at some lonely
atoll and thank him. Then in 1982, I suddenly had doubts
that I'd ever meet Tristan Jones. He might never even go
to sea again in a small boat. I was in Singapore when
news reached me that doctors in New York had amputated his left leg above the knee, the result of a wound
sustained while serving with the Royal Navy in Yemen.

But I was wrong. Tristan didn't give up the sea. The
next news I heard he had been thrown out of a hospital in
New York for organizing a wheelchair race among the
other amputees —"they were much younger, but so miserable. I felt sorry for them." He then raised the money,
outfitted a trimaran and returned to the sea. I did eventually meet Tristan at Phuket in southern Thailand. He had
suffered another tragedy. He had lost his other leg to an
infection, but he still planned to go sailing.

Single-handed sailing isn't solely a man's game. With
Sharon Sites Adams, the first woman to sail across the
Pacific alone, it was just something she wanted to do, or
so the press led everyone to believe.

The story goes that her seafaring life began when she
noted an advertisement for a sailing school run by Al

Adams of Los Angeles. She was intrigued by the possibility of a new adventure.

She took to the sailing life rapidly. She made her first solo run thirty-eight minutes after the first lesson began, and a year and a half later she married her teacher.

Sharon Adams was sailing only a few months when she made her second solo passage, from California to Hawaii. It took her thirty-five days and earned her world attention. "I will never sail alone again," she said at the time. But then something happened.

She did sail alone again, from Yokohama to San Diego, California, in a thirty-one-foot boat. Al Adams went to Yokohama to see his wife off. As she sailed away he blew her a kiss. The voyage lasted seventy-five days. The thirty-eight-year-old mother of two was terrified most of the time. "The boat suffered a knock down in one storm." she said later. "It fell over on its starboard side and that made a mess of my housekeeping. It also scared the daylights out of me. Fortunately the boat righted itself."

Sharon Adams came home a hero. Her husband Al Adams greeted her and was by her side as she stood in front of the microphone to make her welcoming speech. Just before she spoke, she put her hand over the microphone, turned to her husband and said, "When this is over I want a divorce." She got her divorce. She claimed any man that would send his wife out to sea when he knew the conditions was not worthy to be her husband.

Another solo lady skipper was pretty Clare Francis, twenty-seven years old, five foot two and weighing one-hundred-and-seven pounds. She set off across the North Atlantic from Plymouth, England, in her thirty-two-foot *Gulliver G* for Newport, Rhode Island, "just for the hell of it." She sailed in May choosing a route to pass close to the Azores, looking for the more gentle winds.

Instead, she met a continuous procession of depressions that forced her to the south. For most of her nearly four-thousand-mile voyage she was beating into winds of Force Five and often more. She averaged about one hundred miles per day, but had frequent runs of more than one hundred and twenty miles.

After Newport she sailed again, solo, for the Caribbean. "I think I want to be nomadic," she said, "and to be that you really need a boat."

Did she intend to continue sailing solo? "I cannot say I want to continue as skipper indefinitely," she admitted. "On my next big cruise, when I retire from single-handed sailing, I have every intention of going along as first mate—by marrying the skipper."

While Sharon Sites Adams and Clare Francis did it because they wanted to, Larry Nilsen aboard his cutter *Heather* had no intention of sailing alone around the world. In fact, he hates long sea passages. "I just like to go where only a small boat can take me," he admitted.

For several years before he got *Heather*, Larry had been cruising around the Pacific on different yachts. I met him on Tahiti and we shipped out together on a very fine sailing ship called *Nordlys*. One afternoon when we were sitting on the spreaders sixty feet above the deck, Larry explained his views.

Off our starboard bow was Rose Island, laying midway between Bora Bora and Samoa. It's the type of island you see in cartoons in magazines, with sand and palms, where a shipwrecked sailor sits on the beach.

Nordlys was too large to enter the lagoon and our skipper, Captain Ed Dekoning, didn't want to chance standing off shore while an exploring party rowed ashore. We sadly watched the island drift by.

"A small boat," Larry said, thinking aloud, "one that

can take you across reefs and you don't have to worry. That's my idea of sailing, to explore all the islands, visit all the reefs, to go where no other ship dares go."

In New Zealand he found *Heather* for sale, a twenty-eight-foot canoe stern cutter. "It didn't look good but it was sound," he said. "I bought her for fifteen hundred dollars and spent the next year outfitting her."

Larry never intended to sail alone, nor did he have it in mind to sail around the world. His crew member-to-be was his boss' seventeen-year-old daughter. They were to sail together to South Africa, Larry's home. The plan was for her to sneak away and meet Larry in the Bay of Islands, but on the day of their planned departure something happened. Her father got wind of their plans. She did manage to get a message to Larry, telling him to meet her in Brisbane, his next port-of-call.

In the Tasman between New Zealand and Australia he encountered the worst storms he ever had at sea. "For five days the wind blew at full gale force. I was relieved when she was down to Force Five."

In Brisbane he went to the hotel where he was to meet his girl, only to find in the nick of time that her father had checked in and was awaiting him. He had to flee, with the girl's father in hot pursuit. Larry jumped aboard his cutter, tossed off the mooring lines and set sail, alone.

After a long passage at sea, *Heather* sailed into Timor, short of water and provisions. He was in good spirits when he arrived, but not for long.

Since Larry was traveling on a South African passport, the authorities at Timor refused to permit him to land. He talked them into giving him some water, and without an alternative he hoisted sail and set out across the Indian Ocean to Cocos Island, about 1,400 miles away.

There is probably no other navigator in history who

sailed the Indian Ocean with charts traced on bread-wrapping paper. "It's surprising what you can do when you have to," Larry explained. "I never had much money. I got most my supplies by trading for them. But you can't trade for charts. You need money."

Finally he reached South Africa. But after a few weeks on shore he was longing for the sea again. He also missed the isles of the Pacific and especially New Zealand.

He made his preparations, and again he didn't intend to sail single-handed. He chose for his mate a young English girl. He was somewhat skeptical at first. She had no sailing experience

"But I'll learn," she insisted. "I'll do anything. You won't have to cook a meal." He was convinced. At last this was the girl he was looking for.

They cleared harbor with all sails set on a starboard tack. The days that followed were beautiful, with a gentle sea running and a brisk wind. All would have been well but Larry never saw his first mate. She never got out of her bunk. She did no cooking. In fact, she couldn't stand it even if Larry cooked.

The little cash that Larry had saved up went for her plane ticket back to South Africa from their next port. Larry was now a confirmed single-hand sailor.

A few months later Larry entered the South Pacific. Here was sailing he loved. He cruised the prehistoric Galapagos, visited descendants of the *Bounty* on Pitcarin, stopped in the Marquesas and returned to Tahiti.

For the next six months, after a brief stay on Tahiti, *Heather* zigzagged her way across the Pacific, with stops at Cook Islands, Samoa, Fiji and finally after two years eight months and one day after leaving the Bay of Islands was back. During that time he visited some sixteen major ports and forty-two islands.

A few of Schooner *Third Sea*'s crew members over the years.

Chapter 15

GIVE ME A GOOD CREW

In early 1934, Irving Johnson and his wife Electa purchased a ninety-two-foot North Sea pilot boat with the idea to sail around the world with a paying crew of young people selected for skills and compatibility. Irving would serve as skipper and they would have only a paid hand or two, a cook and mate—but everyone else would be amateurs sharing expenses. Each crew member would have regular duties aboard and would stand regular watches. The first and second mates would always be experienced men, but aside from that, sailing experience would not be a prerequisite. They rigged the vessel as a brigantine and named her *Yankee*.

Before World War II began, the Johnsons saw their dream come true and made three circumnavigations. Each voyage took them by a different route. They visited the Caribbean and Central American ports, passed through the Panama Canal and pointed their bow towards Pitcarin Island, home of the descendants of the *Bounty*. Pitcarin was seldom visited by any ships, much less yachts, which was typical of the pattern that *Yankee* followed in all her voyages. The Johnsons had no idea what they would find at Pitcarin, but it turned out to be the first of many visits they had with the descendants of the *Bounty* mutineers.

From Pitcarin *Yankee* sailed to Tahiti, Moorea and Bora Bora, when the only way to get there was by boat, and crossed the Pacific touching the Cook Islands, Tonga, Fiji, the New Hebrides, the Solomons and Borneo. She poked her nose into out-of-the-way places the world had little known. Singapore became their port-of-call on every voyage, and *Yankee* was the first American yacht to sail up the Chao Phraya River to Bangkok.

With her amateur crews, *Yankee* became the Johnson home afloat and a training school for countless young people. The Johnson's two sons were born aboard and learned to walk on a tossing deck. But then came World War II and the world would no longer be the same. In 1941, Irving sold *Yankee* to the Admiral Billard Academy as a training ship for cadets, and then joined the U.S. Navy. He was commissioned and went to sea aboard a survey ship charting the islands where fighting soon became hot and heavy. He saw action at Wallis Island, where he had once sailed *Yankee,* and was captain of the USS *Sumner* at the battle of Iwo Jima. He reached the rank of Captain, U.S.N.R. at his retirement after the war.

In 1946, with the help of movie actor Sterling Heyden, who had sailed aboard *Yankee* on their second voyage, the Johnsons were fortunate to find their second *Yankee,* a ninety-eight-foot schooner the Germans had built and used as a recreation ship for the Luftwaffe during the war. They rigged the new *Yankee* as a brigantine with a grand total of 7,775 square feet of canvas.

Between 1947 and 1958, the Johnsons made four more circumnavigations, all with amateur crews. On one trip, Irving discovered and raised the anchor of the *Bounty* at Pitcarin. Between these voyages, the Johnsons published several books and lectured extensively. Irving Johnson skippered the two *Yankees* seven times around the world. Then, after a quarter century of voyaging to every corner around the world, the Johnsons sold *Yankee.* Soon after it was wrecked by its new owner on a reef at Rarotonga.

Irving and Electa Johnson did not give up sailing, however. They had Sparkman and Stephens design for them a third *Yankee,* a fifty-foot steel centerboard ketch with shallow draft and masts stepped in tabernacles so they could be folded for passage under low bridges. The Johnsons thus began a retirement period cruising the vast canals of Europe.

I was very fortunate to have met Irving Johnson at the *National Geographic* in Washington, D.C. where I was trying to sell a story idea about diving for pearl shells in the Tuamotus. The editor rejected the story but Irving was encouraging when he learned about my building a schooner in Singapore. I was hoping to meet up with him again some place around the world, but when I finally did see *Yankee* she was on the reef in Rarotonga. Still, Irving Johnson was encouraging in another way. I did follow his concept of taking aboard amateur crews, young inspiring people with no experience. It proved to be successful. With few exceptions, those amateurs who signed on were able to adjust easily to shipboard life. The key, I believe, was to keep everyone busy. I learned quickly how essential this is. On our lengthy twenty-nine-day voyage from Singapore to Hong Kong, against the northeast monsoon, I had one crew member so seasick he could not get out of his bunk for days. He became so weak from not eating that I thought he might die. I had to do something. Against the outrage of the crew, I demanded he get up from his bunk and stand his watch, if only for a few minutes. For his first watch he managed to hold on for five minutes; his next watch he did ten minutes. In a few days he was up and around, and acting like sailing was the most natural thing to do.

Also important for holding on to a crew is to not lose the feeling of excitement, and to foster curiosity that comes with visiting exotic places and different people.

Choosing the right crew, of course, is all important. How do we judge people we don't know? I recall when I was in Tahiti, before I had *Third Sea,* there was a skipper who arrived aboard his 42-foot ketch and was the envy of everyone on the island. He handpicked a very special crew—all women. He was on his third Pacific voyage when I met him.

His name was Lee Quinn, no relation to Quinn's Bar in Tahiti. His yacht was a trim, well-maintained vessel called *Neophyte.* Like Erving Johnson, his policy was to sign on inexperienced crew, but in his case it was all young women. But Lee Quinn of the *Neophyte* was not Irving Johnson of the *Yankee.*

Before turning yachtsman, Lee Quinn had made a size-able fortune painting flag poles, enough by the age of forty to buy a comfortable yacht and entice young women to go sailing with him. When I saw him stepping ashore in Tahiti I wondered how he did it. He was short and wiry and looked more like the guy next door than like a stud and adventurer which was the reputation he had acquired.

For eight years Lee Quinn sailed with all-women crews. He had covered forty thousand nautical miles, during a career that saw him sign aboard a grand total of fifty-eight lady sailors from twenty-three nations, rang-ing in age from eighteen to fifty.

Then on October 11, 1970, Lee Quinn cleared the harbor at Yokohama and pointed *Neophyte* to the north-east on a route that would take her some two thousand miles up near the Aleutian Islands and then south to San Francisco, taking advantage of the prevailing winds from the north for the trip down the coast. Aboard were Chozo Saeki Yonko, eighteen; Jamko Kume, twenty-nine, and Pat Seedsman, a twenty-seven-year-old Australian who had made many voyages with Quinn. It was to have been a sixty-day voyage and it wasn't until Quinn and the three women were a month overdue that the Coast Guard trans-

mitted an urgent marine broadcast asking vessels in the
Pacific to report if they had seen the *Neophyte*. After
four days of silence, the Coast Guard mounted a fruitless, six-day air search for the missing sloop. *Neophyte*
had vanished without a trace in the North Pacific at the
height of the typhoon season, one which the U.S. Coast
Guard had noted in weather-bureau logs for the unusual
fury of its winds and the awesomeness of its seas. All
evidence seems to point toward the conclusion that Quinn,
forty-three, and his pretty three-woman crew met their
deaths in a storm too overwhelming for even the stud Lee
Quinn to manage.

I have always felt indifferent about women crew. After
launching *Third Sea*, I signed aboard mixed crews, men
and women alike. But I did learn that I had to be careful.
Third Sea was not modern; no power winches or roller
reefing. She had a bowsprit that jutted far out over the
water, and here deck hands had to stand to work the jib.
Ratlines ran up the rigging, and they were for climbing,
not for looks. Someone had to scamper up them when
called to do so. Everything was manual, even the anchor
windlass. To lift sail, all hands were needed on deck. It
was strenuous, endless work. It was most difficult at night.
A sudden squall and I'd give the call: "All hands on deck!"
As crew came charging up the ladder, I tapped each one
on the shoulder calling instructions—"Release the fore-
main jib sheet!" "Take the fisherman topping lift!" I could
not see faces, only forms in the dark. "Go out on the
bowsprit. Hold it! Disregard that order." I had assigned
the most dangerous position to a woman crew. Morally I
could not do this, endanger her life and the safety of the
ship and crew when I knew she was incapable of carrying out the order safely. I could not order her to do so
when a hundred-and-eighty-pound muscle man comes up

the hatch next and I would have to tell him to take the helm.

What it meant was that the forces I put to work were not equal, and I could not treat them as equals. So the system was sometimes unfair for the male members of the crew, such as when I needed someone to pull up the anchor, row through a rough surf, or go aloft to run a halyard through a block. But what happens when I ask someone to go down into the galley and help cook the next meal?

A captain of a vessel with women crew members aboard has a responsibilty for these women. He has to make them feel that they can be comfortable with the rest of the crew, that they do not have to worry about their own well-being and that no one will take advange of them. And a captain must also assure that women crew maintain a decorum that does not upset the men. I found aboard *Third Sea* this was not always easy to do when the crew was young and robust. We did manage to develop an unspoken moral code that everyone followed.

Mandi, a slight New Zealand girl, could handle the helm as good as any able-bodied seaman. But I could never send her aloft.

I did have one unpleasant experience with a woman crew member. When I was not aboard *Third Sea* for any length of time, I usually hired someone to watch over things. No problem until one day I announced to the crew that I was leaving for a month. Malaysia's chief game warden, and old friend, had invited me on a jungle trek with the game department, and I mentioned I was asking a skipper I knew to take over while I was gone. "What about Suzie?" someone said. "Or are you against women skippers?"

Suzie had been crewing for me for several months. She was tough, much like Tug Boat Annie. She could do most anything, including tracing an electrical short and even taking the engine apart if need be. And I never had to ask; she'd do it on her own. I wasn't being prejudiced. I just never gave thought to Suzie taking over as skipper while I was gone. Why not give her the chance? I thought. So I promoted Suzie to skipper of *Third Sea* during my absence. I must admit, she did prove to be good. She was capable and she ran a good ship. She did so well, I kept her on as skipper after I returned from the jungle. But this wasn't another of those Lee Quinn arrangements. We kept our relationship professional. I was especially very careful about that.

Things went along smoothly until one evening when I invited a lady friend aboard for drinks and dinner. It was obvious from the very start that Suzie wasn't very fond of the woman. Suzie didn't like the way she dressed, the scent of her perfume, or the way I treated her, like any gentleman would treat a lady. The next morning, after my friend had gone, Suzie called her a hussy. I let it pass, but later when I mentioned we had varnishing to do, Suzie said, "See if your girlfriend will varnish for you! She probably doesn't even know what a paint brush looks like." I had words with Suzie.

A few days later Suzie left *Third Sea*. She said she was joining another boat, as skipper, which she did. I understand that she did rather well and is working as a skipper aboard a fine yacht in the Caribbean.

Yachting is a never-ending learning process. There is so much we all can learn from the sea, given the impetus to learn. At sea, especially aboard a sailing ship, we are close to nature, closer than we can ever get anywhere else. We learn to read the wind. We come to know squalls and the power they might pack. We learn to read the clouds. That is a fair weather cloud over there, and that one is a storm cloud on the eastern horizon. We learn to read the texture of the sea, to know when currents are running and when they are not. We are awed by riptides. We learn that the blue in the clouds ahead means we are approaching a low atoll, that the blue is the reflection of a lagoon. We learn the speed of the wind by the white caps on breaking waves. We find that by following the movement of birds we can tell in what direction land might be. We learn to read the stars, and they become friendly. We soon have stars we favor, and we learn to recognize the planets. We learn the moon and all its phases. We know when it sets, and when it rises. We wait for it, and then we welcome it when we see it. We lament when it sets and turns the night into black. We even marvel when we see the moon in the daytime. What landlubbers would do that? Nature to the yachtsman is real and meaningful.

Aboard *Third Sea*, the oceans became our classroom. Our library became our prop. Direction is important. I had a man and wife team who lived in Alaska for many years, and all they talked about was Alaska. It can be heavy when sailing the South Seas and someone continuously talks about the frozen north. Diversion is needed. "What do you think of Somerset Maugham's *The Narrow Corner*?" I asked Matts, my Swedish crew, and handed him the novel. Matts had just finished reading Jack London's *South Sea Tales*. He particularly liked the short story called "The Heathen," about a drifter and a Tahitian who were the only survivors of a hurricane. The next day Matts appeared with Maugham's novel in his hand.

"He just doesn't have it," he shouted. "Maugham was a good storyteller, when he told about district officers and rubber planters. He loses it when he comes to describing a storm at sea. With Jack London it's real!" Soon the rest of the crew are reading both books, and arguing over the merits of each. It's then that I bring out the more obscure writers of Pacific lore—Louis Becke, Robert Frisbe, Frederick O'Brien. A deadly duel begins—"It's my turn next! I'm next!"

Robert Stedman, my nephew who joined the crew his first time in Samoa, and later in Honolulu as first mate, is a case example of what reading can do for one at sea. Robert was a college drop out. He was bored. Our family was very upset, and, of course, they were concerned about his future. They accepted his joining *Third Sea* for his first voyage. It would help him find himself, they all said. But when he joined *Third Sea* the second time, for an extended voyage across the South Pacific to Asia, I became the fall guy. What am I doing to my nephew? Nevertheless, I felt the sea was better for Robert than working for Saks Fifth Avenue in Los Angeles.

When Robert rejoined *Third Sea* in Honolulu as first mate, he discovered the ship's library. From the time he stepped board to the time we arrived in Singapore nine months later, he had read fifty-eight of the ship's five hundred books, and most of them were classics. He received an education far greater than any college or university would have given him. And he got into the reading habit. He is a voracious reader today.

Aside from the reading library, the ship's music library was equally as important. I had it stacked with classical music tapes. We also had a fair collection of music from the South Pacific.

Every afternoon, weather permitting, we had what we called "The Helmsman's Choice." The person at the helm could pick whatever music he or she liked and could play it on deck. When I took an afternoon watch, I introduced the crew to Mozart or Beethoven, and when they could recognize these composers, I would play Shostakovitch or Borodin. Soon they had their own favorite composers. They learned that more than any other music, classical music can fit the mood at sea, and who would ever have imagined, when a squall appeared on the horizon, someone shouted out to put on Beethoven's Sixth. "Play the Third Movement, the one about the storm."

For Mate Robert Stedman, left, *Third Sea* was his college classroom. Dave Loomis, right, made a number of passages aboad the schooner.

I had to be Captain Bligh in some respects. I had forbidden Walkman's with ear phones, for a reason. When I was designing *Third Sea*, I installed an earphone jack at the binnacle to enable the helmsman to listen to his favorite music during lonely hours at night. I removed the jack after the first voyage. For the ship's safety I found it is important that the helmsman be alert. He should not only see what is around him but he should listen as well. He must listen to the sounds of the sea, to the rudder biting in to the waves, to the hum of the rigging, to the moans of the masts, to a call for help that might come at night.

For the first dozen years I sailed *Third Sea*, I was very traditional in every way. We used the sextant and did our own plotting. We had a depth sounder, but we also used a lead line. When we went into port, I had someone stand at the bow and toss the lead line, and call out the depths— "By the mark, five fathoms," or whatever it might be.

We live in times when we depend upon mechanical aids for our very existence. The most difficult thing to teach a new crew was that we had to depend upon wind and sail to get us wherever we are going. It's so easy to say "turn on the engine." We might ask, how did the old schooners and square riggers get into and out of port without engines? Simple, by kedging. In bygone days they had kedging posts or blocks in all the ports and entrances to ports. A ship's crew would row their longboat up to a kedging post and fastened a line from the ship to the post. The crew aboard would pull the ship, either by hand or by windlass, up to the post. In the meantime, the longboat crew would row a second line to the next post and fasten it and repeat the process.

Kedging posts have disappeared but the procedure is still valid. Instead of posts two anchors will do just as well. With each new crew I signed on, I taught them how

Peter at the helm with Elaine at his side epitomize the romance of sailing the South Seas. Peter had been a lone beachcomber.

to enter and leave port without the use of the engine, by kedging with anchors. Another method I followed was to tow the schooner with our dory. Whalers once did it so why not *Third Sea*? The training was a moral boost for a new crew. They learned that we aboard *Third Sea* were self-sufficient, and survivors. I can still see the early-morning risers at the Ilikai Hotel facing the yacht harbor in Honolulu, standing on their balconies, watching *Third Sea* being towed out to sea. I wondered what they thought, that we had no engine, that we were too poor to buy diesel, that the captain was a martinet. What they thought didn't matter; what did matter was what the crew thought.

Over the years, *Third Sea* was host to hundreds of crew and passengers. *Third Sea* changed many lives. I heard it said ever so many times—"I've always wanted to go to sea in a ship like this!" Sometimes they may have left disappointed, but more often they departed with the grand feeling that they had accomplished something in life. They learned something about themselves. I had one man, a Frenchman, who wanted to join the crew in Tahiti for our sail to Hawaii. He was a lady's hair dresser with a shop in Papeete. He was married, but he was in the process of getting a divorce. His wife had already returned to Paris. I was reluctant to take him, as I was with anyone who came aboard to announce they wanted to join the crew so they could quit smoking. Or drinking. Nothing can be worse than putting up with someone who is trying to kick a habit. They can be irritable, and they can make everyone around them irritable. But the hair dresser had a way about him and convinced me that he should come.

The young man, whom I shall call Dominic, confided in me at the helm one night. He confessed that he had always been weak, that his wife had lost respect for him. He had never exerted himself, and he had never revealed to his wife his true feelings. But what his true self was even he wasn't sure. He was hoping the long sea voyage would help him come to terms with himself. Deep down he didn't know what he was capable of doing. At Caroline Island he found out.

Captain Omar Darr had asked us to stop at Caroline to pick up Peter, his caretaker there and carry him to Honolulu. Anchoring at the island was most difficult. There is no lagoon or even a sheltered bay. Omar explained what we had to do. It was risky business. First we lowered the anchor over the edge of the outside reef and then rowed the dory with a line and second anchor towards shore. We secured the second anchor in the coral, tied the line to it, and then pulled the stern of the schooner as close to shore as we could get. As long as the wind blew off shore *Third Sea* would be safe.

To reach the island from the schooner, we had to row the dory through a narrow pass in the coral. It was near dark by the time we got ashore, and it wouldn't be until the next morning that we could depart. We had to keep a close watch aboard *Third Sea* that night for any change of wind. It was after midnight when the storm struck.

It came from the direction of the sea, bringing frightful flashes of lightening and a change of wind. We had no choice but to untie the stern line and motor into the wind, pulling up the anchor at the same time. I had all crew on deck in the driving rain standing by. There was no need to be alarmed. The engine started and I gave word to untie the stern line. We would have to return later for the line and anchor and the two crew we left ashore.

The wind had increased to gale force and I could now hear the anchor chain scraping long the coral. We were dragging with the bow swinging toward shore. I had to put the engine into gear to keep the bow pointed out to sea. The stern line became too taunt to untie. "Cut it then," I shouted above the cry of the wind. Dave and Judy were aboard on that trip. Dave pulled out his knife and hacked at the line until it was cut through. I pushed the lever to full throttle. The engine roared into action, and then suddenly, without warning, it stopped. It stopped with a loud thud! I knew immediately what had happened. When Dave cut the mooring line, the severed end got caught in the twisting propeller blades and stopped the engine dead. We were still fastened to the shore with the mooring line wrapped around the propeller. Someone would have to go overboard and cut the line. But it was not that simple.

That day when I returned to *Third Sea* after having gone ashore, I had found the sea all about the schooner thrashing with schools of hungry, vicious sharks. Dominic and another crew, against my advice, had harpooned a shark. I knew that once you killed a shark while at anchor, others would be attracted by the scent of blood, and they would not go away. The sharks were still there. We could see their shadows slithering beneath the surface. Now I had to send someone over the side. I could only ask for a volunteer.

"I'll go," Dominic said and stepped forward. "It's my fault the sharks are here. I'll go."

"You know what you are doing?" I asked. I wondered if I would be doing the right thing to let him go. I could see the look of terror across his face. He was trembling from both fear and the cold.

"I know," he said. "I still want to go!"

"Tie a line around his waist," I called, and handed Dominic my knife. I then instructed Dave and Judy to unfurl the sails and get them up. Cutting the mooring line would not free the engine. We had to sail off the reef with the anchor over the edge. I took my position at the helm and grabbed the wheel, ready to do what I could when the sails went up. I turned to see how close we were to the reef. With each swell of the ocean we rose high above the reef, but then we would drop and the water rushing over the sharp coral ridges looked like the well of death, and at any minute we would be sucked into its wrath. Blinding flashes of lightening and the sudden claps of thunder added to the feeling of doom. And then when I turned to the other side, there stood Dominic on the boomkin. He was without shirt and wore his sarong pulled up and tied at the waist. A line was fastened around his chest, and between his teeth he gripped the knife. The strain showed on his face. Torrents of rain drove against his bare flesh, and his hair was splattered down against his forehead and over his eyes. He made the sign of the cross and stepped off with his eyes fixed straight ahead. He was gone and we could only wait.

I hadn't noticed until that moment, but the other crew who had harpooned the shark with Dominic was at the port rail near the bow, slapping the water with a white cloth dangling over the side. In doing so, he had attracted the sharks to that side of the hull.

It seemed like all eternity that he was down there. Why wasn't he coming up for air? Suddenly I could feel the schooner lunge and the wheel sprung free. Dominic had managed to severe the line. "Pull him up," I shouted at the top of my voice, and when I looked back Dominic was coming up the side of the schooner. He had a look of wonder about his face.

We heeled far to port, the bow dug into the sea and we inched our way away from the treacherous reef. Once free from the island we had to struggle to pull up the anchor and three-hundred feet of chain. It took hours, and when dawn came the island was far to our stern. Two crew were still on the island, sleeping in Peter's hut, but retrieving them would not be a simple matter. In the turmoil of cutting the mooring line and breaking way from the island, our dory had broken free and was gone—our dory that Don Maclean had built in Rabaul and that had served us so faithfully. We no longer had a ship to shore boat, except for a rubber raft, but that would not do. It would be cut to shreds in minutes on the sharp coral.

We were fortunate to have given the two men on shore one of the ship's walkie-talkies. They had no idea what had happened during the night. When they awoke the next morning, *Third Sea* was gone. They saw the anchor on the reef and the floating severed line. They expected the worse. Relief came only when they picked us up on the phone. We explained what had to be done. Without a dinghy, they had to work their way over the reef by both walking and swimming to the very edge. There they would have to stand and *Third Sea* would make a pass at which time we would throw out two lines. They had to grab on and hold, and make as little movement as possible. Sharks might still be in the area.

By sheeting in the sails as tightly as we could, we caused *Third Sea* to heel far to one side, thus reducing the depth of the keel. Like a baseball player coming into home plate we slid sideways along the reef and snatched our two crew members off the coral to safety. Once clear of the island we shortened sails, lashed the helm, and cracked open a couple bottles of Philippine rum. We all slept after that for almost twenty-four hours.

We arrived in Honolulu two weeks later. Peter flew to London to visit with his mother, and Dominic returned to Paris. Several months later I had a letter from them both. Peter asked if he could rejoin *Third Sea* as a permanent crew. "I'll be content to eat beans," he said. Dominic was pleased to inform us that he was back with his wife. "You know, I am not the same person," he wrote. And at the end he added one word—Thanks. We were able to do what we did because we had a crew that was trained and responded to orders. Taking orders is important, and one must learn to obey and follow them at sea. In our discussions, I always informed new crew there was always more than one way to do things, and both ways may be correct. I wanted no one to contest an order when I gave one, but afterwards we could discuss my reasons for doing what I did. We once had a passenger aboard who thought I was incompetent and actually reported me to the French authorities in Papeete.

We were moored in Robinson's Cove on Moorea, preparing to depart for Tahiti in a day or two when Omar Darr called us from shore. He said he had received storm warnings on his radio and suggested we lift anchor and sail for Tahiti immediately, as the winds were not favorable and would come whipping directly into the bay. I alerted the crew and informed them we would depart immediately. We had a visitor aboard, a middle-aged Englishman, and I told him we would row him ashore. He asked if he could make the short passage with us back to Tahiti. I had no objections. It was only twelve miles and would take no more than three hours at the most.

Twenty minutes later it was all we could do to get through the pass leading out of Cook's Bay. Winds were head-on with seas from the open ocean rolling into the pass in huge swells. The bow lifted high and then dropped with each incoming wave. Half the time the propeller was out of the water.

The crossing was not easy, and we battled every mile of the way. At the entrance to Papeete Harbor, on the far right side, was the wreck of a large ferry boat on the reef.

I had inquired earlier about the wreck and was told the vessel lost control when the skipper decided to chance the wind which was coming from the west. The Sailing Directions said vessels should not attempt to enter the harbor when the wind came from the west. As *Third Sea* approached the entrance, the wind veered. It was now coming directly from the west. "Prepare to tack," I called out. "We've going back out." The crew responded and we swung about and nosed *Third Sea* back out to sea.

"But I don't want to go back out to sea," the Englishman protested. "I want to go into the harbor." I couldn't take the time to explain and gave further orders to reef the main. "Listen," the man continued, "I demand that we go into port." I told him to step aside and be quiet and called the crew together.

"We'll head toward Point Venus and get into the lee of the island and wait out the storm there," I said. I handed over the helm to the first mate and went below deck to get the weather report on WWV. I had the shock of my life when I tuned in. What had started as a gale had now reached hurricane force winds. The winds were beginning to rotate and if they closed their loop it would turn into a full tropical storm, or in other words, into a hurricane. A hurricane means the winds are circular and no direction is safe, except far from land and out at sea. I rushed up on deck. We were already well past Point Venus and going into the lee of the island. "Change course," I shouted. "We're heading northeast, away from land."

"You're mad," the Englishman said. "I demand that I be put ashore."

"You will," I said, "when the time is ready."

For twenty hours the wind blew nearing hurricane force, but they never closed the loop. When they finally subsided we were sixty miles north of Tahiti, and it took us the rest of the day and that night to reach the entrance to Papeete Harbor. The winds had played havoc in the tight harbor. Yachts had pulled free from their anchors and a few were up on the beach. A tug boat before us was pulling a dismasted trading schooner into the port. We dropped anchor and warped up stern-to to the quay. The Englishman stepped ashore and went to the Harbor Master. The next day I was called to an inquest. I was being charged with illegally carrying a passenger. The French Naval officer-in-charge listened to my story. I explained in detail why I had done what I did. I even presented my Thai master's papers. The officer commended me and shook my hand. "You did the right thing," he said. I thanked him, and when I looked around for the Englishman he was gone. I think he knew the next charge against me might have stuck—for assault.

One bad apple in a basket can ruin all the other apples. The same might apply with the selection of a crew. But it's also true that a ship can make the crew. *Third Sea* did that very well.

A happy crew! Keeping busy is important. We stop often to fish or swim, even at sea. Stephens on the right, with two crew members.

Chapter 16

NO PLACE TO ANCHOR

In *The Circumnavigators,* Donald Holm wrote about men and women who sailed in almost every possible size and type of floating device, and who had not only crossed oceans, but had also circumnavigated the globe as well in these vessels. "They have ranged from canoes and rafts to amphibious Jeeps; from lovely little twenty-foot sloops to luxurious one-hundred-foot huge brigantines. They have been motorless sailboats and sailless motorboats; and auxiliary-rigged craft of every description. They have been cutters, sloops, ketches, yawls, wishbone ketches, square-riggers and hermaphrodite brigs. They have been monohulled, catamaran, and trimaran. They have been deep-displacement, light-displacemcnt, and planing hulls. They have had long keels, short keels, fin keels, and centerboard keels. They have been built of wood, fiberglass, steel, aluminum, and even concrete. One at least was hollowed out of a giant cedar log. They have been, when they began their voyage, a century old, and a few weeks old. They have been manned by one person, and as many as twenty-five. Their cost has ranged from as little as five hundred dollars to more than a quarter million dollars."

From the deck of *Third Sea* we had seen much of what was happening in the sailing world of the South Pacific and Southeast Asia. Sometimes we were amused; sometimes appalled. A few times we were completely mystified. To give you an example, we were in the Marquesas Islands when a ketch flying the American flag arrived from California. None of the crew had ever sailed before and Nuka Hiva was their first port of call. Not knowing how to anchor, they lowered the hook a mile out at sea and let all the chain out. When they did touch bottom they were so far away we could hardly see them. But I could see something was wrong, so I rowed out in the dory to see if they might need help. They did need help. We pulled up the anchor and reset closer to shore. "How did you ever manage to get this far to Nuka Hiva?" I asked.

"Nuka Hiva!" one of the crew spoke up. "Isn't this Hanaiapa Bay, or whatever you call it, on Hiva Oa?"

They were not only in the wrong port but on the wrong island. What was even more striking was that they admitted they thought the chart didn't look right, but they found the solution. "What was that?" I asked.

"We turned the chart upside down and it worked."

I thought perhaps they were ribbing me until they broke out the chart, turned it upside down, and showed me how they used it to reach Nuka Hiva. What was even more surprising, they reached Tahiti where we saw them a few weeks later. They sailed right through the low lying Tuamotus without a mishap, which is quite an accomplishment considering the nature of the islands.

Singapore was the place to see weird happenings. Every yachtsman who is on a world cruise generally will put into Singapore to resupply. One afternoon everyone at the Singapore Yacht Club took notice when a beautiful yacht sailed into the club lagoon. The owner invited every aboard for cocktails. Indeed, it was a marvelous ship, with the latest state-of-the-art navigational equipment, all neatly confined in one console unit. Radar and satellite navigation, Loran, radio direction finder, radio telephones, depth sounder, self steering and even their sails were adjusted electronicall. "No sextant?" Ed Boden asked.

"Sextant," the skipper laughed. "We have the most

modern equipment a sailing yacht afloat today can have. Sextants went out with black-and-white T.V." A week later the new yacht sailed; two weeks later it was towed back into port. On their Indian Ocean crossing en route to Madagascar, the entire navigation system went out. Even the compass wouldn't work. Fortunately the radios functioned, and they were able to call for help. Due to the complicated nature of the equipment, repairs couldn't be made aboard and the vessel had to be towed back to Singapore. A technician had to be flown in from Japan. The trouble was found. A plastic pin half the size of a pencil had worked it way loose and was lost. A new one could not be manufactured. The technician had to send back to Japan for a replacement. It took two weeks before the vessel was ready to sail again. The skipper and entire crew flew back to America. We never knew what happened but the rumor was a professional crew was hired to sail the yacht to Europe.

How did early explorers manage to get around the vast Pacific with the crude instruments they had three or more hundred years ago? They had no WWV radio reports, no satellites spinning the earth overhead, no VHF/FM radio, no time ticks and certainly no charts.

Even more baffling, how did the early Polynesians get around the Pacific as they did?

The subject of the Pacific island migrations is usually discussed with heated debate. Many people seem quite knowledgeable about the subject. They can emphatically state how the first immigrants arrived on the islands. And they do it so convincingly.

You hear scholars tell that Hawaii was originally settled by natives from Bora Bora, and they give you the date. They will tell you that these early natives of the Pacific voyaged aboard double-hulled canoes a hundred feet in length with capacities of skimming across the seas at thirty knots. They speak of these early sailors as being masterful seamen and skilled navigators who reached Hawaii by following a group of stars called "Seven Little Sisters." They even know what the islanders carried aboard their boats, from the clothing they wore to the type of food they ate.

How can they be so positive when only recently men of science have begun to unravel the great mystery of the Pacific migrations? Where were they getting their facts? Chances are these people are quoting from James A. Michener's epic novel *Hawaii.*

No other book on or about the South Pacific has done more to influence the general public about the region than Michener's *Hawaii.* Immediately after its publication it reached the best-sellers' list, and it has gone into several dozen printings in dozens of languages. Two epic movies were made from its theme.

There's no question—*Hawaii* is a masterpiece. And so convincing was Michener in telling his tale that those who read it accept it as gospel. They quote its passages as some people quote the scriptures.

There is one fault, however. *Hawaii* is a piece of fiction. In the introduction the publishers admit "it is a work of fiction," but they become misleading when they go on to say, "Yet so true to the spirit and history of Hawaii that it can be properly called the first major chronicle of the land and its people."

In researching his material Michener drew heavily from the Bishop Museum in Honolulu and from the writings of the late Dr. Peter Buck. As director of the museum, Peter Buck was one of the leading authorities on early Pacific migrations. His textbook *Vikings of the Sunrise* is still widely read and quoted. But even Peter Buck admitted that the migration route of the Melanesians and Polynesians is a matter of speculation rather than proven fact. Michener based the substance of his book on these speculations, and that was more than thirty years ago. The fascinating field of Pacific archaeology had barely commenced. Since then, scientific developments in the field of dating the past and further studies in linguistics and botany have shed new light on the subject. It has removed Pacific archaeology from "theory" to applied science.

Up until these modern techniques had been developed—mainly carbon dating—the field of anthropology was much different. It was based on theory alone. It began in the classrooms and libraries and advanced to the field research stage. Theories eventually had to be proven. Those who could back up their theories with conclusive facts became leaders in the field. There was, for example, a theory years ago that the Pacific islanders migrated from South America. One man who held that belief and set out to prove it was the Norwegian anthropologist Thor Heyerdahl.

Shortly after World War II, Heyerdahl visited the islands of the South Pacific and became fascinated with the stone Tiki gods he saw there. These stone idols looked remarkably like the monoliths left by extinct civilizations in South America. Was there a connection?

There was reason to believe there was. An Inca legend declared that the Inca's forefathers had driven out their chief sun god Tiki into the Pacific. Could it be that he made his way, along with his followers, to the islands of Oceania?

And there was the question of the sweet potato.

Scientists have long agreed that the Polynesians' food plants, language and much of their culture are clearly of Asiatic origin—with one exception, and that is the sweet potato. Botanists have determined conclusively that the original home of the sweet potato is South America, and yet it is found in abundance on most of the islands of the South Pacific. These botanists have further concluded that it had entered the islands directly from the east and not from Asia. Heyerdahl's theory was that the expelled Incas carried the potato with them.

Heyerdahl prepared his thesis for publication and took it to New York. It was rejected by what he claims "a big museum in New York" for one very obvious reason—the Incas were not seafaring people nor did they have sailing craft capable of negotiating the far reaches of the great South Pacific Ocean.

But the Incas did have balsa, and it was a known fact that they constructed rafts from their balsa. So why couldn't these Incas build balsa rafts and float with the winds and currents to the isles of the South Pacific? Heyerdahl became so convinced that it was possible that he decided to prove it—by building such a raft and floating across the Pacific. Thus the Kon Tiki Expedition was born.

No one put much faith in the expedition. There were few sponsors and the project was flatly refused by the *National Geographic.* Yet for some reason it captured the imagination of the public. It became one of the most publicized expeditions of the mid-twentieth century. A book that evolved from the voyage promptly became a bestseller. A documentary movie was made that played in cinemas around the world and a dozen other raft expeditions by amateurs and publicity-seekers followed. One old man tried it alone, while another more ambitious and younger man took a crew of five women. They were all failures.

Although the Kon Tiki expedition was successful, it proved nothing, except perhaps, that a raft can float. Today the use of computers has ruled out the drift theory completely.

Furthermore, once the early Polynesians reached the Pacific outposts they had to possess the skills to return. They certainly could not have settled Hawaii, with its more than twenty cultivated plants and domesticated animals, in only one migration. They had to make repeated voyages.

The modern techniques for dating the past were non-existent when the Kon Tiki set out from Peru, nor for that matter, were they fully developed when Michener began researching *Hawaii.* Scientists have completely revised their thinking in regard to these early migrations. It is now conclusive that the Oceanic islands were settled much earlier than previously thought, and perhaps even more important, the Melanesians and Polynesians are direct descendants from the peoples of Southeast Asia. Their migration routes are no longer a matter of speculation.

The breakthrough came with the development of radio-carbon dating. About the time that the Kon Tiki was setting out across the Pacific. Dr. Willard Libby of the University of Chicago worked out the way for using radio carbon for dating the past. All organic matter has a built-in time machine. With carbon-dating the migrations of the Pacific islanders could now be plotted.

The first human inhabitation of Oceania, scientists have now established, began with the Melanesians and not the Polynesians as first thought. Archaeologists have dug up primitive stone tools in New Guinea more than twenty-five thousand years old. When melting snow raised the water level of the sea, these dark skinned Melanesians in the Pacific became isolated from their Negrito cousins who to this day inhabit the deep jungles of the Malay Peninsula and central Australia.

Then about 4,500 years ago, brown skinned Polynesians came down from Southeast Asia in their double-hulled sailing craft and reached New Guinea, New Caledonia and Fiji. The indications are they did not dislodge the Melanesians they found living there. To this day there are pockets of Polynesians living on isolated islands within this Melanesian belt. I used *Third Sea* to explore these outposts whenever the chance came. We visited Tikopia Island northeast of Noumea, Stewart Island in the Solomon Group and Kapingamarangi north of New Guinea. The people here have maintained their culture and are as Polynesian as their cousins on Tahiti and Bora Bora.

These early Polynesian seafarers used the Melanesian islands of Fiji and New Caledonia as kind of staging points for further exploration to the islands of the Pacific. Ethnobotanists tell us they reached the Pacific via the Micronesian route and that they brought with them such important food plants as breadfruit, bananas, yam and taro. The coconut, of course, was already there. Zoologists have long established that the pig, dog and fowl found in Polynesia had their homes in the Indo-Malaysia areas.

There still remains the riddle of the sweet potato. Since the Indians of South America were not island people and had neither the skill nor the craft to make such long sea voyages, we are forced to conclude that the plant was carried by the Polynesians. We know now for certain they had the ability to cross the seas and return. It follows that they must have explored the Peruvian coast and taken this valuable food plant back with them to their home islands. Botanists have established that the plant was in the Pacific islands before Columbus discovered America, thus it couldn't have been the Europeans who brought it.

One of the most significant discoveries in the Pacific has been that of Lapita-style pottery. With the advancement of radio-carbon dating, Lapita-style pottery has become the key to the history of the Pacific.

The first of these prehistoric relics was found in New Britain Island in 1909, and soon after others were discovered in New Caledonia and Fiji. The more recent finds were on Tonga and Samoa. By carbon-dating the scattered finds of pottery it is possible to establish the framework of early migrations. Lapita artifacts clearly trace the visits and attempted settlements of a maritime people who moved along the Melanesian route to Polynesia.

Compared to the dark-skinned Melanesians, the Polynesians were latecomers to the Pacific arena. Carbon-dating shows the islands that they have inhabited the longest are in the Tonga group. It was from here that they set out to colonize other islands of the Pacific.

About the time of Christ they reached the Marquesas, and five hundred years later they reached Hawaii in the north and New Zealand in the south. Certainly by the year 1000 all the islands were inhabited, including far off Easter Island.

The one major question still remains unanswered. Where exactly in Southeast Asia did the Melanesians and Polynesians come from? From the Philippines or Indonesia? From Malaysia? From Thailand or Indochina? The answer will have to come not from the islands of the Pacific but from Southeast Asia itself. Could a fragment of pottery found in a cave in Malaysia or in a mud bed in northern Thailand prove to be Lapita? Carbon-dating and possibly DNA will remove all the "guesswork" in any future discoveries.

Archaeological finds in Southeast Asia are certain to bring up new clues to the Pacific migrations. But where do we look? In the bottom of bays or harbors? In caves or unexplored jungles? We don't know, but one day for certain someone will turn over a stone and there will be a fragment of pottery—and the link will be made.

Balboa named the Pacific from the Spanish meaning "peaceful." When we sail upon the Pacific we know it can be quite the contrary. These early Pacific travelers often ended up where they did because of storms. They were blown off course and could not return.

Captain Cook arrived in Tonga and found two Samoans who had been there for sixteen years, yet Samoa is only a few hundred miles to the north of Tonga. They simply didn't have the ability to return. And as we know, the Maori arrived in New Zealand from Bora Bora in seven canoes. How many hundreds of canoes might not have made it?

We have come a long way since the early Polynesians began their migrations, but still, we who sail the seas in small boats must face the inevitable—storms at sea. And for certain, one of the most awesome and frightening experiences a person can have is to go through a tropical storm at sea. I don't mean as a passenger aboard an ocean liner, or as a crewman aboard a freighter or tanker, although violent storms can make it uncomfortable even aboard these vessels. I am speaking about the ultimate, about experiencing a storm at sea as a crewman aboard a small yacht.

And unfortunately, it's something every sailor who sets out to sea in a small boat must sooner or later face.

In recent years there has been a regeneration of sail. The reappearance of sailing craft on the oceans of the world is rapidly becoming commonplace. However, in comparison to the great square riggers of yesteryear, these modern-day sailing vessels are tiny, manned by four or five souls or less. Science and modern techniques in shipbuilding have made it all possible. With equipment like the pocket computer navigation is no longer a mystery. Our advanced knowledge of the behavior patterns of wind and sea allows the amateur sailor to do what only the professionals could do a few decades ago.

But what has not changed is the might of the wind and sea. Storms and heavy weather are certain. And storms are rarely pleasant experiences, except perhaps from the sense of exhilaration in the early stages, and from the elation when they have passed.

Not all storms are a threat to yachtsmen. In fact, some yachts do better in a Force Four or Five—with winds up to twenty-five mph—than in light breezes. Generally speaking, it's only when winds reach Force Eight, forty mph, that sailing vessels may find themselves in trouble.

Although trade winds and monsoons may reach wind speeds up to fifty mph, they seldom pose a threat to ocean sailing. Since they blow in one direction it means they are predictable. Nor do thunderstorms or line squalls, with winds up to sixty mph, cause much concern for the experienced yachtsman. A squall seldom lasts more than twenty minutes, and can be seen on the horizon, giving the wise sailor ample time to shorten sail. Aboard *Third Sea,* when we had a full well-trained crew, it was a challenge to see if we could run with a squall without reducing canvas. We most always lost.

The real threat comes from tropical storms, which may be cyclones, typhoons or hurricanes, depending where they are. These storms are essentially traveling systems of winds that rotate around a low barometric pressure. Cyclones contain warm and cold fronts whereas typhoons do not. Typhoons throughout the South Pacific are called hurricanes.

A typhoon is the most unpredictable storm we find through-out the Philippines and Southeast Asia. They are the most destructive and strike without warning. Within an interval of twelve hours or less the barometric pressure suddenly drops fifteen millibars or more. By the time the storm reaches maturity it may have expanded to a width of one hundred miles or more.

A tropical storm is termed a typhoon when its wind velocity reaches sixty-four knots or more. Some which devastated much of the Philippines have reached an estimated one-hundred and seventy knots, or more than two hundred mph. The maximum velocity of tropical storms is not known, as most anemometers disintegrate at about one-hundred and twenty-five knots. When such typhoons are on the open seas, waves are likely to reach forty-five to fifty feet in height. Waves up to sixty and seventy feet have been noted, with the highest ever recorded at one hundred and twenty feet. Happily, these are rare.

What does it mean to the small boat sailor caught in a storm? What are his chances of survival? How much pounding and punishment can a small boat take?

The simple answer is plenty. But there does come a point when the skipper and crew of a small boat, no matter how experienced they might be, can no longer retain control of a vessel. When the winds reach Force Ten or more, perhaps gusting at hurricane strength, wind and sea become master. Skipper and crew can do little more than hang on. Even the most simple navigation is impossible.

The sixty-eight-foot schooner *Curlew* which left Mystic, Connecticut, on a winter day is one example of what a sailing vessel can sustain. As she entered the Gulf Stream she encountered a tropical storm with winds at eighty knots. On the second day she suffered a broach-to, and was knocked down on her beam ends for almost three minutes before she slowly righted. The next day a mountainous sea broke over the entire ship, and stove in the main cabin skylight. As a result Mayday calls were sent out to the US Coast Guard which responded with a cutter to their rescue.

Water in the cabin by now was up to the skipper's waist as he operated the telephone giving directions to the cutter. The rescue came twenty-four hours later when the crew were taken aboard the Coast Guard cutter by means of cargo nets, but only after tearing away the schooner's bowsprit and carrying away her foremast and shrouds against the ship's sides. There was no alternative but to abandon her.

Now comes the strange ending to the story. Three days later the schooner *Curlew* was sighted and towed into port. There was five feet of water in the main cabin and everything below had been smashed, but after a survey it was discovered that the hull was undamaged. All her seams and fastenings were as good as new. The boat was virtually unsinkable.

Much more severe than broaching-to and sustaining a "knock-down" is what is commonly called "pitch-poling." This may happen when a yacht gathers speed, even under bare pole, and is pushed along with the wind and the waves. Unless warps or mooring ropes are streamed astern to slow her down, the yacht may lose control and, like a surfboard, skim down the surface of a wave, only to bury her nose in the trough of the wave and go pitch-poling end over end. Without fail, mast and most of the structure above deck will be swept away. One of the most incredible stories of a boat being pitch poled not once but twice is that of the ketch *Tzu Hang*.

While attempting to round Cape Horn from the Pacific to the Atlantic she was caught in one of these survival storms and dismasted in her end-over-end experience. She was jury rigged, returned to port and rebuilt, only to be dismasted on the second attempt. She made it the third time around.

Cape Horn at the tip of South America and the Roaring Forties in the southern latitudes are noted for their almost constant storms, and consequently for the intrepid yachtsman they become the ultimate challenge.

The Roaring Forties, where the winds often reach low Force Seven or Eight, was the clipper ship route during the mid and late 1800s. It was upon this noted "Clipper Way" that grain-carrying ships from Sydney could reach England in less than one hundred days. Today they are the seas which not many yachtsmen frequent and, indeed, few ships of any sort go there now, because with steam and the opening of the Suez Canal the modern route from Australia is quite different.

Sir Francis Chichester found the Roaring Forties something else. It wasn't so much the violent winds that troubled him as the spiritual loneliness. "Down here in the Southern Ocean," he wrote in *Gypsy Moth Circles the World*, "It was a great void. I seemed planetary distances away from the rest of mankind."

Captain Alain Villers, who probably knows more about Cape Horn sailing conditions than anyone else, burst into print when he heard that his friend Chichester was contemplating sailing the Horn, alone, at the age of sixty-five. He described the Horn in an article he wrote for the occasion. "It is a simple thing for a yacht to find herself lifted on some great sea boiling underneath her in its headlong rush towards the Horn, quite out of control in the cross-sea brought up by the shifting winds. Such a vessel as the *Gypsy Moth* can then be rolled over beneath the tumult of ghastly breakers murderous and merciless around her."

Chichester, of course, sailed the *Gypsy Moth* around

the Horn and safely back to England.

Chichester was not without trouble, however. But there are many examples of yachts which have sailed in the Roaring Forties and around the Horn without incident. This was the "impossible route" chosen by Vito Dumas, for the great single-handed voyage he described in his book *Alone Through the Roaring Forties*.

The concept of heading out to open sea in a storm had always puzzled me. Would not an anchorage be better? The fact is, a well-founded vessel stands a much better chance at sea than at anchor or even in a protected harbor.

I built *Third Sea* with the knowledge of what a storm can do to a boat. I experienced my first hurricane aboard a sturdy fifty-seven-foot schooner called *Fairweather*. I shipped aboard the schooner at the Bay of Islands in New Zealand. The Skipper was a lady, Sutie Adams, a most remarkable women. In Auckland her husband decided he had enough sailing, so Sutie took command. With her five children aboard, she completed the circumnavigation.

Captain Sutie Adams aboard schooner *Fairweather*. Sutie skippered her ship though a hurricane, with her children and Stephens aboard.

Fairweather was bound for New Caledonia. If winds permitted we would stop at Norfolk, a lonely and seldom visited island where the descendants of the HMS *Bounty* mutineers were relocated from tiny Pitcairn. I had always wanted to visit the island and now was my chance.

Some five hundred miles north of New Zealand the winds stopped, completely. For two days we were becalmed, drifting idly. None of us had ever seen the seas so calm, or misgiving. We lounged on deck, seeking whatever shelter from the sun we could manage. We avoided going below, where the heat was overpowering. The horizon shimmered and it was most difficult to perceive where the sea ended and the sky began. They were one, and we appeared to be in a void. It was an eerie feeling.

Vern Hansen, our Hawaiian-born navigator, stepped down into the cabin for some reason, only to return with the startling news—"The barometer is falling."

Slowly, almost unnoticed, the winds came. We took sights and checked the charts. We were sixty miles southeast of Norfolk. Could we make it before the storm and seek shelter in the harbor? With reefed main and mizzen we turned towards Norfolk.

At dawn we could see the island, but by now the winds were Force Eight. Four miles from the entrance we were forced to put up storm jib, lash the rudder and heave to. It was 9 A.M. we went below deck to wait out the storm.

At 10 A.M. with the ship pitching violently into the oncoming seas, we heard a loud report, like a rifle shot. Vern was the first to reach the hatch and slide it back. He pulled himself up into the weather and immediately dropped back into the cabin. "I can't, can't look," he said, gasping for a breath of air. "The jib halyard has parted."

Following Vern, all hands scrambled on deck. It was

another world. The jib halyard was standing out horizontally from the mast and the seas were breaking over the bow in fermenting fury. One had to turn his head away from the wind to breathe. There was only one choice of action now: to unlash the rudder, pull down the storm jib and turn and run with the wind. But one misjudgment of a wave and we might broach.

Ray, an Australian surfer, took over the helm. He had experience as a sweep aboard the lifesaving boats at Bondi Beach near Sydney.

We had to shout to be heard above the roar of the wind which hummed in the rigging mournfully. The flapping jib tore at our fingers as we labored to pull it in. In the end our efforts proved fruitless. The winds ripped the jib to shreds and carried it away. The threat now was that as we turned away from the wind we might broach.

From the bow I looked back at Ray at the helm. He appeared to be riding a bucking bronco, up on the crest of a wave one moment and down in the trough the next. When the stern was down we appeared to be in our greatest danger. Toppling seas crashed in a deafening roar behind us and any one of them, it seemed, would splinter us into bits. But each time we rose, only to go skimming down the wave.

We streamed every warp we had from the stern, and when these failed to slow us down sufficiently—we were still doing more than ten knots under bare poles—we tied on bits of sails and fenders to other lines and tossed them astern. It seemed to work.

We learned later that the wind velocity had reached more than one hundred mph. The seas that broke astern of us were taller than our masts, which stood at sixty feet. When a crest did break over the stern, and white water washed across the decks, it took all our bodily strength to keep from being washed overboard.

By afternoon we reached the eye of the storm. Incredibly there was little wind, but the fury of the seas continued, tossing and tumbling and breaking in godawful fury, In the sky above we could see the vast circle of clouds, surrounding us in its web. And caught in the eye of the storm were literally hundreds of thousands of birds, mostly storm petrels, called Mother Carey's chickens. They fluttered wildly to try to land on the rigging but dared not attempt it.

Coming out of the eye of the storm we knew would be far worse than going in. We were fortunate to have light with us and not the blackness of night. We had a chance to do battle against the cross winds and seas which were now opposed to one another. For sixteen hours we fought the full fury of the hurricane, trying everything to survive, including spreading oil over the surface of the sea to calm the waves. It seems almost ludicrous to stand with an oil can in hand, upon a tossing deck and facing a mountainous broiling sea, and shooting a trickle of oil into a cresting wave. But I am convinced it worked, and there are some friends in the South Pacific who will forever remember me as "Steve the Hurricane Oiler."

Two other yachts that left New Zealand when we did were less fortunate. In Noumea they faced an official inquest. The skipper of one yacht told the horrifying story of how one crew member was washed overboard, missed the trailing warps that were streaming astern and slowly disappeared into the distance. It was impossible to turn around, of course. The other skipper reported he came on deck when the ship was behaving strangely and the helmsman was gone. He didn't know what happened. He had simply disappeared.

Jack London, Joseph Conrad, Somerset Maugham,

Robert Louis Stevenson, Herman Melville, all have written about typhoons, hurricanes and storms at sea, and it was Melville who perhaps captured the emotion of the sea in the fewest words. "There is no force, save its own, that can control it," he wrote. It is so true. No one really conquers the sea. It's just that the sea had been lenient to those who survive its worst elements.

The question that remains is still unanswered—"Is it worth it?" All one has to do is be aboard a sailing ship on a moon-filled night, when the winds are favorable, and one will find the answer for oneself. We learned this very early aboard *Third Sea*.

Schooner *Third Sea*, with all her flags flying, anchored in Papeete.

Chapter 17

GETTING OFF THE MILK RUN

Cruising yachtsmen call it "the milk run." They set sail from the west coast of the United States, make their way "downhill" to Hawaii and then drop south to Tahiti. They then sail westward to Pago Pago in American Samoa, perhaps visit Apia in Western Samoa, and move on to Fiji. A few yachts may turn south to New Zealand which usually becomes the turning point. From here most yachts return home across the Pacific. A small percentage continue on through the Torres Strait between Australia and New Guinea and thus continue on around the world. The Pacific voyagers usually take a year to a year and a half for their trip; circumnavigators take much longer, sometimes years. Ed Boden in his *Kittiwake* spent thirteen years while Josh Slocum, the first circumnavigator, did it in three years. The average seems to be between two to three years.

Cruising yachts in the Pacific seldom leave the milk run. They become totally absorbed with French Polynesia, and here they meet other yachtsmen and compare notes. But there's far more to the Pacific than the milk run. To explore these remote islands and forgotten atolls of the South Pacific and Asia was my purpose for building and outfitting *Third Sea*. I had previously made a few Pacific voyages on other yachts, including the schooners *Nordlys* and *Fairweather*. With *Third Sea* the whole world of the Pacifc was now waiting for me. And what a world it was! Considering that there are tens of thousands of islands scattered throughout the seas and oceans all the way from Singapore to the shores of South America—Indonesia alone has some thirteen thousand—one can spend a lifetime and still not see all there is to see.

But there is no doubt the oceans of the world are changing, and how long we can enjoy their beauty is a thing of speculation. Man is doing his very best to destroy our oceans. In the past it was easy for us to think of the world's oceans as merely indestructible bodies of water so deep and so wide that they could absorb anything we give them. But cruising yachtsmen are finding this is not so. Let me give an example.

We were reaching on a port tack, with all sails set, seven days out of Port Vila bound for Pago Pago in American Samoa. It was one of those beautiful afternoons in the South Pacific when the seas rolled in with gentle swells from the northeast and the Trade Winds blew with just enough strength to keep us on course with all sails filled.

Then suddenly came the call—"All hands on deck." What possibly could be going wrong? Before I went below deck there had not been even a threatening cloud in the sky, and the nearest land was at least five hundred miles to our south.

Third Sea lunged violently to our starboard. Then came the shouts of the helmsman, "Reef, reef!" We had to be in trouble.

I hastily scrambled to get on deck. A dozen thoughts raced through my mind. Had an island appeared from out of nowhere? Was it an uncharted reef? Could it be a volcanic eruption as we had seen in the New Hebrides? Or was my navigation that far off? Had I made a terrible mistake and put us five hundred miles off course?

Once on deck I found the schooner pointed into the wind. With the sails hanging slack, the heavy main boom swung dangerously back and forth. The helmsman stood immobile, staring to starboard, like he was looking at a ghost. I rushed to join him at the railing.

There it was, sure enough, a reef. The helmsman had veered just in time to prevent us from crashing into a wall of coral. But then, on closer observation, it looked all wrong. The reef wasn't stationary. It bobbed up and down with the motion or the sea. It stretched as far as we could see, running from north to south in a great sweeping curve.

We waited, and slowly the reef drifted closer and closer. Then came the shock! It couldn't be. It wasn't a reef at all. It was garbage, miles and miles, tons upon tons of garbage, garbage floating at sea in an endless riptide. Plastic bags and containers, bottles, rubber sandals, children's toys, Styrofoam lids, planks, light bulbs, matted netting, shoes, beer bottles and goblets of thick gooey oil. The Pacific Ocean, the vast, wide, blue Pacific Ocean has become man's garbage dump.

Thirty years ago when I first began sailing the South Pacific, there was none of this. In this relatively short time, I have seen many destructive changes caused by thoughtless, uncaring mankind. These desolate shores of uninhabited islands that were once bare of any trace of human activity, are now littered with the refuse of man's civilization, refuse that has drifted with the winds and currents for thousands of miles to their shores. On some coral isles the shores are so strewn with rubble it was impossible for us to walk upon the white sand beaches— broken bottles would have cut our feet to shreds.

Aboard *Third Sea* we explored literally hundreds of lonely islands across the Pacific, and I have yet to find a beach on any shore, even upon the most remote and uninhabited island, that wasn't contaminated with deposits of oil and tar to some degree or other.

As enormous as our oceans are—three hundred million cubic miles of water spread over seventy percent of the earth's surface—we still manage to contaminate all the seas of the world with something like twenty million tons of garbage every day, with everything from unspent ammunition and dubious naval stores to radioactive waste, caustic chemicals, heavy metals and human excretion. If we don't know what to do with something, we dump it into the sea.

But we are rapidly finding out that the oceans are not indestructible. Perhaps they are finally telling us that enough is enough. Could it not be that whales and dolphins fling themselves upon alien land where quick suicide is inevitable rather than endure a slow suffering with the agonies of poisoned water?

We forget that life upon earth began in the sea, and it is still the coastal seas that play the most important role in the chain of life. The waters over the continental shelves are where the majority of marine species spend at least part of their lives. They are also where millions of people earn their livelihood and where far more spend their recreation time. These are the waters that suffer most from the effects of pollution.

When I stand upon a lonesome coral atoll in the South Pacific, and see the dreadful damage man has done to his environment, I wonder what can we do. I look back at my own mistakes, at my naive thinking that mankind can do no wrong. Technology, I used to think, gave us the wondrous and exciting world we have today; technology could get us out of any scrape we get into. I no longer think this is true.

In the 1950s, when I attended Georgetown University in Washington, D.C., I had listened to our professor tell us that science was the savior of mankind. Science can do anything. Science, he claimed, can feed the world's growing population no matter how large it becomes by simply taking plankton from the sea and making it edible. No one realized that science was also poisoning those very same seas.

So we decide to leave the milk run and search for the remote. Let's look at one such place, the Bismark Archipelago.

Ask anyone to locate the Bismarck Archipelago on a map and chances are he will begin looking somewhere in the North Sea. Instead, this fascinating chain of islands which stretches nearly a thousand miles east to west is on the other side of the world in the western Pacific. To be exact, it's north of New Guinea.

Not only is the name unknown to most people today, but the islands themselves are forgotten. Yet it wasn't always that way. A hundred years ago, it was the most talked about archipelago in the southern seas. And the most feared. Uncharted, disease-ridden, inhabited by cannibals, the islands were on the maps only to be avoided. But for the adventurer, there were huge profits to be had.

The first to exploit the islands were blackbirders, or slave traders. Then came traders, followed by zealous missionaries and finally planters and settlers, all of whom were greedy for land. Incredibly, the first really successful settler in these hostile islands was a twenty-seven-year-old American Samoan woman from Apia, Emma Coe whom I mentioned earlier.

Just before World War I, Emma Coe, better known as Queen Emma, sold out to the Germans and from that point the islands became known as the Bismarck Archipelago. The Germans lost possession during the war, and, after the armistice, New Guinea and the islands to the north became a protectorate of Australia.

Then came the grim days beginning in 1941, when the Japanese invaded, and, before long, the names of many of the islands in the archipelago became household words to every G. I. fighting in the South Pacific—New Britain, New Ireland, Cape Gloucester, Manus, Los Negros. The islands became the scene of some of the heaviest fighting in the Pacific war. Then the war ended, the G.I.s went home and the islands again drifted into obscurity. There was an attempt to re-establish the copra industry, but with new synthetics and falling copra prices, it wasn't profitable. With independence a few years ago, the New Guinea government turned its interests in other directions. Most of the islands today have only caretakers. Some have been completely abandoned.

My own involvement with the archipelago came when I sailed *Third Sea* the first time from Asia to Honolulu. I returned a half dozen times after that. My favorite in the group was Hermit Island.

As I mentioned in the chapter "Eastward Across the Pacific," it is difficult to find an opening through the reef at Hermit, but once we did, dark-skinned Melanesians in an outrigger paddled out to show us where to anchor in the lee of the thickly-wooded island. We dropped the anchor in eight fathoms, a dozen yards from shore, took a deep breath, and sighed. The amazing beauty of the place and the perfect stillness of the lagoon were so overwhelming that we dared not speak. Here at last was that perfect island one always dreams about. Here at last was all peace and joy.

Our serenity didn't last long. Other natives in outriggers came out to greet us. As we soon learned, three families, nineteen people in all, lived on the largest island. In Pidgin English, which we found not too difficult to understand, they asked to come aboard. Certainly.

They eagerly told us that another yacht had anchored to visit them three years before, that there was good fishing on the reef, and in the lagoon could be found lobster, clams, shellfish, turtles and even pearl shells with an occasional pearl.

"Yu gat masket?" Joseph the headman asked. When I admitted we had a gun, he told us the islands had wild pigs, cattle and even deer. Fresh meat! We divided up the crew, hunters in one direction, fishermen in the other.

That night on shore we had a great feast, dining upon roasted pig and venison, boiled lobster, baked yams and fresh pineapples and mangoes, washed down with rum from the Philippines. Our hosts stood in the background, watching but not wanting to participate. No matter how much we encouraged them to join us, they refused. Later we discovered why.

Before the white man came, the islanders were all fierce cannibals who never turned down a meal when it was offered to them. Had we arrived by schooner a little over a hundred years ago, they probably would have had us for dinner, and not as guests. In the very spot where we were anchored, the bark *Eliza* had also dropped her anchor, but her crew was not as fortunate as we were. The ship was attacked by the islanders, pillaged and burned, with all hands, including the captain's wife and daughter, murdered and, so it's said, eaten.

The Melanesians we found at Hermit had been converted to Christianity and were Seventh Day Adventists, whose religion prevents them from smoking, drinking alcohol or eating pork, turtle meat and fish without scales. They were now looking upon us as being the savages.

We spent a week on Hermit and over the years I made several other visits. I fell in love with the island and became fascinated not only with the beauty of the atoll but with its history as well. In 1895, the islands were purchased by a young German planter, Heinrich Wahlen, a friend of Queen Emma, who immediately turned Hermit into his own private baronial estate. Nothing was spared. On a high hill on Maron Island—Hermit is actually a cluster of small islands—he built a splendid stone house with pillars and archways and verandahs facing the sea. Many important and interesting people came to his retreat by private yacht from as far away as Bali in Indonesia.

Once their vessels were anchored in the lagoon and the guests had stepped ashore, they were taken by horse and carriage up a tree-lined road that led to the house on the hill. In time, Wahlen's abode on Maron became the most famous home in the South Pacific.

The plantation prospered. It had more than seven hundred workers, five overseers, a row of large godowns, several stores, farms and cattle stations and a string of copra schooners to freight the produce to New Guinea. Today you must hack your way through brush to reach Maron's summit and all that is left of the grand house are a few pillars and the stone foundations. On my last visit to Hermit, even the game had disappeared and most of the fruit and palm trees had been chopped down. I will tell readers what hapened to the island in a later chapter, "Return to Asia."

In the other direction, two days' sail to the east, is the biggest island in the group, Manus Island, with its capital at Lorengau. Sailing into Seeadler Harbor, we were surprised to be aboard the only ship in sight. Lorengau is no more than a slumbering town in the tropics and Seeadler Harbor a far cry from its World War II days—described in James Michener's *Return to Paradise*—when it was one of the most important deep-water ports in the South Pacific. It was this small, almost unknown island to which General Douglas MacArthur pointed on the map and said, "Here we begin our offensive." Manus was the turning point of the Pacific war. Two marine divisions stormed ashore on February 29, 1944 and before the week was out, the island was recaptured from the Japanese forces. Then came the changes.

"At Manus the U.S. Government assembled one of the greatest naval establishments in history," wrote Michener. "Overnight Lorengau became a city larger than Sacramento. It had native stores worth half-a-billion dollars. I was at Manus when MacArthur was preparing for the invasion of Leyte, and in the endless roadstead I saw twenty-six carriers, dozens of battleships and actually hundreds of lesser craft."

Others who had been there reported seeing no less than one thousand ships at anchor at any one time, post exchanges by the score, dozens of movie houses, fuel depots, electric power plants, two dry cleaners and three huge laundries, a radio station, a telephone exchange, miles of paved roads, six airfields and storage sheds that covered acres of ground.

After rowing ashore, we found mostly jungle with concrete foundations where buildings once stood. Natives still uncover storage tanks filled with petrol in the hills. A week before we arrived, the body of a Japanese soldier was found in the jungle, sitting with his back against a tree in the same position as when he had died almost half a century before.

Lorengau, although only a shadow of its former self, is an interesting tropical port, right out of a South Seas novel. It has one hotel, a fish-'n'-chips shop, a Burns Philp store, two smaller Chinese shops, a movie house and a World War II brass cannon in the town square.

One of my favorite islands in the archipelago is Lou Island, a day's sail southeast of Manus. Lou is volcanic, with black, rich soil that can grow anything. And they do grow everything. It's truly a garden paradise. We anchored in a cove, rowed ashore and asked where we could buy fruit and vegetables. "At the marketplace when the sun is overhead." They said someone could come and lead us to the market the next morning.

We were on shore early the next day and followed a group of youths down a trail to a nearby village. Like the tributaries of a river, small paths led to larger ones, and on all the trails natives were making their way to the marketplace. They carried their wares, bananas and mangoes, pandanus sacks of oranges, clusters of coconuts, yams, taro, and fruit and vegetables we had never seen before. Others carried suckling pigs and chickens hung on poles, and still others led young goats, geese and ducks.

The marketplace lay before the village on a green lawn. Fishermen were already there with freshly-caught lobsters, crayfish and tuna. The display of food was unbelievable, enough to feed a couple of villages. But where were the customers?

The chief of Lou Island leads Stephens by hand through his village.

One can imagine our surprise at learning that we were the only customers. "But we only need a little food," we explained. They understood. But nevertheless, it was most difficult buying from one and not the other. For a few dollars we had more food than our crew could eat in a month.

While Lou is my favorite island, Rabaul on New Britain is my favorite port. It became a kind of second home for *Third Sea*. It is strangely beautiful. When you sail into the harbor you find yourself surrounded by smoking volcanoes. When I climbed one volcano and looked down into the bay, I could see that the harbor itself was the crater of a large volcano that had exploded aeons ago. The view was spellbinding.

Sailing charts show hundreds upon hundreds of islands that would take a lifetime to explore. And there's something exhilarating about sailing among them. I spent hours scanning their coasts with my binoculars. What secrets do they hold? Heavy jungles. No roads or trails. No towns, not even a village. On many, man has not yet marred the pristine beauty of a primeval existence. It is here, among the islands of the remote Bismarck Archipelago, that I can feel and know the deep beauty of the world. There's still hope. And there's still so much to discover and learn.

The Solomon Islands are no less interesting. I was most anxious to take *Third Sea* to that part of the Pacific to see if we could recapture a bit of history that took place on a dark moonless night in August 1943. On that night a young U.S. Navy lieutenant stood behind the helm of Motor Torpedo Boat *No. 109* and entered Blackett Strait east of Ghizo Island in the Solomons.

It was his first command, and his name was John F. Kennedy, who later became the thirty-fifth president of the United States. Thirty-five years later, almost to the day, I stood at the helm of *Third Sea* as we entered the same waters. Lt. Kennedy had been under orders to search out four Japanese destroyers reported by coastwatchers to be operating in the area. We were looking for the remains of Kennedy's *PT-l09*.

At 2:30 a.m. on that ill-fated night, a Japanese destroyer suddenly knifed out of the darkness and before Lt. Kennedy could give the orders to fire torpedoes or to turn the wheel to avoid collision, his vessel was sliced in two by the destroyer. He and the deck crew were thrown into the sea.

Those who survived later climbed aboard *PT-109*'s hull and awaited dawn. The next afternoon, fearing the hull might sink, Lt. Kennedy and his men decided to abandon ship and swim to one of the many small islands bordering the strait. They were rescued several days after being rammed.

What became of *PT-109*? Did it float out into open sea and eventually sink, or did it drift into one of the shallow lagoons and break up on a reef? Finding the wreckage could lead to a great seafaring adventure, and it would certainly be an achievement. It never occurred to me to make an attempt to find *PT-109* until we were sailing in the northern Solomons.

Anyone who sails the seas in a small boat has to admire PT boats and the men who sailed them. Before the war no one thought much about them. On the morning of December 7, 1941, six PT boats were moored at Pearl Harbor submarine base. In a matter of seconds after the first Japanese bombs dropped all machine guns in the PTs were firing. They claimed first Japanese blood of the war by shooting down two low flying torpedo planes.

On December 10, three days after the attack, they saw action again when the Japanese made their first attack on

Manila Bay. A squadron of six boats commanded by Lt. John Bulkeley had arrived in the Philippines four months before. PTs were successful at Pearl Harbor but no one gave them much hope against high-flying dive bombers which were beyond the range of their .50 calibre machineguns.

Skeptics soon changed their minds.

Five Japanese bombers peeled off deliberately and started to dive on the PTs which were under weigh in the harbor. Lt. Bulkeley had a plan and ordered other commanders to follow suit. He waited until the diving planes reached their release points, and then gave the signal to put their helms to hard port. Not one bomb came close. Two PT boats shot down three planes.

PTs could outmaneuver enemy planes and escape but their land bases could not avoid destruction. And with the Philippines cut off, supplies became drastically short. One of the more serious problems was gasoline. The supply was not only short but the quality was bad. Gas strainers on the Packard engines were constantly clogged and cleaning carburettors became an hourly task.

In spite of the lack of spare parts, and damaged hulls held together "by jury rigs of wire and braces," PT boats proved to be reliable. Recommendations for overhauling engines were every six hundred hours; they more often went beyond twelve hundred hours. And more than once boats came limping in with several feet of water in the engine rooms, the engines almost submerged but still running.

Bulkeley's Squadron Six continued to fight the invading Japanese. However, when defeat was evident, the squadron received orders to proceed to Corregidor. The high command had to be evacuated, by orders of the President of the U.S. General MacArthur, his wife and their son were taken aboard *PT-41*, with Lt. John Bulkeley in command. They made rendezvous with three other boats from the squadron at the entrance to Manila Bay and together proceeded south. It was not an easy voyage.

A strong easterly wind made the going rough, with sheets of water crashing over the bows. Before the night was over the boats became separated. Passengers and crew alike aboard *PT-41* were drenched and exhausted when they reached their destination, but they had made the trip of six hundred miles through Japanese-patrolled waters and had arrived precisely on time. Later that day the other boats reached port.

Lt. Bulkeley returned with *PT-41* to the fighting in the north. They fought until there were no more torpedoes available. In the end, *PT-41* was set afire by its own crew to keep it from falling in the hands of the Japanese.

Lt. Bulkeley escaped to Zamboanga in the south and was ordered by General MacArthur to take a personal letter to Washington, D.C. The message was a request for a hundred or more PTs for operation in the Pacific. "With enough PTs," MacArthur wrote, "hostile Japanese could be kept from invading an island or even a continent, and kept two hundred to three hundred miles off shore."

For his service, Lt. Bulkeley was awarded the Congressional Medal of Honor and given command of PT operations in the Pacific.

Lt. Bulkeley was requested to pick his crews. He recruited the biggest, toughest athletes that could be found. They included all-American tackles from top colleges and pro football teams. Others were Olympic swimmers, world record sculling champs, lacrosse players and many more. Among them was a young officer named John F. Kennedy.

PT boats in the Pacific were proving their worth. They

had completely disrupted Japanese shipping in the Solomons and certainly helped avert an invasion of New Zealand and Australia. The Japanese forces were halted at the Battle of the Coral Sea and the First Marine Division stormed ashore at Guadalcanal and on the neighboring islands of Tulagi and Florida. Tulagi became the major PT land base. From here and later on at New Georgia, PTs patrolled the seas in an effort to stop the flow of Japanese shipping southward.

We sailed *Third Sea* through the same waters. At Guadalcanal we anchored in one small cove and the natives wanted to show us something very special. They led us to an old B-29 landing field where several planes were piled up at the end of the runway. The more we saw of the old battle fields the more we became intrigued. We tried to imagine the difficulties PT boats had operating at night in these treacherous waters. If enemy planes didn't get them, the reefs would.

Barge hunting was PT commanders' chief occupation. The Americans had neither sea power nor air power to counter all the thrusts by the Japanese to regain Bougainville. The Tokyo Express had to be stopped somehow; it was the PT boat commanders who were given the near impossible task.

An all-out encounter with the Tokyo Express came on the night of August 2, 1943. A coastwatcher high in the mountains on Guadalcanal reported that four Japanese destroyers escorting barges and large landing craft started their run south through Blackett Strait, better known as "The Slot."

It was apparent the Japanese knew that PT boats would be their only opposition. Just before dawn on August 1, Japanese bombers made a strike on the PT base at Lumbari Island. Two PTs were lost, leaving a fleet of fifteen to meet the destroyers. With many of their bases knocked out, the PT boats really had no place to anchor.

The northeastern patrol of Blackett Strait was given to the command of *PT-109*, with Lt. John F. Kennedy in charge.

In the briefing before the operation, *PT-109* was to lead *PTs 106* and *169* on a slow southern sweep. At ten p.m. on that black moonless night they set out, three frail plywood boats with instructions to attack on sight four powerful heavily-armed Japanese destroyers. It was Lt. Kennedy's first combat mission. A little past midnight the boats made contact with the enemy. PT boats and destroyers opened fire.

The sky became alight with flashes of guns firing from the destroyers and PT boats, and from torpedoes exploding as they hit their marks.

Aboard *PT-109*, Lt. Kennedy was standing next to the helmsman when the destroyer rammed it at full speed. Gasoline burst into flames immediately. *PT-106* had to swerve to avoid collision with the destroyer. *PT-109* fired two torpedoes but at one hundred and fifty yards the missiles did not have time to arm themselves. The two PTs then made a zigzagging escape while laying down smoke. They reported that *PT-109* was lost in battle and no survivors were seen.

Six days later eight natives arrived at base in a canoe and brought word from a coastwatcher that a few of the survivors of *PT-109* were on Cross Island near Ferguson Passage. Two PTs went and rescued those of the crew who were still alive. They were brought back to base; Lt. Kennedy was among them.

Lt. John Kennedy was required to make an intelligence report of the loss of *PT-109*. He made the report and filed it on August 22, 1943. It tells what happened aboard

PT-109 after it was rammed.

Scarcely ten seconds elapsed between the time of sighting the enemy ship and the crash. *PT-109* did not sink, at least immediately. The fire which *PT-106* saw and reported was gasoline burning on the water's surface. It was at least twenty yards away from the remains of *PT-109* which was still afloat, bottom up. Lt. Kennedy ordered all hands to abandon ship when it appeared that the fire would spread to it, but they all crawled back aboard when the danger passed.

When daylight arrived, eleven survivors were still aboard *PT-109*. In his report Kennedy estimated that their half-submerged hull lay about three miles north and slightly east of Ghizo Anchorage and about three miles away from the reef along the northeast of Ghizo.

What followed in the report became the center of my attention. On the morning of the second day after they had been rammed, Lt. Kennedy made the decision to abandon *PT-109* for fear that it would sink. The vessel was drifting close to a small island about four miles to the southeast of Gizo. Just before dawn and still under cover of darkness, the crew abandoned *PT-109* and started swimming towards the island. They found refuge in the underbrush.

During the course of the next few days they changed their locations to three different islands. In each case, Kennedy reported swimming was difficult because of the strong currents.

In all probability after the survivors abandoned the bottom-up hull of *PT-109* it would remain afloat and would drift in the same direction as the currents. I studied the charts and read the pilots for the month of August. Currents varied not only from month to month and day to day but from hour to hour. The depths of the seas among the islands were beyond the reach of normal diving operations, but if *PT-109* did not sink it would then be carried to one of the reefs by the prevailing currents at the time. But which currents and what reefs?

Charts could help locate the many islets and numerous reefs but it would be no help with the currents. The only sure way was to go to the area in the early days of the month of August and as close to the same hour that *PT-109* was rammed and let the current be the deciding factor. We set sail aboard *Third Sea* from Rabaul bound for Ferguson Pass between Rendova and Gizo Islands in the Solomons.

We had a compressor and diving tanks aboard and could do limited undersea exploration. What I really wanted to do was to prove my theory that *PT-109* did not sink in deep water but was wrecked on a reef. If we found anything, we could return later with a full diving expedition. We had to be quick. We could not linger long in the area for I was aware we did not have the necessary permits nor the authorization from the newly independent Solomon Islands Government.

Ten days later, on August 1, we sighted Gizo Island. Now came the difficult part of tricky navigation. During daylight hours we felt safe and secure since we could take bearings on land marks and fix our positions. But at night it was another thing. Unless we had a sky full of stars we could not take star shots and get a celestial fix. Here in the Solomons I gained a great respect for PT boat commanders and their crews; they had to operate mainly at night. How any of them managed to survive is a miracle.

We couldn't linger but on the other hand neither could we be reckless. We sailed with shortened sails, edging our way among the maze of small islands. They appeared menacing on all the horizons.

Instead of starting at the spot where it was believed that *PT-109* was rammed, we worked backwards. We went to Cross Island where Lt. Kennedy and his crew were rescued and studied the island and the passes in the area. We determined if our drift carried us to the same islands and reefs, we would know a little more about them.

After two days in the area, while anchoring off reefs at night, we sailed to the pass north of Gizo Island. An hour after midnight on August 3 we lowered our sails. We were in the area where *PT-109* was rammed.

It was a strange feeling, indeed, to be floating upon that black empty sea knowing that thirty-five years before it was a holocaust of flame and death. Then when flashes of lightning filled the sky and reflected on our masts and rigging and the damp faces of our crew, we had the uncanny feeling that we were treading upon a sacred grave. We came very close to calling off our expedition.

During the night we could not determine in which direction the current was carrying us—towards Cross Island or out to sea. There was a considerable chop and also a ten-knot wind. Fearing that our masts and rigging might affect our drift, more so than a hull half-submerged in the water, we decided to lower the dory and follow her drift. Three crew with signal lights and a walkie-talkie climbed aboard and we cast them off.

By 4 a.m. we were more than a mile apart, almost beyond the range of the signal lights. It was risky. I didn't want to risk losing our crew. We started the engine and motored over to them.

When dawn came Cross Island was in sight. We took bearings and discovered we were in the very same drift pattern as *PT-109* had been. We were, however, somewhat farther to the south. We calculated by afternoon, when the *PT-109* was abandoned, we would be about eight miles from Cross Island rather than the four miles esti-mated by Lt. Kennedy.

With the dory in tow we sailed to the point where *PT-109* was abandoned, and again followed the drift of our dory. It was a nerve-racking night that followed. We did not let the dory drift more than a hundred meters dis-tance. By dawn we were in sight of a reef six miles south of Ghizo.

Not wanting to take any more chances we anchored outside the reef. The reef stretched for miles, mostly sub-merged but in places it broke surface. We wished we had a magnetometer or similar device for detecting metal un-der water but we didn't. It had to be trial and error.

During the next two days we discovered not one but four wrecks on the reef, all in less than fifteen feet of water. Any one of them could have been World War II vintage. From one we brought up a telephone from the radio shack. It appeared to be a U.S. Navy type.

Without a permit from the Government and proper sal-vage gear we couldn't remain longer in the area. We did not find *PT-109* but I'm sure it can be located. A magnetometer would be necessary, and things like shark cages and bang sticks would be helpful. Each time we were in water for twenty minutes or more, sharks came. They didn't look friendly.

The fact that *PT-109* was still afloat when it was aban-doned makes me believe that it did not immediately sink, and if it did stay afloat, then the current would have carried it onto one of the many reefs south of Ghizo Island. We did find two anchors in fairly shallow waater but we were unable to bring them to the surface with only our small dory.

I intended to take *Third Sea* back one day, and this time, I was certain, we would locate *PT-109.*

When you do find a place to drop anchor in any one of the exotic ports of Southeast Asia, there always arises the challenge of diving on wrecks. Someone is certain to approach you with a wild idea or a scheme that will make you both rich. Some are too far-fetched to believe; others you have to make up your own mind as to whether they are real or not.

I once had this problem, deciding whether what I was hearing was true or not. It happened when *Third Sea* was anchored on the Chao Phraya River down from the Oriental Hotel, before they constructed the Sathorn Bridge. A yachtsman, who had just arrived in Thailand, dropped anchor nearby and rowed over to introduce himself. He talked at length about his Pacific crossing and then began telling me about something that happened to him in the South China Sea.

Outriggers gather around *Third Sea* even before the anchor settles.

"I swear, the entire sea bottom is littered with wrecks, Chinese wrecks, old junks, you can still see their outlines," he insisted. "They're covered with coral but you can still make them out."

All the while I had been building *Third Sea* in Singapore, I had been listening to strange tales of sunken wrecks, buried treasure, lost Manila galleons, about shipwrecks with priceless porcelain, gold, silver. Rumors mostly, wishful fairy tales. Hopeful thinking, I called it. Landlubbers want to strike it rich in the lottery. Yachtsmen want to find sunken treasures.

But for some reason, the man who was telling me this tale seemed reliable. He had nothing to gain or lose. He was only a yachtsman sailing with his wife and their two children from America across the Pacific to Asia on a pleasure cruise.

I questioned him further. "It was late afternoon," he said. "We left the Philippines and were halfway across the South China Sea heading to Thailand when we saw water breaking on what appeared to be a reef. It was impossible, I thought. My navigation couldn't be that far off!"

At this point, he said, they dropped sails. A quick glance at the chart indicated they were on course, but he had no time to ponder their situation. "My sons, both teenage boys, began jumping up and down," he said. "A reef, dad, a reef. That means good spear fishing, maybe even lobster," they kept shouting. They wanted to put on scuba gear and go investigate. At first I was against it, but they persisted and I finally gave in. It was when we dove overboard that we discovered the wrecks, scattered across the bottom. Darkness forced us to leave before we could do any serious exploring. The next morning the weather turned foul and we had to leave."

I asked the yachtsman about the location. "I couldn't find any reef marked on the chart, but I swear it was there," he said. To emphasize his point, he gave me the coordinates. We went to my chart table and took out the chart I had on the South China Sea. We checked both the latitude and longitude that he gave me but we could find no reef where he indicated. I was having my doubts, but then I remembered some old charts I had tucked away in a bottom drawer of the navigation table. We were in luck. I found an old yellow chart of the South China Sea, and there, sure enough, was a reef exactly where he said it was. It was marked Whalebone Reef. For some reason it had been dropped from modern hydrographic charts. That does happen. Reefs, shoals, even islets appeared on charts and then disappear at the next printing.

The yachtsman was contented to know he wasn't dreaming and a few weeks later he and his family sailed off. I intended that one day I would go and dive on Whalebone Reef, to see what I could discover. But I made one mistake. I told too many people about my secret, about the reef with sunken ships, and soon every sailor in Southeast Asia knew about it. I joked along with everyone when they asked about it, but one thing I didn't do was give away its location. I kept that to myself. I still figured that one day I would take *Third Sea* and we would dive on Whalebone Reef.

Time passed, perhaps six years after I met the yachtsman, when things began to happen, sudden like. I was anchored in the Dindings, up the maze of channels that lead to Port Klang on Malaysia's west coast. It's a quiet place, and in the cool of evening you can hear Muslim imans calling prayers from mosques on shore. I was enjoying the night, sitting on the aft deck under an awning, when a skiff with two men aboard came along side. A man sitting in the bow stood up, grabbed hold of the taff rail and introduced himself. I'll call him Mike Radder.

I knew him instantly, not by person, by name. He's a treasure diver, a ruthless, notorious man. I had heard he stops at nothing. "I have a proposition to make you," he said. He didn't come aboard but asked if I would come to his home and he would explain at dinner. He said he would send a car for me, and to be on the shore at six p.m. I had an inclination it was about the reef but I wasn't sure. Curiosity got the better of me. I accepted his offer and he sped off towards shore. The next evening I had one of my crew row me ashore, and sure enough, a car was waiting there for me.

He lived in an old Colonial home outside Kuala Lumpur. The dinner was excellent, shared by Mike, three other men and me. I gathered they were business partners. Finally, over Hennessy VO, he said, "We know about your secret reef." I nodded but made no comment. At least he was being direct. "I'll make you a deal. Fifty-fifty. You tell me where it is and we split it down the middle. I have my crew ready to depart immediately."

I knew Mike Radder was not a man to be trusted; yet I was curious to see how far he would go. "Fine," I said, after bantering back and forth, "Fifty-fifty, but I'm afraid all my information is in an office in Bangkok." I was hoping this would put matters to an end. It didn't.

Mike poured another cognac. "Maybe if you look at some charts that will help," he said, and led me into another room. On a table in the center of the room was a stack of charts. The stage had been set. More charts were stacked on other side tables. Mike had it all planned; he began peeling charts from the pile and dropping them one by one to the floor. "Maybe this one," he repeated again and again. I kept shaking my head. More Hennessy VO was poured. More probing.

Having gone through the stack, and somewhat irritated now, they turned to another table. The charts there were older. Then came one chart, faded and yellow, like the one I had aboard my schooner. Mike ran his fingers over the longitude and latitude lines. Suddenly the name leaped out at me—Whalebone Reef. "Maybe here," he said.

"No," I replied, holding my breath, "that's not it." My heart beat so loud I thought the pounding would give me away. Mike turned to the next chart. I studied it closely, like I had seen it before. I made sure it didn't have Whale-bone Reef on it.

"This is it," I said pointing to an area marked *Caution: Uncharted.* Many pre-World War II charts carry such markings.

Mike Radder didn't offer to drive me back to my schooner. He left that to one of the other men. I knew I wouldn't hear from him again, but that didn't matter. I had pulled the great hoax over Mike Radder, the treasure diver no one could trust. I pictured him setting out for the South China Sea on a voyage that would lead him to nowhere.

About six months later the news broke. They said it was the biggest treasure discovery in history. Mike Radder was news. His photograph appeared in newspapers and in *Time* and *News Week.* He appeared on television. Christie's in London estimated his Beijing Cargo to be worth millions. An auction was held to a record crowd.

I went into a rage. I found it hard controlling myself. No doubt he had found treasure in the "uncharted" area I had pointed out. Maybe it wasn't my intention that he found treasure there, but he didn't know that. He could have cut me in like he agreed. He was a scoundrel, in deed. I waited for the day I would see Mike Radder again.

I was capable of murder.

I didn't know what good it would do but when I saw his salvage boat anchored in Singapore I jumped into my dinghy and rowed over to his vessel.

"You are a thief and a liar!" I shouted, waving a fist, when I climbed aboard. I expected him to come after me with a belaying pin. But I was prepared. Two crew came rushing up to his side and stood there.

"A thief," he stammered. "Why do you say that!" I was surprised how calm he remained. He wasn't ruffled at all. Before I could answer he continued. "Your location, that uncharted area, it proved nothing. We spent a couple weeks there. Nothing. Wasted so much time."

He looked directly into my eyes. "It was near there," he calmly said, "at a place called Whalebone Reef that we made our discovery." He leaned back against the railing, smiling. "Now don't tell me," he continued, "don't tell me you are going to say you knew about Whalebone Reef too. You even denied it was the location when you saw it on my chart that night we had you to dinner."

I didn't say anything after that. I rowed silently back to my *Third Sea*. I looked for another place to anchor.

Chapter 18

THE SOUTH CHINA SEA

Consider Indonesia, an island republic of more than thirteen thousand islands. Think what possibilities there are here for the cruising yachtsman. Let's take any one of the islands. Take Sumatra.

Sumatra is a challenge. No yachts have cruised its western shores, yet imagine what rich rewards it must hold for the adventuresome sailor. The great Acheh ports of old are in the North, where the first trade routes between East and West were established. There are the romantic sounding off-shore islands along the west coast like Nias and Mentawai. Anthropologists tell us that Mentawai is inhabited by distant cousins of the Polynesians. Can there be some tie?

Far to the south is the great port of Bencoolen. The port was once destined to be the greatest in Asia, but then came Sir Stamford Raffles who founded Singapore, and twenty years later the Dutch traded Bencoolen for Malacca with the British.

Then there's Krakatoa, the volcanic island that literally shook the world when it erupted with sudden and uncontrolled fury a hundred years ago. It changed the climatic conditions the world over for several years afterwards, with fallout reaching as far as London. The island was completely destroyed, with not one living thing left. What secrets does the island hold today? We anchored *Third Sea* off shore and any minute thought the island might explode once more.

Today in Southeast Asia it's possible to visit all these places. Twenty years ago it would not have been. The reason is that Southeast Asia, at last, is becoming yachting conscious. More and more cruising yachts from abroad are finding new pleasures in Asian waters, and Asians themselves are discovering that boating can be as much fun at home as it is in the Mediterranean, and cheaper.

Tourism to Southeast Asia has done much to bring about a sudden awareness of what Asia really has to offer. Other than temples, massage parlours and good shopping. The sea is one. Those things that once frightened would-be sailors away—mainly pirates and typhoons are no longer considered valid. As one intrepid visiting yachtsman said. "Pirates! You find more in Florida and Hawaii."

As for storms, we learn that typhoons exist in belts which can be avoided. Hong Kong and the northern Philippines are in that belt and are unsafe during the typhoon season, approximately four months out of the year. The area below that is free of typhoons and includes the southern Philippines, all of Borneo, Singapore, Indonesia, Malaysia and Thailand. That's a lot of cruising ground.

Same for monsoons. When the northeast monsoons blow, it's time to sail to the west coasts of Malaysia and Thailand, and all the way to Phuket in southern Thailand. In April or May, when the southwest monsoons move in, the wise yachtsman moves to the east coasts and perhaps up to Pattaya and Bangkok or he sails to Hong Kong and the Philippines. It's all a matter of studying charts with depths and currents, and the seasons.

The big advantage of yachting in Asian waters is if you want to change your environment, or culture, the distances you have to travel to do this isn't that great. Where else can you find half a dozen cultures within a thousand-mile radius?

Other than blue water and lovely sandy beaches, there are some added attractions to yachting in Southeast Asia that you don't find in the Pacific, the Mediterranean or the Caribbean.

The number one attraction is islands in the sun. In Southeast Asia alone, to visit all the tropical isles would take not one but several lifetimes. Charts of the Philippines list some seven thousand islands, many uninhabited, while, as I mentioned, Indonesia is a chain of more than thirteen thousand islands that stretch for three thousand miles from one end to the other. Thailand and Malaysia are dotted with islands on both their coasts, and even tiny Singapore has fifty-two islands.

The stark beauty of some of these story-book islands is legendary. When MGM needed an idyllic isle to film James A. Michener's imaginary Bali Hai for the musical "South Pacific," they chose Tioman Island off the East Coast of Malaysia.

Tioman, one hundred and fifty miles from Singapore, is beautiful. It has two excellent bays for anchoring and a path across the mountain that connects them. Several other beautiful islands neighbor Tioman. Rawa has a white sand beach and a resort where yachtsman stop for cold beer. Tinggi has the shape of a perfect cone.

Farther to the north of Tioman along the Malay coast are two more islands that capture the hearts of dreamers. They are Perhentian and Redang. My favorite is Redang, where I encountered my first storm aboard *Third Sea*. It appears like a picture postcard. The water in the bays— there are two—is so clear you can see the white sand bottom at forty feet. At one of the bays is a Malay fishing village, unchanged since time's beginning. There are, of course, no accommodations on the island.

In the Gulf of Thailand farther to the north is Ko Samui. It has some excellent coves with good anchoring. North of Ko Samui are two smaller islands, Ko Phangan and

Ko Tao. Thais here live in scattered villages. There are
no roads, only trails connecting the villages. No hotels,
no electricity, no shops, no food stalls. But you can get an
insight to Thai life and the coral reefs around Ko Tao are
alive with sea life.

The west coasts of both Malaysia and Thailand are
ideal during the northeast monsoon. Pangkor is popular.
Penang is Singapore fifty years ago. Yachtsman can anchor right downtown in front of the clock tower in old
Georgetown.

The Langkawi Islands lie sixty miles north of Penang
on the Thai border. They number ninety-nine, and like
the fiords of Norway they create an exciting labyrinth of
waterways and passages. Sheer granite cliffs drop abruptly
into the sea, their walls worn and serrated by weather and
the passage of time. One island, uninhabited, has a fresh-
water lake with a white crocodile, more legend than real,
while still another has a waterfall that cascades down the
granite rocks to form seven pools. Each one of the smaller
islands can be a paradise in itself, without facilities.

Sailing among the many lovely islands around Phuket offers some
of the best cruising grounds for yachts in all of Southeast Asia.

Phuket is Thailand's most popular island resort; for the yachtsman it is an island surrounded by a hundred smaller islands, each one more magnificent than the other one.

At the southern tip of Phuket is Ko Racha Yai, a small sun-drenched uninhabited island where you can watch your anchor settle to the bottom thirty feet below. Farther to the east are the Phi Phi islands, the most beautiful of all the Phuket isles. So powerful is the sight as you approach that they are certain to leave impressions that remain etched in your memory forever.

Sheer limestone cliffs rear up like contorted dragons, forming the larger of the two islands, Phi Phi Don. Phi Phi Lay, the smaller of the two, lingers in the background. At Phi Phi Lay, uninhabited, take your dinghy and explore Viking Cave. So called because of curious, inexplicable ancient paintings of boats on the wall. Swim into tiny grottos and caves where the dappled light creates endless pictures. In another cave you can marvel at the wooden scaffolding where energetic Thais scale flimsy bamboo structures to gather birds' nests for making the famous Chinese soup.

Ko Rak Nok, uninhabited, has a waterfall nearly a thousand feet high and a beach of phallic carvings where Thai fishermen come to give alms in hope their barren wives can give birth.

Southeast Asia also offers river cruising. One of the great rivers of Asia is the Chao Phraya, the River of Kings that flows down the very center of Thailand.

At one time the Chao Phraya was navigable all the way up river to Ayuttaya. Back in the early 16th century Europe first heard about this magnificent city called Ayutthaya, an Eastern kingdom located far up a river in a land known as Siam. What tales these first visitors to this strange land had to tell. Imagine, they said, palaces and temples—more than four hundred of them all within the city walls, great soaring rooftops turned up at the ends, glittering with gold and multi-colored tiles and mosaics. Princes and princesses who moved upon lotus-covered waterways in stately royal barges, and enormous war elephants with jewelled harnesses returning from the northern provinces, bearing treasures from their victories, marching upon paved roads.

Here, these visitors realized with awe, was a capital of great riches, a city which had ruled for centuries, its population greater than that of London, a port more magnificent than Genoa and Venice combined. And upon this river called the Chao Phraya, which linked the kingdom to the sea, were sea-going ships, ships from the Indian subcontinent, from as far away as Persia, from Java and dozens of other ports in Southeast Asia.

And from China there were junks by the score. One early visitor reported that these huge Chinese vessels lay at anchor below Ayutthaya, stretching for more than two miles downstream. All sorts of other boats—junks, sampans, prows, river scows—waited to load and unload the precious goods. And what cargoes they were: ivory, camphor wood, teak, peacock feathers, cinnamon, peppercorn and cloves, fine porcelains, lacquerware and bolts of silk. And there would have been cargoes lesser known in the West, such as birds' nests, agar-agar, and trepang.

They all came to trade; and Siam, with her capital at Ayutthaya, had what they wanted. She was the greatest trading center the East had ever seen.

Time was when a yachtsman could sail up the Chao Phraya and anchor in front of the Oriental Hotel, as Conrad once did. A new bridge down the river has put a halt to that. But one can still sail up the River of Kings for nearly eighteen miles and either anchor or tie up to docks and wharfs. We mounted an outboard on the dory and made a river trip all the way to Ayutthaya. It was tempting to try to make it all the way to Chieng Mai but we left that to another crew member who sailed aboard *Third Sea*— Steve van Beek. Steve, a long-time Asian hand, actually started at the headwaters of the Chao Phraya and paddled a canoe all the way to the mouth, more than five hundred miles. Steve later sailed with *Third Sea* from Singapore to Zambonaga in the Philippines.

There are dozens of other rivers that will accommodate deep draft yachts, even the tiny Malacca River. I already mentioned taking *Third Sea* up the narrow river to Malacca—impossible, old salts said—and tied up where Dutch and Portuguese ships moored four hundred years ago.

In Borneo it's easy to sail upriver to Kuching, but the real thrill is the Rejang River into central Borneo. It's navigable all the way to Kapit, the last outpost. We sailed *Third Sea* up to Kapit and felt like the White Raja of Borneo. Tattooed tribesmen whose ancestors were once headhunters brought us river trout and fresh jungle fruit to trade for old clothing.

Not actually a river, but very close to it, is the Klang Estuary, a maze of waterways, where the jungle reaches to the water's edge, that leads to Port Klang. Countless small islands, some too tiny to name, make up the estuary. None seem more than a dozen feet above water. Casuarinas and scrub brush blanket the land down to the water's edge where the mud flats and mangrove swamps begin. There's one island above the others that I like to visit. It's called Ketam. It's a settlement, with sixteen thousand Chinese inhabitants, ninety percent of whom are engaged in fishing. The settlement, constructed entirely of wood, is built high above water on stilts, and when you walk the planked streets, you have little idea that the sea is below.

The real excitement of cruising in Southeast Asia is to be sailing through history. China was trading with the Indian subcontinent when Rome was still an outpost on ancient Greek maps. Both Tioman Island in Malaysia and Phuket in Thailand were part of the Indian-Chinese trade route. Unearthings on Phuket have produced Greek and Roman earthenware, golden Arab coins and Chinese Ming pottery.

Tioman Island which lays thirty-five miles off Malaysia's east coast, is an unopened history textbook. On the southern end are twin peaks called Ass's Ears, a landmark for seamen for two thousand years. A thousand years before the arrival of Europeans, Chinese merchants made Tioman a port of call. Ming pottery has been discovered in caves in the hills, and one recent visitor reported finding a gold chain of uncertain Chinese origin in a stream bed in one of the rivers.

Malaysia's Pangkor island has an old Dutch fort, and Malacca is one of the oldest European settlements in Asia.

Diving is another good reason for cruising in Asian waters. It all depends upon one's interests—diving for lobster and looking at pretty coral formation, or diving on thousand-year-old Chinese wrecks and World War II battleships near by. In Southeast Asian waters both these options are possible.

Yachtsmen in Southeast Asia are forever arguing which island or which reef offers the best water for diving. Is it Phuket, Tioman or Palawan? They are all excellent, and no one can possibly win.

For diving on wrecks, that's something totally different. Ships of a dozen eastern powers plied Asian seas for centuries, and how many tore out their guts and spilled their treasures on uncharted coasts and submerged coral reefs can only be a matter for conjuncture. The future for marine archaeology in Southeast Asia is limitless.

All you need is a ship and scuba gear. You might find the *Flor de la Mar* which ran aground off the coast of Sumatra.

The ship was never found, nor its cargo recovered. Its captain was D'Albequeque, the Portuguese admiral who sacked Malacca. Three days out of Malacca bound for Europe the ship was lost in a squall off the coast of Sumatra. The wreck has never been found, nor, to my knowledge, has anyone ever looked for it.

Or there's Sir Stamford Raffles' ship. He founded Singapore, and sent to England a cargo of historical riches aboard a British merchantman. The ship ran aground and caught fire somewhere off the coast of Sumatra and was never recovered.

The discovery of a Dutch ship that sank in 1724 only a few miles offshore from Mersing on Malaysian's East Coast made history in 1984 when divers brought up elephant tusks and tin ingots worth millions.

But we don't have to go back that far in history. A German submarine carrying eighteen tons of valuable mercury was lost during the war off the coast of Penang. Two British divers found the sub and salvaged most of the cargo, but not all of it. The sub is still there.

Or you can go diving on two British battleships, the *HMS Repulse* and *HMS Prince of Wales*, both sunk by Japanese torpedo bombers off the East Coast of Malaya during the opening days of the war. The *Repulse* is in one hundred and eighty feet of water, still intact, the tomb of more than five hundred sailors who were trapped inside when the Japanese sank it. We dove on the *Repulse* from the deck of *Third Sea.*

And there's a romance of sailing in the East that can't be denied. It can be sheer excitement, sailing through the Conradesque world of Southeast Asia. Consider, for one, the Dindings and the Klang Estuary that I mentioned. You drop anchor in front of a village, and in the evening when the harsh noonday glare of light is reduced to softness, you become subtly aware of skyline silhouetted by onion domes and minarets of Muslim mosques. And when you have your evening meal on deck under the awning, with the sun setting in a blaze of oranges and reds behind the village, you can't help but feel Asia to the very tips of your fingers. It's the combination of many things—smells that come from the village, and that of sounds, the imans (Muslim priests) calling out evening prayers. You feel then that the world, your private world at least, is at peace. This is what cruising in Southeast Asia has to offer.

A quiet Malay village as at dusk seen from the deck of *Third Sea.*

Chapter 19

TALES OF PIRATES

"Pirates! Aren't you ever afraid of pirates?" The question was asked everywhere I went—wasn't I afraid of pirates. I have to admit, in the beginning, when I first launched *Third Sea* and began sailing Asian waters, I was a bit apprehensive about pirates. And I good reason for being so. All I had to do was pick up one of the English language newspapers in Asia—*Straits Times* , *Bangkok Post* , *The Nation, The South China Morning Post*—and the headlines told the story: "Ships warned to expect more pirate attacks." "Group to visit Malaysia for talks on piracy," "Mariners on alert after pirate raids," "Piracy on the Chao Phraya on the rise." The papers were filled with horror stories of piracy on the high seas. I was concerned but I also knew if I wanted to sail these waters this was a problem I would have to overcome. There were a numer of precautions I could take to reduce the risk of pirate attacks. Most important, I reasoned, was not to make *Third Sea* look like an easy target. No shiny, white-hulled, super foreign yacht. I painted her hull brown, the color of mud, and I had our sail maker in Hong Kong fabricate dark maroon-colored sails. Not until years later, when I began chartering in Phuket, did I paint the hull white and change *Third Sea*'s appearance. I must admit, she did look much better with her white hull.

What developed with the hull painted brown was not what I had expected. When we sailed into small harbors and visited distant islands, and even met other vessels upon the high seas, we were the ones taken to be pirates. With our jutting bowsprit, ratlines running up the rigging and tall masts flying strange-looking pennants, I must admit, *Third Sea* did very much look like a pirate ship right out of the movies. When we sailed to some islands, the islanders fled from their homes, and at sea we found when we turned toward a vessel, especially fishing boats, they were the ones that fled. Of course, it did have its drawbacks. When we wanted help at sea we couldn't always get it.

My concern was not so much at sea as it was when we were at anchor in a secluded cove or forgotten bay. The trouble arose when the crews of passing fishing boats saw us peacefully at anchor and decided to come and drop anchor near us. These crews were often scruffy, loud and boisterous, especially after they began drinking. In the beginning we thought it best to be neighborly. As soon as we did, they lowered skiffs into the water and rowed over to us. They invited themselves aboard and we couldn't likely say no. And some fishing boats have dozens of crew members. We found it best to avoid them completely when they came near, even eye contact. No waving; no friendly smiles. Another policy we developed was when more than two boats came and anchored near us, we lifted anchor and moved to another location.

At anchor at night we always kept a watch on deck. Joshua Slocum, the first solo circumnavigator, solved his problem by scattering tacks around on deck when he anchored at night. I often wondered after reading his book *Sailing Alone Around the World* what would have happened had the wind come up at night and he had to lift anchor and set sail. Anyway, that was not our problem. Aboard *Third Sea*, we always had an ample crew to stand watch, an advantage a bigger boat has.

Our problem, of course, was nothing like ships of bygone days had when they plied Asian waters. Aside from pirates they had to battle uncharted reefs and shoals.

The sea lanes in Southeast Asia were deadly, especially the waters between the southern tip of the Malay Peninsula and the islands of Indonesia. Ships had to contend with winds that were unfavorable and currents which were swift and strong; navigators had to pick their way through a maze of islands, around shallows and over innumerable reefs and partly-submerged rocks. The Chinese traders had good reason for calling the waters around Singapore the "Dragon Teeth Gate."

Only after the British laid claim to Singapore were some of the rocks blasted away to provide safe passage. Even today, with lighthouses and marked buoys, up-to-date charts, radar and satellite navigation, ships continue to go up on the reefs around Horsburgh Light and Lima Channel.

The navigational hazards of rounding Singapore to reach the Indian Ocean were only the first obstacle. The other was pirates. Merchant ships were virtually at the mercy of these brigands. They plundered at will, without fear of retribution or reprisal. They hid out in their shallow-draft prows in small coves and bays, and swooped down upon helpless merchant ships which had lost their wind. They could move at incredible speeds, with as many as a hundred sturdy men at their paddles, and they attacked without mercy.

Piracy until the turn of the century was an aristocratic profession practised by many a Malay prince. They enlisted their crews among the head-hunting Dyaks of Borneo. An equitable arrangement existed between master and crew: the Malays took the booty; the Dyaks the heads. We will never really know how many thousands of vessels were lost to pirates.

The first time we sailed into friendly Tongareva in the

Cook Islands, the natives were actually waiting for *Third Sea* to pile up on the reef, and our ship and everything aboard would have become theirs. We didn't learn this until much later, another time when we visited the island. The islanders had prepared a feast for us, as they usually did, and we all went ashore to meet at Papa Beer's house. We had just sat down and as the food was being brought out we became aware of a commotion somewhere in the background. Suddenly everyone began jabbering and before we knew what was happening the men and young boys vanished. There were no explanations; they just picked up and left, while we were left with the women and children. The women insisted we eat and not wait for the men. We did as they bid but it was a rather solemn affair. We returned to *Third Sea* wondering what could possibly have happened. It was not until we came ashore the next morning that we found out.

It seems that in the dark of night, a Korean fishing boat had crashed into the reef at the other side of the island. To reach the wreck the men and boys shoot across the lagoon to find the boat high and dry on the reef. With the first light of dawn, they could see the fishermen and crew huddled together on shore. No lives had been lost.

It sounded like a very magnanimous move on the behalf of our islander friends to help the shipwrecked crew, but to help them was not their motive at all. From what it sounded like to us, these peaceful, god-fearing Tongarevans had turned into marauders. They pounced upon the stricken vessel like vultures. They took axes and smashed in the doors and pilfered and removed anything and everything that wasn't attached. They were fortunate for the vessel had a full cargo of fish and had refueled and restocked in Tahiti a few days before for its passage home. Apparently the crew were partying when they hit the reef. The vessel was a total loss. The islanders took everything they could carry and returned to their village, leaving the crew behind.

That happened on a Friday. On Sunday everyone went to church, and listened to the preacher give thanks for their plentiful bounty. They then remembered the crew, how unfortunate they were. After church, boats set out across the lagoon and brought the eleven crew members back to the village and fed them. The food had come from their own vessel. That evening the radio operator reached a passing Korean fishing boat. The vessel stopped long enough to pick up the stranded crew and sail off.

The islanders thought nothing unusual of what they had done. They then casually mentioned when they first saw *Third Sea* they secretly hoped she too would run aground. The man who told us the story led us to the cemetery. Here was history carved in stone. Head markers told of sailors whose bodies washed ashore after being wrecked, and there were more markers of castaways who spent years on the island, and were never rescued.

After that experience, I felt often uneasy about the seemingly peaceful islanders of the Pacific. When we sailed among those seldom-visited islands did they consider us their "cargo cult" like the natives of New Guinea do? The natives there build runways in the jungles and construct fake airplanes, to entice planes to land on their landing field so that they can confiscate them.

When I was in Bangkok I mentioned the Tongareva incident to Steve van Beek, a writer on Asian matters, and a little later he sent me a copy of *The Travels of Marco Polo* with a passage underlined. When Marco Polo began his return journey to Europe after spending seventeen years in the Far East, he traveled by ship via Japan and the East Indies. He visited numerous river ports in the Malay Archipelago and noted that "should a vessel be accidentally driven within the mouth of its river, not having intended to make that port, they seize and confiscate all the good she may have on board, saying: 'It was your intentions to have gone elsewhere but our gods have conducted you to us, in order that we may possess your property.'"

After reading the passage I better understood the motive of island people, but the question remained—are they right in praying that every passing ship will become a wreck? We would be faced with the same dilemma when we reached the western Pacific on this return voyage.

We picture pirates brandishing swords and swinging aboard captured vessels on rope halyards. Far-fetched? Some things don't change.

The vessels that these modern-day pirates use are often quite primitive, some even with outriggers, but they are fast. With powerful outboards they can clip along at excess of thirty miles per hour. They hit fast, at night, and may go undetected. They sneak up on vessels from the stern, throw hooks with boarding ladders attached to the railings above and climb aboard. I remember one incident that was told to me by a ship's officer when I was in Singapore. The vessel he worked aboard was a luxury cruise liner.

One evening a lady passenger went screaming hysterical to the captain who was dining with guests at the captain's table in the main saloon. She said she had been robbed. She confessed to have seen the culprits. The captain led her away, and when he asked where the thieves gone, and she replied over the side, he nodded and had the ship's doctor give her a sedative. He went to his own cabin, still chuckling, only to find that his quarters were looted. The phone was ringing. He picked it up. It was the bridge. Pirates had cleaned out a few of the officers' quarters too. Not one of the officers or men on the crew had as much as a glimpse of the pirates nor the vessel on which they made their escape. The report never hit the newspapers. Such news could be devastating for the cruise industry.

Tales of raids upon private yachts are endless. Secret U.S. Coast Guard files occasionally leak information to the press and articles appear in *Time* and *Newsweek*. The serious cases seem to be more in the Florida Keys than in Southeast Asia. There it's called "yacht-jacking." Stolen yachts are used to smuggle heroin and marijuana from Central and South America into the U.S. Smugglers commandeer yachts, slay the occupants and then use the pleasure crafts as contraband cutters.

Among many of the cases that were made public, the seizure by drug pirates of the sailboat *Kamillii* is the most bizarre. Hijackers boarded it at Honolulu and dumped the three crew members 140 miles at sea in a life raft without food or water. Luckily, the castaways were picked up by an Italian freighter.

A Coast Guard C-130 aircraft spotted the stolen craft and ordered it back to Honolulu, but the yacht continued on its course. A Coast Guard cutter armed with machineguns intercepted *Kamillii* and subdued the heavily-armed hijackers. They were taken back to Honolulu with the yacht in tow.

During interrogation, the three modern-day pirates confessed they were taking the yacht to Thailand to pick up a load of heroin.

On several occasions I had been approached to engage in hauling drugs in Asia, and I was always able to back away. One concern was when I took on new crew. I was aware they could bring drugs aboard without my knowing it. To help lessen the chance, I would instruct any joining crew or passenger that they had to leave their baggage on the dock for a government inspection. The method appeared to work for I never had a drug problem aboard.

It's impossible for the navies of the nations of Southeast Asia to provide total safety for private yachts and larger shipping vessels even within their own territorial waters. In Singapore alone more than a hundred thousand ships enter through Dragon Teeth Gate. Even the entire British navy had a tough time protecting the waterways, and now with the U.S. out of the Philippines, piracy is on the increase. Fortunately, private yachting is not a target.

Chapter 20

RETURN TO ASIA

When William A. Robinson sailed the South Pacific in 1928, he made repeated references in his book *Ten Thousand Leagues Over the Sea* to how friendly and generous the islanders were. When he went ashore, all he had to do was admire an object and it was his. Every time he set sail he was loaded down to the gunwales with stocks of bananas, taro, jams, coconuts and even live chickens and suckling pigs. The world Robinson knew certainly doesn't exist any longer and we can only lament its passing. But we could hardly expect the same conditions to exist under present day conditions. When *Third Sea* was in Papeete on her last voyage, the harbor master revealed that he had checked in nearly four hundred yachts that year, and it was only July. We counted over a hundred yachts at anchor along the waterfront. Thirty years before, when I first arrived in Tahiti, there were less than half a dozen. When Robinson arrived, his was the only yacht in the harbor.

But the surplus of cruising yachts doesn't have to detract from the pleasures of sailing the South Pacific. There's no question about it, French Polynesia is still a great cruising ground for wayward yachtsmen. The sad part, as always, is leaving, and leave I had to do. It was Herman Melville who wrote in *Moby Dick*, "Push not off from that isle, for thou canst never return." The island, of course, was Tahiti, and Melville didn't follow his own advice. Once he left he never returned.

So was I to listen to Melville and never leave, or would I take my chances? Leave I had to, like the countless others before me. I would have to take the chance that one day I would return behind the helm of *Third Sea*. After six years of cruising the Pacific, *Third Sea* was in need of repairs, and I missed her when I was in Asia. My reporting for the *Bangkok Post* required that I spend a couple months a years in Asia, and, it seemed, the flights across the Pacific were getting longer and longer. It wouldn't be easy to say goodbye, and the thought of the long and difficult voyage ahead began to weigh heavily on my mind. Would I have to pay a penalty for the easy life, the good sailing we had in the Pacific? The answer, unfortunately, was a harsh and cruel Yes. The sea that we found so kind was to become mad and merciless and, as Melville said, "with no power but its own to control it." It was to be schooner *Third Sea*'s struggle for survival. But there was more than typhoons and raging storms. There were pirates this time. You read and hear such things, that others have faced, but you never believe it will happen to you, until it's happening. Dying, I'm sure, is the same.

Third Sea was anchored in Hawaii when I made plans to return. It meant recruiting and training a new crew and taking on supplies that could carry us for eight months across the Pacific to the Philippines and then to Hong Kong and finally Singapore. It meant planning a course to take advantage of the currents and winds and to avoid the hurricane seasons in both hemispheres .

My plan was that we would sail to Tahiti in time to arrive for the Bastille Day Fete, bid our last goodbyes, and depart for the leeward islands—Moorea, Huahine, Raiatea and Bora Bora. Then to Tongareva in the northern Cook Islands, and northwest to the Samoas—Pago Pago and Apia. From there it was the long haul past the Ellice Islands and the Solomons to Rabaul in the Bismark Archipelago, and finally to the Philippines and Hong

Kong. We expected to reach Manila by Christmas—ten thousand miles in six months—not an impossible endeavor—and the last three thousand from Manila to Hong Kong and then to Singapore, another two months.

I considered recruiting Don Perkins to be my first mate again, but I heard he was back with his wife and I didn't want to tempt him away. Besides, I had someone else in mind, my nephew, Robert Stedman. When Robert was still in his teens, he had toured Asia with me, and he crewed aboard *Third Sea* on our first voyage from Samoa to Honolulu. He had adapted well to the sea and proved to be invaluable. I could use him now. He was a jack-of-all-trades and could fix most anything. He had that rare, innate ability to fathom the workings of the most complicated machinery and electrical gadgets. He understood radio waves and the meaning of things like decibels; navigation to him wasn't an orange but spherical triangles with graphical solutions; and electricity was more than alternating and direct currents—it was resistors, transistors and capacitors.

Robert had been a terror around the house when he was growing up. He took everything apart. One Christmas, his mother received one of those perpetual motion clocks mounted beneath a glass dome. They put the gift on the mantel above the fireplace for all to see. Curiosity got the best of Robert. When his mother and father returned home one evening, they noticed the clock was missing. They found it in Robert's room, hidden in a drawer. It was in a dozen pieces. Even the watch repairman couldn't get it back together. But the most trying time was when Robert's mother bought an upright piano so that Robert could "learn how to play." It was an old piano and Robert convinced his mother that he could refurbish the antique instrument. Unfortunately, how the

319

thing worked was more interesting than just sanding and varnishing so and he took it apart piece by piece, and couldn't get it back together again. When his mother called in a piano technician, the man simply looked at all the parts that were once a piano and said to forget it. But, for sure, it was all part of the learning process. Fortunately, he was well advanced when he joined the crew, although when he appeared with a screwdriver in his hand, I had sudden flashbacks.

"You sure you want to take Robert?" my mother asked the first time I took him to sea. I was hard on Robert that voyage. I didn't want to show favoritism with a crew that had been with me for so long. Robert took it all and responded without a grudge, but I felt sorry for him when he returned home. He had a great story to tell, about sailing the South Pacific before the mast, trading with natives for pearls, dancing with long-hair island girls on a coral beach, fighting storms, rowing through a surf to bring needed supplies to the schooner, and so many more things that teenage boys dream about but never do. He did all these things, and the sad part was no one cared. His peers were more anxious to tell him about the new sets of tires they got "at a good price" for their sports cars and the wonderful time they had at a local disco. "You should have been there!"

Robert started college but dropped out after a couple years. He planned to return to his studies, but instead ended up with a job, an apartment, a live-in girlfriend and credit cards. He found himself getting further and further into debt, and he was bored.

Our family was against Robert joining me the second time. "He has to face his responsibilities, not go running off to the South Seas." I wonder if someone had given the same advice to Herman Melville, Robert Louis

Stevenson and Jack London? If they had, and these men had heeded their advice, today we wouldn't have *Moby Dick, Treasure Island* and *The Cruise of the Snark.* Nevertheless I too wondered if I might be doing the right thing. Working against Robert was his age. He was barely twenty-one, the drinking age in California, and now I was giving him the responsibility of serving as first mate aboard a hard-driven schooner, a responsibility that was not only for the safety of the boat but also for the well-being and lives of everyone aboard. In his favor was his experience. He was the the only crew who had sailed aboard *Third Sea* before. But more important than anything else, I could put trust in him. I was sure he wouldn't bail out when the going got tough.

No sooner had I sent Robert the cable from Honolulu than he responded. "I'll be there as soon as I can get ready," he replied. He gave up the lease on his apartment, quit his job, sold everything he owned and found an excuse for his girl friend. Two weeks later he was covered with muck, scraping barnacles from the bottom of *Third Sea* at the boat yard in Keehi Lagoon. He may have regretted his move but he never mentioned it.

The new crew began to arrive. From Washington came Ken Sippel, an old friend whom I knew when I was living there. Ken had somewhat the same dream as I had, to one day sail the South Seas. Instead he went into law and was nearing retirement after twenty years' service with the Department of Land Management. He had traveled with his wife to Bangkok a few years before to make the maiden voyage aboard *Third Sea* to Singapore but we were running behind schedule. He did present *Third Sea* with a heavy brass ship's bell that the watch ceremoniously rang every two hours at sea. Ken had eagerly waited, until now. He would sail with us to Tahiti.

Another crew member was Eric Rimby, an enthusiastic young man from Florida. Eric arrived in Hawaii with two mates who were looking for passage aboard a sailing boat to to Tahiti. During a shakedown cruise in the rough Molokai Channel, Eric's mates changed their mind and backed out. But not Eric. His had the type of determination that would later see us through some trying and difficult hardships.

A third member was Matt McCoy from Bakersfield, California. Others joined and dropped out at various ports along the way. Some came for short passages only. They had jobs back home to return to, college to finish or families waiting. And there were the few who found sailing the bounding main not exactly what they had envisioned.

With four tons of fuel, water and tinned and dried goods stored aboard, we left Hawaii on our stern and pointed south on a beam wind to Bora Bora, 150 miles to the west of Tahiti. It was a happy moment for everyone aboard. In a grand and proud gesture, I handed the helm to Robert as we were leaving Ala Wai Yacht Harbor. "First Mate," I said to him, "take her to sea, and back to Asia."

It's nearly three thousand miles, from Hawaii to Tahiti. Usually to break the passage, I make island stops en route—Christmas Island discovered by Captain Cook; Fanning, inhabited by Ellice Islanders; and Caroline, an uninhabited atoll.

But now time prohibited us from lingering at any one place for too long. Currents and winds in the western Pacific could change on us. With Tahiti an exception we would remain no more than three or four days at any stop.

Then twenty-five days out of Hawaii we sighted the jagged mountain peaks of Bora Bora. That night with a full moon lighting our way we entered the narrow pass through the reef and dropped anchor with the darking our background. Dawn brought the loveliest sight that could befall any sailor. For most of the crew this was their first tropical landfall, and for certain one that could never be equalled.

That morning we hiked up a high promontory and located a World War II gun emplacement with a five-inch brass canon. We climbed out over the long barrel and looked down at the schooner. So clear was the lagoon the schooner seemed to be floating in mid air.

We sailed from Bora Bora and three days later brought up the peaks of Moorea. She appeared more like a mirage, a never-never land. Was she more beautiful than Bora Bora? Visitors will forever argue that point. No one will ever settle it.

Beyond Moorea loomed the undulating hills of Tahiti, her tallest mountain peaks bathed in clouds. We sailed into Papeete Harbor and tied up stern-to along the quay. Immediately friends began to arrive. The fete was about to begin.

Third Sea, with all her flags flying, anchored in Papeete Harbor during the Tahitian Fete, while outriggers prepare for the start of the race.

We were greeted by happy Tahitians. They came and gathered under the awning on the aft deck. They came with demijohns of red wine and gigantic meals they had prepared ashore, and with bundles of fresh flowers for making leis and guitars for background music. Sometimes the music never stopped.

From Singapore came my old friend, Dr. Goh Poh Seng. Author of half a dozen novels and a wonderful poet, he held several poetry readings in the main saloon of *Third Sea*. Yachtsmen came from all their boats, and with Poh Seng sitting on a stool, the glow of candle lights reflecting on his face, he read from his own works. I never would have thought that poetry reading on Tahiti would have the effect that it did. Poh Seng was a success and added a new dimention to *Third Sea*. When Poh Seng returned to Singapore, he sent us a poem he wrote—"Song of the *Third Sea*." It was later publsihed in his book of poems, *Bird with One Wing*.

Left, a lovely long-hair Tahitian dancer prepares for the competitions at the National Day Fete. Right, a dancer during the competitions.

The frenzy of the fete builds with each passing day. What excitement! The dancing competitions are the most dramatic. A team may have fifty or sixty dancers and a dozen drummers. Teams compete for six days, and on the seventh the best dancers are chosen.

Competitions last for seven nights, and in keeping with customs of old, dance teams present themselves before Queen Pomare, the last reigning queen of Tahiti, and the French Lord Admiral, the governor of French Polynesia. The role of Queen Pomare, who died in 1877, is reenacted, always, by a lovely Tahitian woman. She is seated in a fanback rattan chair at the edge of the stage, and seated next to her, in white naval uniform, is the Lord Admiral. The greatest honor I could have had was to be asked to play the part of the Lord Admiral for the fete. For seven nights I sat with the beautiful queen, in our rattan chairs, while the dancers and drummers made their presentations to us. Who could ask for a better honor, or a better seat?

From Captain of *Third Sea* to Lord Admiral. With a seat beside Queen Pomare, Stephens played the part during the National Day Fete.

Homer Morgan's dance team won the competitions that year, and they celebrated their victory aboard *Third Sea*. Wine flowed and the music and drums continued all night. When the last visitor stepped ashore we untied the mooring lines and pulled up the anchor and set sail. No ship had a more glorious departure!

Before leaving we signed on new crew. Among them was an Englishman and a young German, John and Tony. At Moorea and Huahine we anchored for the night and then sailed through the narrow pass between Raiatea and Tahaa to reach Bora Bora. The pass was exciting. A lookout in the rigging called instructions to the helmsman. We glided past coral heads and reefs, so close we could have touched them with a boat hook.

We cleared French Polynesia from Bora Bora and with a following wind and a current in our favour, sailed direct for Tongareva in the northern Cook Islands. We sailed not only forward over leagues of sea but backward through passages of time. Again, so striking was our approach to this lovely, forgotten coral atoll, so powerful, that some of the crew wept. Imagine, seeing the speck of island at the first light of dawn, and as we close the distance, the island takes shape and form. Palms line the shore, swaying gently, and white sand beaches glitter in the morning sun. We followed the coast, all so familiar to us, searching for the opening in the reef, and when we found it, we cautiously edged our way into the lagoon. The white coral church appeared, and further along the lagoon was the village nestled among tall palms .

Then the islanders saw us. They recognized the schooner. A launch set out with half the village aboard, threatening to swamp the vessel. They came alongside, shouting and waving, and then they all tried to scamper aboard *Third Sea*. More outriggers arrived. Young boys swam out from the shore. Papa Beer, my old friend, a barrel-chested pearl diver, gave me a bear hug that almost broke my ribs. He recognized Robert and grabbed him. We were back! We had a feast that night that topped all feasts. Food baked in an earth oven included chunks of *kape* wrapped in banana leaf and *lu ika*, fish drenched with coconut milk and sealed into a taro leaf. All this was served on raw banana leaf with an assortment of mullet, kape, papaya and breadfruit. We were also served chicken, bananas, and *lu pulu*, a boiled confection of sweetened taro greens. Young pig, roasted on a spit, was the prime delicacy.

I wanted to trade for pearls, but an Australian buyer by the name of Peter was on the island. Papa Beer told me about him. He arrived on the island with a suitcase filled with money and bought up most of the pearls. The islanders were no longer interested in trading with me for an undershirt or a pair of shorts. I met Peter in the village and he invited me to his house. I was anxious to get to know him. I said I'd come visit him the next day.

The hut where he lived was away from the village along the windward shore. He was sitting on the verandah when I arrived. He now wore a large straw hat, and I must say, he even looked the part of a pearl trader. On a table in front of him was a small weighing scale. He explained how he paid the islanders a fair share by the carat weight for their pearls. He had arrived with a quarter of a million dollars in small bills, most of which had been paid out by then. He pointed to a shoe box on the table. It was half filled with pearls. "More than eight thousand of them little babies," he said proudly. "Bought up nearly every pearl on the island."

For certain, the contented islanders would no longer be interested in trading with me. They had money and were waiting for the trading boat to arrive any day.

Peter, the buyer, hadn't seen a white man in months. It was obvious he was a shrewd trader, and I had the feeling the islanders weren't too fond of him. He did have an arrogance about him that set him apart from the natives.

He was pleased to have our comany, and he admitted he hadn't had a drink in months. When he heard we had rum aboard, he suggested we come for dinner and have a party in his hut that night. We accepted. I brought a couple bottles of rum from our ship's stores.

Peter, an Australian pearl trader *Third Sea*'s crew met on Tongareva Island, carefully weighs pearls which he bought from the islanders.

We all got a bit tipsy after dinner, but Peter got wildly drunk, singing and shouting, and falling off his chair. He had one more week to go on the island and he was as happy as any man could be. A ship was coming to pick him up and take him back to Sydney. "One more week," he shouted. "One more week and I'll be away from this bloody place and these bloody people. Let's have another drink." He reached for the bottle, but while leaning forward he knocked the shoe box off the table. Pearls rolled under the table and chairs and into the cracks in the floor. I expected Peter to go into a rage, but instead be began laughing. "Well look at that," he shouted and laughed louder. "Never mind. They're not going any place. I'll pick them up in the morning. How about another drink." He was totally drunk now.

It was hard to believe. Perhaps two million dollars worth of pearls were scattered around the room and under the house. I looked at Peter, swilling down his drink, and I realized at that moment the wild and rambunctious days of the Pacific are still with us.

The next morning we were having coffee under the awning on the aft deck, hashing over the details of the night before, when we heard shouting from the shore. A young boy who I recognized as having been at Peter's the night before, was motioning to me. He seemed very excited. I quickly rowed ashore.

"Hurry, hurry," he shouted when I stepped from the dinghy. "Something terrible has happened," he kept saying over and over as I followed him down the beach. I couldn't imagine what could be more terrible that hadn't already happened. Had someone come during the night and taken the pearls?

Peter was draped in a sarong and sweating profusely when I reached his hut. I could see a look of terror on his face. Standing at a safe distance behind him were dozens of natives.

"Pay us, pay us," I could heard one of them shouting. Pay them for what? Hadn't Peter already paid them?

"No," he shouted when I asked him. "No, not for the pearls. I told you I already paid them. Now they want to be paid for their chickens. Twenty Australian dollars each chicken."

"What are you talking about?" I asked. Had he gone rock crazy?

"The chickens," he said. "The checkens came this morning and ate all the pearls that fell through the cracks."

For the next few days we ate well aboard *Third Sea*. We dined on baked chicken, fried chicken, barbecued chicken, chicken a la king, chicken fricassee and chicken cooked ways you've never heard of. Peter ran out of money buying up chickens and had to re-sell some of his pearls. I must say the natives were honest about it. They could have kept the chickens.

The day of our departure came. Trader Peter was due to leave a few days later. Papa Beer and family came aboard, and with their outrigger in tow, to guide us through the pass. Our ship's log sums up our mood. "Robert has the helm. Papa Beer on the bow pointing out the direction. We enter the pass. The tide coming in. White water churning everywhere. We crashed through and found ourselves in calm water in the lee of the island. Cut the engine and drifted. Bid our good-byes to Papa Beer and his family. Both Papa Beer and I broke down in tears. They placed flower leis around our necks and then climbed into their outrigger which we were towing. We hoisted the main jib. It filled and pulled us away from the island. We then tossed our leis into the sea, the custom in these islands. As the flowers floated upon the blue swells, Papa Beer and his wife picked them up, kissed them and threw them back into the sea. We hoisted more sail and turned southeast towards Pago Pago. I leaned against the rail until their little canoe blended into the island and the island into the horizon. The boat and Tongareva were gone, much like a dream goes, and I wondered if I did dream it all."

I never saw Peter the pearl trader again.

Papa Beer had prepared a meal for us, wrapped neatly in banana leaves. We ravishly opened the packets but never touched a bit. It was baked chicken.

In tropical downpour we anchored in Pago Pago, which is nothing unusual. It rains all the time there. We intended to resupply here. Three days at most. But there was no cooking gas on the entire island. We had to wait eighteen days for a ship to come in from Honolulu. The delay was to cost us dearly.

From Pago Pago we made an overnight passage to Apia, Western Samoa. We visited with Aggie Grey again and climbed to Robert Louis Stevenson's grave. In Apia a few crew dropped out. We were now down to six, shorthanded but still enough to handle the schooner safely.

Now came the long sail, from Apia to Rabaul in Papua New Guinea. The passage took thirty-three days.

It takes a long passage to feel you've come to grips with the sea. You forget the outside world. Nothing matters except what is happening around you and your ship. You stand your watch, you cook or help with the cooking, you eat, you read. You might go for a swim over the side or change the lures on the fishing lines. You respond to the call "porpoise" or "whale," and you might go up on the bowsprit and sit. Or maybe even climb the rigging to get away. You become relaxed and a bit lazy. You don't want things to change. You want to finish that book, and begin another. You have five hundred more to choose from in the ship's library. Maybe you might decide to bake bread, or write a poem. But reading is the most desirable.

We crossed through the doldrums, where there might be thunder and lightning storms, or else no wind at all. At the equator, with the sun overhead, the heat became unbearable, burdensome, like a weight. The sky was lacquered. The horizon floated. For exercise, when we were becalmed, I lowered the longboat and had the crew take turns rowing, with the schooner in tow. Or if fish came in close we speared them, until the sharks caught the scent of blood. Then it was back to reading. In the afternoon we had a concert hour on stereo, maybe Tchaikovsky, and after that an hour of the helmsman's choice, most likely the Beatles' "Sergeant Pepper." In the evening, after sunset, we listened to the "Mystery Theater." The manager of the Bora Bora Yacht Club gave us several dozen taped radio programs, all classic dating back twenty or thirty years.

Once we were out of the doldrums, the schooner sailed herself. No tending sails, not even touching the helm. The wind carried us across the northern Ellice Islands, a few miles south of Naumea. We looked up the island in the Sailing Directions: Population 1,200. Micronesians. No vehicles, no electric power, no port facilities. Not even a doctor. A trading boat comes once every six months, but maybe as seldom as once a year. Why not visit them! What an experience!

We altered course. Before noon we were running north along the lee shore, a half mile from the reef. The main village came in view. Lovely. Very South Seas. Set back from the beach among palms. A massive stone church with a bell tower. It looked Spanish. Houses constructed from thatch, saddle-back roofs with a high pitch at both ends. We sailed closer.

Nothing happened. We saw not a soul. Still closer. No one. We could have sworn the village was abandoned but smoke rose from several chimneys. Suddenly an outrigger came from around the island. We waved but the two people aboard ignored us, almost like they didn't see us. Soon we were past the village. We tacked and made another pass, and now the outrigger had disappeared. What was it? Didn't they see us? It was all so strange, like we are in a time machine. We left the doldrums and sailed into another era. Disillusioned, we hoisted all sails and turned toward Rabaul, another 1,500 miles distant. For the first time I wished we had a radio aboard. I had a navigational set for receiving time ticks and weather but none for broadcasts. We seriously wondered if something might not have happened in the world. An atomic blitz! Were we all that was left?

Things do begin to work on your mind at sea, and this was only a forerunner of what was to come.

The difference between the eastern Pacific and the western Pacific is like night and day. We found ourselves sailing from one world into another.

Tahiti and the other islands of French Polynesia are in the eastern Pacific, and they lie outside the hurricane belt. Even gale-force storms are rare. The islands here are lovely, and free from most tropical diseases. And the Polynesians are the most fun loving and generous people in the South Seas.

The western Pacific can be the complete opposite. Hurricanes, or typhoons, rage uncontrolled for half the year below the equator, and above the equator the other half. They originate mostly in the Caroline Islands above the equator.

Navigators find the western islands a nightmare. Many reefs are uncharted. Ships are compelled to stay in shipping lanes. Islands appear and disappear overnight. I asked natives about islands we could see but couldn't locate on the charts. Their answer: They rose up from the sea.

The reason is no secret. The western Pacific is in the most active volcanic region on this planet. Islands of the Pacific are themselves tops of volcanoes sticking up out of the water. Rabaul, where we were heading, suffers two or three earth tremors a week. When I was anchored there before we could actually feel shock waves through the water. From one undersea eruption our schooner became engulfed by a sea of floating stones—pumice stones. We came out of it without a fleck of paint on the hull.

Diseases are another drawback. Malaria. Yaws. Ugly skin ulcers. Most everyone has some type of intestinal parasite. You must be careful with the water you drink and the food you eat.

The Melanesians, called Kanakas, are not always friendly. Some groups live in the Stone Age, and you hear tales about cannibalism. The Sailing Directions warns sailors to steer clear of their shores. At one island I visited in the New Hebrides on a previous voyage, I asked about a missionary who presumably lived there. "Him go," I was told. When I asked where he had gone, the headman patted his stomach and replied, "Him belly full up." If I understand my pidgin correctly, the poor devil was eaten by his hosts.

But still, there's something exhilarating about sailing among these strange islands. After leaving Samoa we sailed schooner *Third Sea* along the northern Solomons. One by one islands slipped by—Santa Isabel, Choiseul, Bougainville, Buka. How we wanted to stop but we were far behind schedule, and unless we kept moving we would lose our wind and current before reaching the Philippines.

Nevertheless, I spent hours scanning the coasts with

my binoculars. What forlorn islands they are. Heavy jungles. No roads or trails. No towns, not even a village. Man has not yet marred the pristine beauty of this primeval world. But you know savages live somewhere in those hills. You wonder about being shipwrecked. Could one survive? I found myself constantly checking the charts.

But there are things you can't check, things that aren't in the book. We discovered this when we entered St. George's Channel for the final run to Rabaul. It was a calm night with little wind. Shortly after midnight the watch called me on deck. I expected a squall but it was nothing like that. The night was totally black, but on the horizon we could see a dark, flat object hanging over the water. What was it? I had never seen anything like it before. Then we noticed the black "thing" was moving slowly towards us. Fearing another encounter with a floating pumice island we motored away as fast as we could. By dawn the "thing" was gone. Then came another fright.

We were ghosting along under light sail when dead ahead a bank of white fog rose up from the sea. Then it spread out in all directions, and now the sea began to bubble. It was like being in a kettle. Fish floated to the surface. We were over an undersea eruption. But which way do we run? We couldn't start our engine for it was cooled by sea water. It would boil over. All we could do was wait, and hope another eruption didn't put *Third Sea* on a mountain top like Noah's Ark. We were more fortunate however. The current carried us away and that evening we sailed into Rabaul.

The crew setting the main jib and the flying jib from the bowsprit.

Chapter 21

TYPHOONS, PIRATES AND STARVATION

It was great being back in Rabaul again, visiting with Buka and his family and other old friends, but it was very discouraging when it came time to buy supplies. Prices were astronomic. They had skyrocketed. We had to cut short our rations and the amount of fuel we could take on. We estimated three weeks to the Philippines. We bought food for five. We took aboard one hundred gallons of diesel.

We decided to stop at Hermit Island to stock with fresh meat. Before I had hunted wild cattle and pig on Hermit, and we were able to collect bananas and tropical fruit, oranges included. A German planter once owned the island and had turned it into a tropical paradise. With New Guinea's independence the island reverted to Melanesian ownership. Nine Kanakas lived there the last time *Third Sea* sailed through. We had spent two weeks on Hermit and I came to know Joseph, the headman. When he became ill, we carried him to a hospital at Manus 350 miles away. I was sure he'd let us hunt again and stock up with fresh food.

The five-hundred-mile voyage took a slow thirteen days. We had current with us but little wind. I dared not use up our precious diesel. We arrived to find Joseph was on another island, and to our horror, all the cattle and pigs had been slaughtered. Not only that, but the fruit trees and many coconut palms had been cut down. One lone Kanaka caretaker who was living on the island with his wife told us what had happened. A fleet of Korean fishing boats stopped at the island and killed all but a few of the animals. They found it easier to cut down the fruit trees and palms rather than attempt to scale them to collect the fruit and nuts. Gone too were the banana stocks. We could hardly ask the caretaker to let us take any of the remaining cattle. With little food, we found ourselves in a desperate situation. The caretaker mentioned there were deer on a neighboring island. A couple hundred pounds of venison would add to the ship's table. Robert and I took a rifle and set off across the lagoon in the dory to Luff Island. The caretaker offered to guide us. We had to cut through a low marsh land before we could reach higher ground. Waste deep in the swamp, with Robert carrying the rifle high above his head, we stopped short. We heard a thrashing in the swamp ahead.

"What's that?" I sang out.

The caretaker turned and looked at Robert and me. "Mi ting hem bigfala fis."

I knew enough Pidgin English to understand what he was talking about. If I was correct, the big fish he was referring to was salt water crocodiles, noted to dwell in the rivers of New Guinea and the off shore islands. We didn't wait around to find out. What took us a half hour to wade through on our way in to the hunting grounds took us less than five minutes on our way back to the dory.

No fresh meat, no fruit. We finally settled on a hundred coconuts.

Our most dreaded fear became reality when we left Hermit. Outside the pass a black cloud moved in. Winds reached 35 knots. We sailed hard all that afternoon and night, and when dawn came we were still in sight of Hermit. We hadn't gone a dozen miles. The current was against us. It had changed from one direction to the other in the few days we were anchored at Hermit. To reach the

Philippines we would have to fight for every mile. However, by heading north we could cross the equator at 8° North and thus pick up the Equatorial Current which would be in our favor. At that latitude we would also have the northeast trades. There was one problem. It was the height of typhoon season at those latitudes. To turn back and wait out the season in Rabaul, we would need six months. The other choice was to gamble that we wouldn't encounter a typhoon. I talked it over with the crew. We decided to go for it. We cut rations to one meal a day and turned north.

The sea changed, its very texture. It was ominous. The water lost its blue tint and became dismal gray. We saw no whales, no porpoise and few birds. Nor did we have strikes on our lines. When we needed fish most we never caught them. And we suffered from the lack of a proper diet. We had little energy and it took twice as long to get sails up and down. Our reflexes became slower.

At 6° North latitude our world fell apart. The barometer was falling. No words can strike more fear into a sailor—the barometer is falling! I tuned in WWV. The weather report confirmed it. They called it Typhoon Kit; it was coming down on us.

We quickly double-lashed everything on deck, closed the seacocks and put storm windows in place. We strung safety lines along the deck. Swells arrived before wind. They were mammoth and by nightfall reached thirty feet. Then the wind came. The first gust hit at fifty knots. It knocked the schooner sideways bringing the crew on deck. They thought we had gone over. I had to shout at the top of my voice to be heard, and when I faced the wind I could hardly breathe.

I knew from experience we had to keep to the storm's southwest quarter. If not we might get thrown into the center and never get out. It meant we had to keep sailing. We lost sails, one after the other, and kept patching torn ones. Eventually every sail went. We ran the engine until we were down to our last few gallons.

We plotted the storm's center. We could expect the full fury the next afternoon, at 170 knots. The wind speed was now incalculable, the wave height indeterminable. At the helm I felt like a rider on an untamed steed. And all the time we knew it would only grow worse.

And then Typhoon Kit veered. The morning weather report stated the typhoon was heading northwest. We were spared from its direct onslaught. A sun fix the next day put us ninety miles off course. With patched sails it took us a week to make 150 miles west. Christmas Day came and we had but a few cans of food left. No rice. No cooking gas. And we had three hundred miles to go to reach the Philippines. But luck was with us.

We noticed fish swimming in the shade beneath the schooner. Eric took a mask and spear gun and went over the side. I was nervous. On the way to Hermit Tony was in the water when a giant whale shark made an appearance. Tony fended to hold him off and was pulled under the water. Fortunately whale sharks are harmless, so the book says.

But Eric was cautious, and being a good diver he speared two mahi mahi. We feasted well on raw fish Japanese style. Other hunks we wrapped in tin foil and cooked on the engine manifold. The rest we threw into the salt barrel.

We were down to our last two tins of beans when we sighted the coast of Mindanao in the Philippines. We dropped anchor behind the protection of a reef at Maribojoc, a small fishing village on the coast. I sent Eric and Tony ashore with a bag of clothing to trade for food.

I watched them with my binoculars. No one came to greet them. The very same thing happened at Nanumea in the Ellice Islands. The villagers fled. Then a child appeared. There seemed to be some conversation, and suddenly the beach filled with people. Eric and Tony became lost in the crowd. A half hour later they rowed back, followed by outriggers filled with smiling Filipinos.

When *Third Sea* first appeared on the horizon, upon seeing our red sails and old-fashion rigging, the villagers thought we were Indonesian pirates. Some even went so far as to believe we might be the Portuguese returning, in the wake of Magellan. When Tony spoke English to them, they lost their skepticism. That night we had our first full meal in many weeks.

Maribojoc is a frightfully poor Christian village on a predominantly Muslim island. They traded rice and fish for clothing but fuel was a problem. We could only get twenty gallons, barely enough to take us forty miles up the coast to a larger port—Tandag.

Tandag was a miserable choice. The anchorage was dreadful. We had to drop anchor in twenty fathoms, a half mile from town. We were exposed to the open sea, and could not see the town for a small island blocked our view. We sent Eric ashore in the dinghy for fuel and food. He returned with news that the pass was treacherous. He almost swamped and only with the help of a fisherman in his outrigger did he save the dinghy. Garcia, the fisherman, offered to transport our fuel and supplies aboard his outrigger.

The next morning we attempted to reset our anchor but when we threw the gears in reverse they jammed. Something snapped. We tried forward but nothing happened. Horrors. Unless we had an engine we couldn't possibly fight the current with sails alone to make the pass north of Tandag. To run south meant sailing two thousand miles around Mindanao to reach Manila. Baslin Strait at Zamboanga was sure trouble. We heard that the Sulu pirates were acting up again. We simply had to make repairs. Robert set to work.

With the raging sea tossing and pitching, and the bow rising and dropping with each swell, Robert dismantled the engine. He worked all that day and into the night with only candles for light. He found the trouble. Flanges on a drum had sheared off and had to be welded back on. The next morning we wrapped the drum in plastic and Garcia took us ashore in his outrigger.

Only an experienced navigator could have gotten us safely through the pass. There was no room for error. We shot through unscathed, only to see a mob waiting on shore. Half the town was there. We then noticed three Red Cross women and a press cameraman. They greeted us with a flash of strobes. We had no idea but we were the object of a massive air-sea search that had lasted a month. It was called off a few days before. We were feared lost at sea. The U.S. Embassy in Manila wanted a full report. The Red Cross wanted to give us hot coffee. We wanted to get our welding done before a storm came. We had little time. The sky looked menacing.

The welding and buying parts took the entire day. Robert worked most of the night putting the engine together. He fell asleep exhausted. At dawn black clouds warned us a storm was coming. Swells were more than ten feet and with each lurch of the bow the anchor chain threatened to break. We had to get away, but we needed fuel and supplies first. Matt, John and I rowed the dinghy ashore to pick up the supplies.

The storm hit an hour later. The sea was a mass of churning foam. We couldn't see the schooner. I had to get back out but could never make it in our dingy. Garcia offered to take me in his outrigger. Matt and John looked at the outrigger and then at me. I knew they had something planned. They announced they were dropping out. We had three crew left aboard the schooner, and I made the fourth. We needed every hand we could get to fight the storm, but Matt and John had enough. I didn't have time to argue nor plead with them. Leaving the dingy and all the supplies behind, Garcia and I set out in his frail outrigger, and when we rounded the island my heart leapt. *Third Sea* was still riding her anchor, but the sea was so violent we could only get within twenty feet of the schooner. I had to jump into the sea and let the crew pull me aboard with a rising swell. We waved goodbye to Garcia.

I conferred with the others. We had to take *Third Sea* out to sea even if it meant cutting the anchor loose and tacking back and forth without engine power to clear the pass. Robert wasn't about to quit, nor were Eric and Tony.

The agony began, getting the anchor up. Robert started the engine and put her in gear. To our great relief she worked. He motored into the wind, easing the pressure on the chain. But suddenly in one mighty surge the bow dropped and rose, shattering the windlass. Shackles and pins went flying. A single safety line held the anchor chain. Eric and Tony rigged a block and tackle system and began hauling in. The sea became more violent, breaking over the bow. Then we began to lose engine power. Dirty fuel! Robert labored in the engine room. He got the engine started again by bypassing the filters.

When the anchor lifted from the bottom we began drifting, toward the small island. With Robert still below deck we hoisted sails. We hardly had them up when smoke shot up from the engine room. Robert stumbled up the ladder choking. He extinguished a fire that began when an over-heated exhaust set fire to the woodwork. I had to send him below again for sail power was insufficient to keep us from smashing on the rocks.

Eric and Tony went back to pulling up the anchor.

After seven hours of continuous labour we got the anchor aboard, and just in time. The storm engulfed us and with sails set and engine running full power we cleared the edge of the island with only a few feet to spare.

The storm raged wildly but it didn't matter. We gave a shout of victory. We were safe! We had taken on little food and only a few gallons of diesel, our dinghy was ashore and two crew members deserted us but we were happy. We had succeeded. We hove to for the night and let it blow.

By morning we were thirty miles down the coast. We could never make it north now. Our only hope was to head south around Mindanao to Zamboanga and worry about pirates when we got there. We had food for four days. We turned south and by the next morning held a record. We covered 186 miles in twenty-four hours. We rounded the cape and turned west towards Zamboanga. Then the wind stopped. Completely. We were like Coleridge's "painted ship upon a painted ocean." Three days later, with still no wind, our food ran out. To make matters worse, we had drifted into Indonesian waters.

Any kind of death is horrible; it's just that some are more noble than others. Death in a bullring would be gallant, or fighting a duel, or anything except a slow death by starving. And we were starving. I knew it. There was no one to help us. At Tandag when they didn't see the schooner at anchor after the storm, would they not think we had perished! No one would look for us. And all the attempts we made to get help were unsuccessful. We sent up flares to attract passing ships. None would stop, or even acknowledge seeing us. We tried to flag down fishing boats but when they saw us waving they headed in the opposite direction. We looked like a pirate vessel. Ships at sea were afraid of us. We spelled trouble.

We began suffering from severe headaches. It was an effort to get up. Dreams were nightmares. We stopped reading. Talking. The sun parched our skin the color of mahogany and cracked our lips. We continued to drift south, and in a daze one afternoon we found the schooner was out of control. We were spinning like a top in a giant whirlpool. Were we in another Bermuda Triangle? Then as suddenly as it began it was over.

The next morning a motorized fishing outrigger with two Moslems aboard came into view. We signalled to them and they made a circle. They stood their distance. If I could get a note to them. They would return to their village. Someone there, perhaps a teacher, might understand English. It was worth a try.

I wrote a note: PLEASE HELP US. WE ARE DESPERATE. OUT OF FOOD. NEED DIESEL. PLEASE PLEASE HELP. Eric slipped over the side and swam the note over to the outrigger.

We watched them head south, towards a faint outline of an island on the horizon. We were drifting in that direction. We studied the chart. The island was Maroe. It was steep-to without an anchorage. It was large enough to have a village.

Before dark two fast outriggers appeared from the direction of the island. We recognized one when it came closer; it was the outrigger we gave the note to. They were coming to help us. We shouted with delight. We were saved. The boats came closer. It was now dusk and Robert went below for a search light. Two shots rang out.

The fishermen were armed. They were shooting at us! Robert shone the light. Men stood in the outriggers brandishing rifles.

Our riffles were locked up below deck. But it didn't matter. If we used them we were doomed. More outriggers with armed men would come from the island. We had no escape. But what did they want? Moments later we found out. A voice boomed out of the dark. "Follow me," it shouted in a harsh voice. "Follow me, NOW," it called again.

There was no way we would follow them. The island meant destruction, ending up on the reef, which is exactly what they wanted. It was now obvious. We were their catch, their prize. But we were no good to them unless we ran the schooner on to the reef.

We tried talking to them. "Tomorrow, when it's light," I shouted. "Tomorrow we will come." The answer came in another burst of shots. We hit the deck and waited.

They were as confused as we were. We heard them conferring. Again they shouted, "Follow me." And again I yelled, "Tomorrow." They didn't fire this time.

The situation became worse. We were drifting directly for the island. The night was black. The island was a mere silhouette, but getting closer. We had two hours before the moon rose. Two hours to make a move. If we started our engine they would open fire again. And how long could we run with our limited fuel?

I put our passports and ship's papers in a plastic bag. We would remain aboard until we hit the reef and then abandon ship. I planned to open the seacocks the moment we hit so *Third Sea* would sink outside the reef: I wanted to make sure they got nothing.

The outriggers motored around us several times and then headed for the island. Apparently they went to announce their victory.

So imperceptible was the breeze at first, so lightly did it arrive that we were unaware it was there. Our first breath of air in days. Maybe! "The main jib," I whispered. We crawled along the scuppers to the foredeck, and in the black of night slowly raised the jib. She filled with air. The schooner began to move.

The breeze freshened slightly. The silhouette of the island slid by. We had another hour before the moon would give us away. We then heard engines. The outriggers were coming back. They returned to where they had left us, and now we could hear them circling in a wild melee, searching for us. With their engines running they wouldn't be able to hear our engine.

Reason told me that sooner or later they would figure out that the wind was carrying us in a southerly direction. I had a scheme that was wild and crazy. I gave the orders to start the engine. I took a sight for the southern end of the island and gave Robert the course to steer strait for the island. No one would suspect we were heading for their island. We threw a blanket over Robert at the helm so the binnacle light would not reveal our position. We raised more sails. We heard the outriggers pass and run south. We continued westward barely skimming the southern reef of the island. We could see lights on shore. We ran until the moon appeared and then cut the engine, to save our last few gallons of diesel. By dawn Maroe was only a speck on the distant horizon. The wind died and again we drifted.

Another Indonesian boat appeared over the horizon from the direction of the Celebese. It altered course to come up our stern. I watched through my binoculars. It looked like an overcrowded Afghani bus. Moslems sat on the cabin roof while heads protruded from all the cabin windows. They all wore head wrappings of some sort; two men at the bow were armed. The captain looked like Arafat.

This time I made up my mind. We wouldn't give in. At sea we had a chance. Robert loaded the rifles and passed them up to us on deck. The boat came up and one of their crew threw a hook on our stern. I held a shotgun cradled in one arm. The captain spoke some English. Who were we, and were we having trouble?

"No trouble," I said. "Just waiting for a wind."

He asked other questions, like what religion were we. I answered Christian. "You are lucky," he said. "Some of us are Christians." We said nothing, only looked at them down the ends of our rifles. How many did we have aboard? I said ten. He asked where everyone was. I said below, waiting. At last he smiled. "We will pray for wind for you," he said. I lifted the hook from our stern with my foot, keeping my eyes upon them, and they departed.

I don't know which god they prayed to but the wind came. It came fresh at ten knots. We hoisted sail and pointed *Third Sea* towards Zamboanga. She sailed as though she had a rendezvous to keep and nothing could stop her. Moreover, she sailed herself, like through a dream. She seemed to sense we were too weak to help.

Inside Philippine waters a fishing boat saw that we were in distress. I was asleep on deck when I became aware that two Filipino fishermen were aboard. One departed and came back with cooked rice, fish and coffee. They gave us cigarettes, a small bottle of rum and saw us on our way. We gave them some blankets. A week after our Indonesian experience we dropped anchor in the outer roads at Zamboanga.

I looked for the toughest Moslem Sulu sailor I could find on the waterfront and hired him. I put him in charge.

We were in safe hands and no one dared bother us. In two weeks we had recovered sufficiently to continue our voyage. I wired friends in Singapore and we now had money to buy the supplies we needed. We departed Zamboanga, sailing through the Palawan Pass and along northern Borneo to reach Singapore. The 1,400-mile passage took us twelve days. *Third Sea* arrived back from where she started seven years before. She was a bit worn, with bullet holes in her sides and with torn sails, but no matter, we had made it. The question now, what was next? Some drastic changes were in the wind.

After her ordeal, *Third Sea* gets a new coat of paint in Singapore.

Chapter 22

SEARCHING FOR THE RAINBOW

Now that *Third Sea* was back in Singapore, where would we sail next? Since launching the schooner ten years before, we had sailed nearly 150,000 miles. We had crisscrossed the Pacific several times, touched upon islands and atolls where few yachts, if any, had dropped anchor before, and explored many of the rivers and waterways of Asia. *Third Sea* needed a rest, and I needed a place where I could settle down and catch up on my writting assignments. But where?

Like many people who have the dream of living on a boat and finding peace and contentment, I was no different. But contrary to what most people think, sitting aboard a yacht is not the place to run a business, or to do any serious writing. When I built *Third Sea* I thought it would be the ideal place for such activity. Away from people, no telephones or TV, no salesmen knocking at my door. After I began sailing it didn't take long to realize that Joseph Conrad couldn't have written *Lord Jim* or *Typhoon* while aboard ship. In fact, he didn't write a single line while he was at sea. Nor did Jack London write *The Cruise of the Snark* sitting aboard. He wrote the book after the voyage was over and he got back to California. Those who have never lived aboard might have romantic notions about this. Dr. Gog Poh Seng, the Chinese poet who visited us in Tahiti, had this same idea when I first met him. He learned that I lived aboard a yacht and he expressed his desire to do the same. "What an ideal place to write," he lamented. He learned differently when he accepted my invitation and came to Tahiti while we were moored at the quay in Papeete. It was during the National

Day Fete when happy, fun-seeking Polynesians come from all the islands to compete in dancing, javelin throwing, singing, horse racing and just plain carousing. The Fete is not the place to find solitude. To do the writing that he planned, Poh Seng took a ferry to Moorea and spent a few days at the One Chicken Inn.

We shouldn't blame the Fete in Tahiti, nor any such celebration. It's more than that. We can call them distractions. Bear me out. We anchor in a lovely cove, far away from villages and other boats. How many times has it hapapened? I set up my typewriter in the main saloon, take a seat and attempt to concentrate upon a blank page. Suddenly a voice, one of the crew, rings out: "Look at that, over there! Look!" Another voice joins in, "Wow, look at it, unbelieveable." Of course, I have to rush on deck to see what it is. A mantaray is circling the schooner. We watch until he vanishes into the depths below. It's difficult now to return to the saloon. Maybe a quick, refreshing swim before I do, and while I'm in the water, why not take a spear gun and see what I can get for dinner. The writing can wait until later. That's the way it happens.

Then there's always the question of finding the perfect anchorage. What is the perfect island? Where is it? I remembered being anchored at Robinson's Cove on Moorea. It's a magnificent spot. Your anchor is out in deep water, and you warp the stern up to the shore and tie off to coconut palms. The lagoon is glass still, except for an occasional fish that breaks the surface. The water reflects the mountains that rise up sheer from the bay at the opposite shore, and their peaks are shrouded in clouds. A few people from other yachts are aboard. "We plan to sail to Asia," one yachtsman says. "Tell us about Asia." I tell them about sailing up the Chao Phraya River through Jospeh Conrad's world to Bangkok, about the golden temples all along the banks and sampans and long-tailed river boats scurrying back and forth, and then I tell them about anchoring off Phuket where you can watch your anchor settle to a sandy bottom five fathoms below. They hang on to every word, and they swear that's where they want to sail next. They can't wait.

Some months later *Third Sea* is anchored in Phuket on the Andama Sea, and yachtsmen from other boats anchored nearby come over and join me for drinks under the awning. "You've sailed to Tahiti?" someone asked. "What's it like?" I find myself telling them about Moorea, about the beauty of Robinson's Cove. They want to sail immediately for the South Seas. They can't wait.

We continue to search for the perect island, the one we might call paradise, for whatever reason we might have. It is possible to find that isle. Many islands, like Tahiti with its influx of tourists, have changed. Visitors come now and stay in first class hotels, shop in luxury stores with glass fronts and dine not on wild pig but filet mignon prepared by French chefs. But let's look beyond Tahiti. A short fifty miles away are untouched isles that visitors seldom see. And still further, a few hundred miles to the north are islands so remote they are uninhabited and no ship ever touches upon them.

The romance one finds in these islands comes in many shapes and forms, and wherever you look adventure is there, beyond the next reef, in every rumor you hear and have the courage to check out. When you knock around the Pacific long enough, you hear, for example, tales about shipwrecks, some ancient, some modern. Portuguese explorer La Perouse was lost somewhere in the Santa Cruz Islands four hundred years ago, a Korean fishing boat ran high upon reef a week ago. You go search for them. La Perouse is a gamble; the fishing boat is a sure thing. Or you might be intrigued by the war stories, like John F. Kennedy's *PT-109* that I mentioned. It's somewhere in the Solomons, run down by a Japanese destroyer. You dive in the area, and by God, you think you found it, and then government patrol boats run you out. You make an oath that one day you'll sail back and this time would will find it.

Or there are those wrecks you stumble upon quite by accident. A brass cannon from an old wreck protrudes from the sand on an uninhabited island in the Line Group between Tahiti and Hawaii. It's too heavy even to budge. Or you hear a rumor when you are in the Solomons that deep in the jungles on a mosquito-ridden island there's an old World War II airfield, overgrown and forgotten, and you decide to investigate. When you hack through the bush, you find a squadron of B-29 bombers waiting to take off. I swear, they still have fuel in their tanks.

Robert Stedman inspects a forgotten Japanese gun on New Britain Island. In the Solomons we found the remains of American bombers.

And there's other excitement, the wild cattle you hunt and turtles you spear to feed your crew, the sharks you battle to pull a tuna aboard, the whales as long as your little ship that come along side to look you over with a beady eye. And there's more, so much more.

Some yachtsmen do find their islands in the sun; other are forever looking. Robert Louis Stevenson chartered a schooner out of Hawaii and searched the Pacific from one end to the other before he found an "earthly paradise" where he settled down and penned *Treasure Island* and and a few other masterpieces. He found what he was looking for in Western Samoa. The Samoans called him Tusitala, teller of tales, and here he became much loved by the people. When he died they carried his body to the summit of Mt. Vaea overlooking Apia harbour and buried him in a crypt that bears the inscription, "Home is the sailor home from the sea, and the hunter, from the field."

James Brooke, the British poet, thought much the same about Samoa when he was there. "It's sheer beauty, so pure it is difficult to breathe," he wrote.

Writer James Michener had his own ideas about the perfect island. In his *Tales of the South Pacific* he wrote about an island paradise which he called Bali Ha'i. Well and good, except there is no map, nor any sailing chart of the South Seas that shows an island called Bali Ha'i. Was it only a creation by Michener? It was. He admitted the Bali Ha'i that he knew was a dirty little village high in the hills of New Guinea. He liked the sound of the name.

In later works Michener did describe what he believed were island paradises. He listed two—Moorea twelve miles from Tahiti, and Bora Bora some one hundred and fifty miles to the westward.

"Nothing is so majestic as the island of Moorea," he said. "To describe it is impossible. It's a monument to the prodigal beauty of nature."

But clearly his favorite was Bora Bora. "By most judges," he wrote, "it's considered to be the most beautiful in the world." He explains how he saw it for the first time from the air, about the fingers of land reaching out to sea, the ring of coral that forms the many lagoons, the white beaches, and the outer reef. "That was Bora Bora from aloft," he wrote. "When you stepped upon it, the dream expanded."

It's interesting to note that when MGM decided to make a musical from Michener's *Tales of the South Pacific* they did not go to Bora Bora, nor any magic islands in the South Pacific. They went to Southeast Asia. They chose the island of Tioman, a sparcely inhabited island thirty-five miles off the Malaysian east coast to shoot "South Pacific."

No doubt, Tioman is a strikingly beautiful island, with several coves and bays and lofty mountains poking up into the clouds. It captured my imagination the first time I had seen it, from aboard a costal steamer sailing from Bangkok to Singapore. It captured my imagination every time I sailed by aboard *Third Sea*.

The attractions of Tioman are more than its beauty. On the southern tip of the island is a small inlet with a concrete jetty, the only one on the island. Rising up to a lofty height directly behind the inlet are the famous twin peaks called Ass's Ears, a landmark for seaman for two thousand years. Probably what was the first guidebook to Malaysia was written by an Arab trader who noted that fresh water was available in the stream beneath the twin peaks.

For thousands of years the Chinese also made Tioman a port of call. Ming pottery has been found in caves in the hills, and one recent visitor showed me a gold chain of uncertain Chinese origin which he found in a stream bed near Gua Serau.

The islanders, who number about fifteen hundred, remember little of their dim past but they do recall with excitement when Hollwood's MGM was on location on Tioman. "Up that beach," an old man explained, "they built a whole new village for the movie." Then sadly he explained how they tore it down when the filming was completed. A minute later hc pointed to the hills. "And up there, near the trail to Juara, we helped them carry their cameras."

The trail the old man mentioned is still in use. It crosses the mountains, from one bay to another, and if you are not prepared, it can be difficult, especially if you get caught hiking it at night and can't find your way. The trail is no ordinary hiking path. It's a mountain climb, through some incredible primeval forests, so dense in places the sun's rays cannot penetrate through the foliage. There are tall waterfalls and streams to wade and mud

Tioman Island seen from the deck of *Third Sea*. The interior is thick and green, with a fresh water supply that made the island an important landmark and stopover for ancient seafarers sailing the China Seas.

banks to climb. The mountains teem with game: wild pigs, barking deer and creatures that flutter past in the dark shadows. Once, they said, there were tigers on the island but there are no signs of them today.

Tioman lies to the east of the Malay Peninsula; to the west of the Peninsula on the Andaman Sea is the jewel of all islands–Phuket. And like Tioman, it, too, has more to offer than its beauty alone. Phuket was once part of the Indian-Chinese trade route. Unearthings on the island have produced Greek and Roman earthware, golden Arabic coins, and Chinese pottery. And on an island some fifty kilometers to the east are some wall murals that are said to have been left by the Vikings. The name, as we might guess, is called Viking Island, or Ko Phi Phi.

These petrolyphs on the cave walls of Viking Island, are indeed, strange figures of what could be sketches of sailing boats used by the Norsemen a thousand years ago.

A human skull found on a lonely island. Ship wrecked sailor, or pirate?

Was it possible that the Vikings did reach Southeast Asia? If not, what other strange craft sailed the Andaman Seas around Phuket in prehistoric times?

Also high within the very same caves are bamboo scaffoldings which reach up some two hundred meters to the ceiling. The Thais have constructed flimsy platforms to enable them to gather the prized bird's nests which form the basic ingredients for the world famous Chinese Bird's Nest soup.

And so for *Third Sea* the quest continued. I could sail back to beautiful Tongareva where the natives dive into the lagoon and swim out to the schooner to greet us, even before we can drop anchor. They are certain to give us black pearls for gifts and serve us roasted pig while we dance with long-haired island beauties, to the beat of shark skin drums and wood blocks. We could sail to the Trobrian Islands where the natives there paddle out to the schooner and the women boldly ask if they can borrow the men in the crew for the night.

Or we could remain in Singapore.

After schooner *Third Sea* returned from the South Pacific to Singapore, the trauma we experienced on our return voyage had some far-reaching effects on all of us, both mentally and physically. Foremost, after being afloat with little food for seventy-two days, we couldn't seem to satisfy our hunger. No matter how much we ate, it was never enough. We thought about food, and we talked about food, from the moment we got up in the morning until we turned in at night. Even after a heavy meal, on our way back to the schooner, we planned our next meal. Tony was the worst. He weighted no more than 120 pounds but he was able to consume half his weight in food every day. A few days after we arrived, Tony signed aboard another yacht sailing via Suez to the Mediterranean. Lucky

Tony. He had free passage home to Italy, but before the ship departed the skipper sent Tony back to us. "I can't afford him," the man said. "He eats more than all the crew put together." Fortunately for Tony, we were able to find him passage aboard another vessel sailing the same direction.

Robert and I found our own solution to the problem. In Singapore where all the cultures mix, food is a specialty—Chinese, Malay, Indian, European. Hungarian and Russian as well as Italian and French. Even McDonalds. We found our liking in Serangoon Road in Little India, at the Apollo Banana Leaf Restaurant. Here we dined on banana leaves, just as the name implied, and we ate with our fingers. Hindu waiters in soiled aprons scooped rice from buckets and stacked it mountain high on banana leaves, and from huge caldrons they laddled out hot spicy curry with massive dippers. We couldn't resist the specialty at Apollo's—fish-head curry, with all the condiments. We could eat as much as we wanted. Seconds, thirds, fourths. Robert and I consumed gigantic proportions, night after night, and still we were never satisfied. The management was more than thrilled when we found another restaurant and took our appetites there.

With Eric the problem was much more serious. He refused to leave *Third Sea*, even to go ashore to the yacht club. We soon discovered the reason. He had gotten into the ship's liquor supply. Before leaving Zamboanga, we had stocked up on a couple dozen cases of rum. We had discovered, after cashing a money transfer, we could not exchange pesos back into dollars when leaving the country. We had no alternative but to spend our pesos. After purchasing supplies and fuel, we spent the remaining pesos on rum. And with the price for a bottle of rum less than a dollar, we found ourselves ferrying back and forth from shore to schooner with cases of rum.

One evening when we were back in Singapore, Robert and I went ashore and remained for two restful days with Goh Poh Seng and his family at his home. We returned to the schooner to find Eric was dead drunk and near to a coma. We managed to get him to a hospital and when he had sufficienlty recovered we flew him back to the States. A few months later tragic news reached us that Eric fell from the rigging of another vessel and died instantly. Robert and I still mourn his death. He was a great crew, and due to his efforts and daring we were able to get *Third Sea* through the pirate-infested waters of the Sulu Sea and back to Singapore.

I thought Robert might want to return home and continue with his college education but he elected to remain in Singapore. He was interested in photography and took it seriously. He worked for a while as an apprentice with another photographer in his studio. He gained experience shooting photographs for advertising agencies and doing designs for them. Eventually he set up his own graphic and design studio. Soon photographic assignments were taking him all over Asia and as far as Turkey and Africa. In a few years' time he had half a dozen people working for him. Singapore has become his home.

For me and *Third Sea*, we weren't quite ready yet to return to the South Pacific. It was time that I halted for a while and concentrated on my writing. I had a number of assignments. Mike Gorman, the editor-in-chief of the *Bangkok Post*, heard about our plight and contacted me. He asked that I write a Sunday feature piece about our experience with the pirates of the Sulu Sea. "I'll make it worth your while," he said. He kept his word, and paid the highest the *Post* had ever paid for a single article— 100,000 baht, or U.S.$4,000. The *Bangkok Post* renewed my contract to write a weekly column and I found myself with another book assignment from a publisher in Singapore.

In Singapore I found a great colonial apartment with twelve-foot high ceilings and revolving ceiling fans. I finished my book and had a few others dancing around in my head. I sent my articles to the *Bangkok Post* and commuted regularly to Bangkok. I bought my first Apple computer.

I found a good, secure anchorage for *Third Sea* at Ong's Marina in Sembawang in the still waters of the Johore Strait between Singapore and Malaysia where the mighty battleships HMS *Repulse* and HMS *Prince of Whales* once anchored, before the coming of the Japanese. I spent my weekends there aboard *Third Sea.*

Then came some changes I never expected. I hired an island girl to be my secretary, fell in love, and married her. Her name was Michelle.

Chapter 23

THIRD SEA GOES CHARTER

So, in Singapore, I found an apartment and moved ashore. Michelle, who was an inspiring writer, came to work for me, typing manuscripts and doing research, but ended up spending as much time helping aboard *Third Sea* as she did sitting behind a desk. We did weekend charter trips around Singapore and made short voyages to Tioman and other islands along the Malay coast. Michelle's three young sons, Tom, John and Paul, from ages six to nine, came to live with us in Singapore. The boys loved the schooner, which, almost overnight it seems, became a "family boat." The schooner was their second home and they made a number of passages with us. Before long they were climbing the rigging and making high dives from the masts. Mr. Peterson would have had some competition.

A year after we were married, another change came about; Michelle was hired as a staff writer by the *Bangkok Post* and she and I signed a contract with the newspaper to write the travel page for a their new Outlook section. It meant moving from Singapore and taking an apartment in the Thai capital. We found ourselves traveling all around Asia and then to Europe, America and Australia, gathering material for our weekly columns. The boys lived with us in Bangok for a while, traveling with us when we could take them, and enjoying *Third Sea* when she was in Phuket, but eventually we had to send them to America for their schooling. We bought a ranch in northern California, where they could live and study and where Michelle and I could establish another home. Michelle's

363

mother and father moved to Califonria to watch over things. It was a satisfactory arrangement.

As for *Third Sea,* I felt like a traitor. She had been more than a boat, and more than just a home to me. In the beginning she was a goal, a dream that kept me motivated. Later when we sailed, and got to know each other, she became an extension of myself, and my teacher. She taught me about people, that life is precious, and has to be handled with caution. I came to know her every whim. I talked to her, and she spoke to me, as boats do to their owners. She told me when I was needed on deck, and when I could go below. She was my provider and carried me to those places I longed to see, to where stories were waiting to be told. When checks from publishers were late, I didn't have to worry. She carried passengers and served as their hotel in port. She made money for us. She helped me raise three boys and gave them an education no school could provide. She was my best friend who

Michelle's three sons, from left to right, Tom, John and Paul, shown here as young college students on vacation in Thailand, spent some of their childhood and got their early education aboard *Third Sea.*

gave me shelter, and sanctuary at times when all I wanted was peace and solitude. She was my pride; she pacified that urge, the one we all have at times, to show off. She was my joy. There were moments when nothing else on earth mattered, except *Third Sea*.

What I hadn't reckoned, however, was that Southeast Asia, like the South Pacific, was changing, ever so rapidly. The entire region was going through a transition. Tourism was rapidly becoming a foreign-dollar earner for most Asian countries. But foreigner visitors now looked for something more than temples and good shopping. They called it eco-tourism. Emphasis was on the outdoors. Yachting and scuba diving became big calling cards. Phuket was soon the "in" place for fun in the sun. *Third Sea* was a natural, but to participate, she needed a crew. In Singapore I went through a series of skippers to do charter and watch over her, but none of them worked out for very long.

Michelle came up with the idea of bringing her brothers and a sister from the Philippines to operate and maintain *Third Sea* for us. It sounded like a fine idea, and soon I had all the help I needed, a half dozen Filipino crew, male and female.

In Singapore we installed a new engine, ship-to-shore radio and a satellite navigation system. In a dry dock in Phuket we changed her color to white. She looked great, but some of her character was gone, and her spirit. I could feel it, for she seemed to protested the hordes of tourists who came aboard demanding air-conditioning, European cuisine and perfection. What did they care that this gallant ship could fight storms and pirates and sail up forbidden rivers where other ships dared not go. It meant nothing to them that she could explore reefs and shoals that others feared. But most important, gone was the devotion that I and a few others had given her. To Bong, her new captain, she was a merely a shelter that provided food, a little spending money, and an escape from the Philippines. Nothing more. The exception was Ruddy, Michelle's older brother. He was a carpenter by trade who would later prove his worth.

I found I was becoming more obligated to the crew than to *Third Sea*. Bong became the issue, but there was a solution. It would take a bit of planning. The underlying factor was that yachting wasn't what interested Bong. He had been skippering *Third Sea* for two years doing charters around Phuket and he continuously had difficulty keeping a crew. He had the nasty habit of punching out crew members when things didn't work out as he wanted. What he failed to realize was *Third Sea* was not the *HMS Bounty* and he was not an officer in the British Navy governed by the Articles of War. I even tried bringing one of Bong's close friends from the Philippines, at a great expense, to crew with him, but after a month the man quit and went back home.

The truth was Bong had no real love for yachting. Given the choice, he favored using an engine rather than putting up sail. Under his command, *Third Sea* had never sailed with her full complement of sails. He had never used the fisherman, that large tri-sail flown midships with the support of a wishbone. He had never felt the thrill of leaving port with all sails billowing in the wind. I once tried to tell him about the time we left Raiatea in French Polynesia. We were tied to the dock, having taken on supplies, and were ready to depart for Bora Bora. There was a stiff breeze, and those on the dock who had come to see us off expected us to cast off, motor away and raise sails once we were through the pass. Not *Third Sea*. I had a competent, well-trained crew who responded to orders.

"Unfurl the sails," I shouted, and immediately they knew my intentions. They unfurled the sails and stood by. "Up main!" I commanded next, and then, "Up main staysail!" With alacrity they raised the main and main staysail, followed by the jib and fisherman. Even the flying jib went up. *Third Sea* responded. She heeled to port. I swung the rudder, and she caught the full force of the wind. With all sails flying we sailed through the narrow pass and on to Bora Bora. It was a great feeling. The story didn't impress Bong. He'd rather have motored out of port.

What Bong really wanted was to go to America.

Aboard *Third Sea* it was possible, perhaps his only way. We struck an agreement. Bong and Ruddy would sail *Third Sea* to Honolulu where Bong would remain aboard until I could refurbish her and find another crew. With satellite navigation, they could sail her safely across the Pacific Ocean. No sextant needed to shoot the sun or stars, no tables to read, no time checks to make. Just switch on the nav set and push a button.

I further agreed to accompany *Third Sea* from Singapore to Zamboanga in the southern Philippines. I signed on a crew, an American couple, Jack and Bev from California, Michelle's sister, Charmaine, and her boyfriend Madd, and my good friend Steve van Beek and his lady friend from New York.

Steve planned to sail to Zamboanga, leave the ship there, and rejoin later when they reached Rabaul. He had made a passage before aboard *Third Sea*, from Phuket to Singapore, and was keen on sailing the South Pacific. He was interested in *Third Sea* from the moment I began building her and gave me encouragement and moral support when it was most needed. Aside from being the fine writer that he is, he proved to be an able seaman. He was curious about everything. Robert Stedman, my ex-first mate and nephew, was there to help us outfit in Singapore and wish us bon voyage.

It was not an easy passage to Zamboanga. We battled our way across the South China Seas fighting harsh winds and difficult currents along the northern coast of Borneo. But now that we had satellite navigation, gone, was the difficulty of negotiating the treacherous Palawan Pass. How frightening it had been each time we went through. On our last passage, Robert, Eric, Tony and I had to pick our way through by following the lights of freighters at night.

In Zamboanga, after making a few repairs and filling the tanks with diesel, I bid my good bye and saw *Third Sea* on its way to Rabaul, their first planned stop, fifteen hundred miles distant. I returned to Bangkok with Steve and his friend.

Less than two weeks later, Michelle and I had a phone call in Bangkok, from friends in the Philippines. Local newspapers there were carrying the news that an American yacht had entered the Philippines illegally and was being held by the authorities in Davao, a port some four hundred miles east of Zamboanga. They gave its name: *Third Sea*. Michelle and I caught the next flight to Manila and a local flight to Davao.

Third Sea was riding out her anchor in the bay at Davao. Bong and Ruddy were putting up in a fishing village by the sea shore. All the crew had left. The newspaper had been correct. The schooner was being held and charged with illegally entering Philippine waters. What had gone wrong?

After leaving Zamboanga, *Third Sea* ran a full gale that lasted for nearly five days. Instead of heaving-to and riding out the storm with a sea anchor, Bong kept the engine running and motored into the wind during the storm. He used up much of their diesel and decided to put into Davao to get more. He hadn't considered that since he had checked out of the country, he had to check in again.

The authorities weren't very understanding and it took two days of negotiating—and a few pesos–before the charge of illegal entry was dismissed and *Third Sea* granted a port clearance. Our next problem was far more grave. Once again we didn't have a crew to continue the voyage.

In the village Bong found three fishermen who agreed to help crew *Third Sea* to Honolulu. A few weeks later when Michelle and I were in Bangkok, we had another call from Bong, this time from Rabaul. He was stranded again. The Filipino crew had abandoned ship and caught a freighter back home. I went to Singapore where Robert helped me recruit three English backpackers and flew with them to Rabaul. Again I saw *Third Sea* off, but her time of troubles was only beginning. While sailing through the New Hebrides, *Third Sea* struck a log at sea and had to put into Santo for repairs. The three Englishmen abandoned ship and Bong and Ruddy were once again alone. Michelle and I flew to Port Vila, the capital, and hired a bush plane to fly us north.

The plane was a four-seater that tossed wildly about when we encountered any turbulence. We had to make several island stops, touching down on grass landing strips where bushmen came out of the jungle with bones in their noses, and their bodies marked with wierd designs. I felt sorry for Michelle; she was in terror when these savages looked at her as if she might be their next meal. Indeed, there was some need for concern. Cannibalism might be outlawed but at one island we learned laws for natives might be difficult to enforce. Old habits don't easily die. A Kanaka was in jail serving a two-month sentence. It appeared that one evening shortly before we arrived, the man's wife returned home to find him cooking dinner— their infant daughter. We were assured the story was true.

Since the last time *Third Sea* had visited Santo a dozen years before, the Japanese had moved in and established a fishing industry which included a shipyard and dry dock facilities. The Japanese foreman agreed to slip *Third Sea*, but at the same price it would cost for a large vessel. He wouldn't negotiate nor listen to reason. We had to pay the full price, in advance. In the next two weeks we completely rebuilt the bow. We left Bong and Ruddy with a paid crew to take them to Vila where they could hopefully recruit a new crew. They couldn't. The next call from Bong was urgent. He had lost the dingy and reported he had discovered serious dry rot in the foremast. I flew from Bangkok to Singapore and convinced Robert to give me a hand. Together we flew to Sydney and from there to Vila. Our work was cut out for us. We had to construct a dingy and a build new foremast. We had to accomplish the impossible. Vila had few supplies and no cranes to step a mast.

With the help of the expatriate community we were able to locate material and supplies. At an old rubber plantation we found a stash of lumber stored under the French planter's house. He once intended to use it for making furniture; we were fortunate he never had. He agreed to sell us enough lumber for the mast. We then found a wood shop that would scarf the joints, and from a dozen other shops around town we borrowed several hundred clamps, important items for mast construction. The Vila Yacht Club was generous and let us use an area under the club house to construct the mast. It was now Ruddy's turn. He labored for endless hours with a chisel, shaping and fitting the timbers together. While the mast was curing, we constructed an eighteen-foot dory that broke down into two parts, similar to the one Don McClean built years before in Rabaul. Without the use of a crane, stepping the mast was the most difficult task we had to face. We solved the problem by tying up to the dock at high tide and letting the schooner settle into the mud with the ebbing tide. We were then able to position the mast into place.

We found three Kanakas for the paid crew. With Bong and Ruddy, *Third Sea* now had five crew to sail to Honolulu. Bong gave instructions to his new crew. "You can have all you want to eat," he said, and then tapping his chest, he added, "but no eat me." They agreed. A month later *Third Sea* arrived in Honolulu. The very next day it was Bong who abandoned ship. He caught a plane to California. He never saw *Third Sea* again.

Ruddy waited aboard until I arrived. We found a Hawaiian and his *haole* wife and their two children to watch over *Third Sea,* as kind of caretakers. Michelle and I were in California, making plans for *Third Sea*, when we first heard about a hurricane approaching the islands. We had been excited about spending a few months aboard, cruising the islands, and looked forward to getting back to *Third Sea.* But the hurricane got to her first. Perhaps had she known about our plans, she might have held on till we arrived. She always did in the past and never once let a storm beat her.

Top, the aft deck of *Third Sea* was the favorite gathering place for other yachtsmen whenever we were in port. Bottom, Goh Poh Seng, poet and author from Singapore, and Leonie, one of the leading ladies from "Mutiny on the Bounty" chatting in the main saloon.

372

Chapter 24

THE LAST VOYAGE

Ships outlast their owners and masters, and I often wondered this about *Third Sea*, when and how might we part company when the time came. Most men who own boats have such thoughts from time to time. They might try to put them aside, but they are always there, lingering in the back of their minds. I knew such a day would come with *Third Sea* and me, but what I never expected, ever, was that the end would come as it did, in a sheltered anchorage in a peaceful lagoon in the Hawaiian islands. But then I never expected the likes of Hurricane Iniki.

Still, I never stopped hoping, even after arriving in Hawaii and hearing that *Third Sea* was breaking up on the reef near the seawall at Ke'ehi Lagoon. Maybe they were wrong. Maybe it was another vessel they saw. My mind refused to accept it, and I strained hard, looking across the lagoon, trying to see my schooner. I even imagined I saw her, standing at the edge of the reef, defying the storm, the winds, the sea. I had to get to her, somehow. I began running down the beach.

Among the debris that littered the shore I saw a battered dinghy. It had no seats and one of her gunwales was stove in. Beneath her, half burried in the sand, was a broken oar. I grabbed the oar and pushed the boat into the water and stepped aboard. She floated, but barely. Once away from the shore the wind picked up and began blowing us across the lagoon towards the seawall. I could see the towering surf shooting high in the sky, piling up upon itself, only to come crashing down in dreadful fury on the other side of the wall. I feared my frail little boat would go down before I reached the wall. I hadn't noticed but two men in a Boston Whaler had seen my predicament and came to my aid. I explained that I had to go out to the seawall. One man threw me a line. I had nothing to secure it to so I held fast to the end as they towed the dingy, with me sitting at the bow, towards the wall. As we drew near and I looked up my heart stopped. I thought I would die there. *Third Sea* was down on her side; only the starboard side of hull, the main cabin and the tops of the masts remained above water. We came in close and I let go the tow line.

Third Sea was dying, lying on her side, wounded, waiting for me as I paddled up alongside. As I came close, and saw her there, so helpless, I couldn't stop the flourish of tears. I never thought her loss would effect me as it did. I was devastated. The two men had left and I was glad that no one was with me; I wanted to be alone with her, for the last time.

I tied up the dingy and scampered aboard, and crawled along the cabin side. At any minute I feared she would slide into deep water. I could see things floating—books, charts, clothing—all beneath the closed windows. It was eerie, a death ship.

Third Sea breaking up at the seawall at Honolulu's Ke'ehi Lagoon.

I made an attempt to swim into the main cabin but the way was blocked with floating debris. Through the grime and oil I could see Theo Meier's wood carvings beneath the surface. Theo's beautiful carvings!

It was a matter of time and she would be gone. No help came, and already looters were climbing over the wrecks of other vessels long the seawall. I counted more than dozen. Some vessels could be salvaged; others were beyond help.

Darkness came but I couldn't leave. I had to sleep aboard, for the last time. I curled up on the cabin side and remembered my friend Robin Dannhorn. He helped me launch *Third Sea*. She was bare hull without bunk or furnishings, but Robin insisted upon sleeping aboard that first night. Now I would be the last.

I attempted to sleep, curled up on the side, until the cold and rising water drove me into the dingy. But the worst came that night, as I lay on the wet bottom, shivering, half delirious with fever. The nightmare became real. Now instead of clothing and books floating in the cabin, I could see faces, faces of all those who sailed with me—somehow they were trapped inside.

There was Leonie. Lovely Leonie. She starred with Marlon Brando in *Mutiny on the Bounty*. When we were moored at the quay in Papeete she asked if she could make use of *Third Sea*. How could I refuse! She needed a dressing room for her dance team during the Fete. Leonie passed away last year.

There was Adolf Knees, manager of Triumph in Bangkok. He had flown to Tahiti with a dozen German friends to spend two weeks sailing the leeward island, and while at Bora Bora we were warned of an approaching storm and were advised to head out to open sea. Adolf's friends checked into Club Med on the island, and Adolf stayed aboard while we went to sea. He then helped me sail *Third Sea*, after the storm, back to Papeete.

There was that pretty Dutch girl. She came aboard when we were in Phuket, wanting to charter *Third Sea* for a day. She came back aboard the next morning with all her friends, happy and smiling; immediately they began peeling off their clothing, down to bare flesh. She hadn't told me they were nudists. How difficult to concentrate on sailing a boat when everyone is naked.

There was Eric, always smiling Eric who had stood on deck and defied the pirates, and helped me sail through the treacherous Palawan Pass to Singapore. Poor Eric, a few months later he met his end when he fell from the rigging of another vessel.

There were the faces of the kids from the American School in Singapore who sailed *Third Sea* up the Malacca Strait, and Dominic who risked sharks at Caroline Island and dove overboard to cut a line to set the schooner free. And Joseph the island chief at Hermit Island, and caretakers Dave and Judy Loomis, and poet Dr. Goh Poh Seng.

There was my son, Peter. *Third Sea* had brought us together. And it was aboard that Tom, John and Paul, my three sons with Michelle, learned the basic values of life.

There were the noted yachtsmen Bernard Moitessier and Tristan Jones and Omar Darr, and the many hundreds who were faces without names.

The next morning, at the first light of dawn, I climbed aboard *Third Sea* again. Torn with agony, I crawled along the cabin side, and then slid into the dingy. I took nothing from my doomed ship, not a belaying pin, not a shackle, not a piece of line. I wanted her go down as she was, untouched. I let the current and wind carry me away, and I didn't look back. I couldn't.

The nightmare still has not gone away. *Third Sea* went down and all that is left is memories. One of those memories stands out in my mind far above all the others. It's that of an old man who came aboard when we were anchored in Zamboanga. He was an ex-G.I., a soldier who went to the Philippines during Word War I and never left. With a cane in one hand, he walked about the deck, glancing up now and then at the rigging; he made his way out on to the bowsprit. He stood there for the longest time, and finally he turned around to face me and he crew. Half muttering, he said, "I want to go with you. I want to sail with you!" We looked at him dismayed, and at that moment he knew. He turned away, and looking at the sky, with a clenched fist, we heard him shout, "Why, God, why does a man have to grow old." And when he was leaving the schooner, he put a hand on my shoulder and said, "Never live in the past. Now, not tomorrow or yesterday, now is important. And above all, always keep that dream alive."

I always have, old man. Believe me, I have. *Third Sea* was that dream, and she shall never die, for she lives in my heart forever, and in the hearts of all those who loved her and sailed with her.

Crew members returning by dinghy to schooner *Third Sea* anchored a half mile offshore on Malaya Peninsula in the South China Sea.

EPILOGUE

The loss of Schooner *Third Sea* is not mourned by me alone. Letters, cables, faxes, e-mail, phone calls—they came by the hundreds, from all over the world. I hadn't realized the impact the schooner had on the lives of so many people. Some of my newspaper readers were so taken back, and not knowing what to say, they sent money, hundred-baht notes, five-hundred baht notes. Robert Stedman sent me an express letter when he heard the news. Robert was first mate during some of our most memorable voyages. He wrote: "The only comfort I can offer you is the thought that *Third Sea* gave me and countless others the most wonderful adventure of a lifetime. *Third Sea* may have met her fate but the ideal and spirit she represented will live on in all who sailed on her—of that I'm certain. It was your dream that made the adventure a reality."

Taking his time from a busy schedule after being elected the first civilian president of Thai Airways International, Chatrachai Bunya-Ananta wrote a warming note: "I was very sorry to hear of the loss of your schooner in the hurricane. It must have been a terrifying experience . . . I hope that it will be possible for you to replace your schooner which has played such a major role in your writing career."

Dennis Grey, Bureau Chief for Associated Press in Southeast Asia, wrote: "The loss of the *Third Sea* moved me to tears."

Robin Dannhorn, my enduring friend who help me plan, launch and sail *Third Sea* on many voyages to distant ports over the years wanted to know if what he heard was true: "I just heard that *Third Sea* was lost in the Hawaii typhoon. My God. Say that it isn't so."

Alan and Karen Dyers, two friends who had never seen *Third Sea* but heard so much about her, sent a heart-felt letter: "The memories of those who had sailed with you will live on forever."

Steve van Beek, writer and loyal friend, who followed *Third Sea* from the drafting table to crew aboard her on a voyage from Singapore to Zamboanga, wrote: "My condolences . . . I hope you were able to salvage her logs and that you are now considering putting her life's story into print."

Tristan Jones, who was living in Phuket and completing the manuscript on his 17th yachting book, wrote: "I heard about your loss. I am so sorry. I have enjoyed reading your stories and newspaper articles; now I want to hear about this last chapter." Tristan did not live long enough to read the last chapter. He died of complications from an operation after having his second leg removed in Phuket.

My faithful friend Robin Dannhorn who couldn't believe the news, wrote a second letter when the loss was confirmed: "A dramatic end to a dramatic phase of your life. You must write about it, from beginning to end. You owe it to your readers; they have been involved in so many stages of the whole thing . . . ."

Perhaps, more so than anything else that prompted me to sit down and re-tell the story of schooner *Third Sea* is the biggest mystery of them all. I have no explanation; it just happened. A year after the tragic event, a large brown manila envelope arrived in the mail at my home in California where I was spending some time. There was no return address, and no letter of introduction inside, only a very tattered log book. It was one of the many logs of *Third Sea*. Obviously, it had been fished up out of the sea, or else found on windswept shore, for its pages were streaked and many were falling apart. I was able to piece together much of the log, including a section for comments from crew and visitors who had been aboard. Some had jotted down their address, and many of these were still readable. How strange to receive this book, without explanation. Was it by some strange fate that those who had entered their names wanted to be told?

A copy of another log came from Ken Sipple. When Ken completed the voyage from Honolulu to Papeete, he asked to borrow the log so that he could make a copy. He did and sent the original back which was later lost with the ship. When he learned I was compiling a book about *Third Sea*, he sent me his copy. And fortunately on record were the many hundreds of newspaper articles and magazine stories that I had written. Together, along with letters sent to friends and family, they all pieced together the story you have just read.

Stephens and Michelle sitting at the helm of schooner *Third Sea*.